Enlightenment
in Ruins

TRANSITS:
LITERATURE, THOUGHT & CULTURE 1650 — 1850

Series Editor
Greg Clingham
Bucknell University

Transits is the next horizon. This series of books, essays and monographs aims to extend recent achievements in eighteenth-century studies, and to publish excellent work on any aspects of the literature, thought and culture of the years 1650-1850. Without ideological or methodological restrictions, Transits seeks to provide transformative readings of the literary, cultural, and historical interconnections between Britain, Europe, the Far East, Oceania, and the Americas in the long eighteenth century, and as they extend down to the present time. In addition to literature and history, such "global" perspectives might entail considerations of time, space, nature, economics, politics, environment, and material culture, and might necessitate the development of new modes of critical imagination, which we welcome. But the series does not thereby repudiate the local and the national, for original new work on particular writers and readers in particular places in time continues to be the bedrock of the discipline.

Titles in the Series

The Family, Marriage, and Radicalism in British Women's Novels of the 1790s: Public Affection and Private Affliction
Jennifer Golightly

Feminism and the Politics of Travel After the Enlightenment
Yaël Schlick

John Galt: Observations and Conjectures on Literature, History, and Society
Regina Hewitt

Performing Authorship in Eighteenth-Century English Periodicals
Manushag N. Powell

Excitable Imaginations: Eroticism and Reading in Britain, 1660–1760
Kathleen Lubey

The French Revolution Debate and the British Novel, 1790–1814: The Struggle for History's Authority
Morgan Rooney

Rococo Fiction in France, 1600–1715: Seditious Frivolity
Allison Stedman

Poetic Sisters: Early Eighteenth-Century Women Poets
Deborah Kennedy

Richard Brinsley Sheridan: The Impresario in Political and Cultural Context
Jack E. DeRochi and Daniel J. Ennis

Studies in Ephemera: Text and Image in Eighteenth-Century Print
Kevin Murphy and Sally O'Driscoll

Developments in the Histories of Sexualities: In Search of the Normal, 1600–1800
Chris Mounsey

Enlightenment in Ruins: The Geographies of Oliver Goldsmith
Michael Griffin

For a complete list of titles in this series, please visit http://www.bucknell.edu/universitypress

TRANSITS

Enlightenment in Ruins

THE GEOGRAPHIES OF
OLIVER GOLDSMITH

MICHAEL GRIFFIN

LEWISBURG
BUCKNELL UNIVERSITY PRESS

Published by Bucknell University Press
Copublished with The Rowman & Littlefield Publishing Group, Inc.
4501 Forbes Boulevard, Suite 200, Lanham, Maryland 20706
www.rowman.com

10 Thornbury Road, Plymouth PL6 7PP, United Kingdom

Copyright © 2013 by Michael Griffin

All rights reserved. No part of this book may be reproduced in any form or by any electronic or mechanical means, including information storage and retrieval systems, without written permission from the publisher, except by a reviewer who may quote passages in a review.

British Library Cataloguing in Publication Information Available

Library of Congress Cataloging-in-Publication Data

Griffin, Michael, 1974–
 Enlightenment in ruins : the geographies of Oliver Goldsmith / Michael Griffin.
   p. cm.
 Includes bibliographical references and index.
 ISBN 978-1-61148-505-9 (cloth : alk. paper) — ISBN 978-1-61148-506-6 (electronic) 1. Goldsmith, Oliver, 1730?–1774. 2. Authors, Irish—18th century—Biography. 3. Irish literature—18th century—History and criticism. I. Title.

PR3493.G75 2013
828'.609—dc23

2013015895

∞™ The paper used in this publication meets the minimum requirements of American National Standard for Information Sciences—Permanence of Paper for Printed Library Materials, ANSI/NISO Z39.48-1992.

Printed in the United States of America

CONTENTS

	List of Illustrations	vii
	Acknowledgments	ix
	List of Abbreviations	xi
	Chronology of Goldsmith's Life and Career	xiii
	Introduction	1

PART 1: COMPARATIVE VIEWS OF RACES AND NATIONS

1	The Cultural Climate: Natural Histories of National Character	31
2	The Lie of the Land: Liberty and Travel	51

PART 2: POLITICAL LANDSCAPES AND BODIES POLITIC

3	Delicate Allegories: Ireland and the East	87
4	Geographies of Ruin: Ireland, America and Auburn's Absentees	113
	Ill Fares the Land: Conclusion	147
	Notes	153
	Bibliography	181
	Index	203
	About the Author	209

ILLUSTRATIONS

2.1 James Barry, *Part of the Palatine Hill from the steps of San Gregorio* (1769). 60

2.2 William Mulready, Illustration of a scene from *The Vicar of Wakefield*. 75

2.3 Arthur Rackham, "A Favourite Song of Dryden's." Illustration of a scene from *The Vicar of Wakefield*. 76

ACKNOWLEDGMENTS

THE SUPPORT OF THE National Endowment for the Humanities and the Keough/Naughton Institute for Irish Studies at the University of Notre Dame, where an enjoyable and stimulating year were spent working on eighteenth-century Irish writing, is greatly appreciated. While there, and since, Seamus Deane and Breandán MacSuibhne read early drafts of this work and improved it. My thanks also to the anonymous reviewers of the manuscript at Bucknell University Press for their helpful comments, and to Greg Clingham and Pamelia Dailey for all of their guidance in the book's production. Special thanks also to Michael Gloster for technical support.

An earlier version of a segment of chapter 3 was published in *Eighteenth-Century Ireland: Iris an Dá Chultúr*; I am grateful to the editors of that journal for permission to rework some of that material in this book. Equally, a section of chapter 4 was debuted in *Edmund Burke's Irish Identities* (2007); thanks to Lisa Hyde at Iris Academic Press, and to editor Seán Patrick Donlan for the opportunity to expand on those ideas here.

This book was researched with the kind assistance of several libraries and librarians: in Special Collections at the University of Limerick library Ken Bergin and Jean Turner put up stoically with my repetitive requests for Friedman's Goldsmith as everything was checked. Gearoid O'Brien at the Westmeath County Library in Athlone enabled me to enjoy the extraordinary Aidan Heavey collection. A Mayers Research Fellowship at the Huntington Library, San Marino, California, was of tremendous assistance. I am also grateful to Marti Kallal and Steve Sawyer at the Morris Library, Southern Illinois University at Carbondale, and to the staff of the Hesburgh Library, University of Notre Dame. The staff in the Upper Reading Room at the Bodleian Library in Oxford were extremely helpful. The warmth and generosity of the late Vera Ryhajlo is greatly missed by many, not least by Oxford's Irish scholars.

ACKNOWLEDGMENTS

For advice, sense and sociability in and around this research, I owe debts to Ruth Clifford, Keith Duggan, Charles and Fran Fanning, David Fairer, Eoin Flannery, Christopher Fox, Luke and Dolores Gibbons, Maura Kennedy, John Kenny, Enda Leaney, Roger Lonsdale, Tara MacLeod, Brian Ó Conchubhair, Diarmuid Ó Giolláin, David O'Shaughnessy, Patrick O'Sullivan, Frank Shovlin, John Shovlin, Jim Smyth, and Fiona Stafford. For their collegial indulgence of this research I am grateful to University of Limerick colleagues in English and Irish studies and in the School of Languages, Literature, Culture and Communication, and to fellow members of UL's Ralahine collective and Eighteenth Century Research Group.

There is some speculation in this book about Goldsmith's Catholic ancestry. But then Goldsmith's teacher at the Diocesan School at Elphin was the Reverend Michael Griffin. As my father hails from that region, the issue which thus arises is not whether Goldsmith's family was, at some stage, Catholic, but: was mine Protestant? With this very eighteenth-century-Irish conundrum in mind, I thank my family for their support and encouragement and dedicate this book to Mick Griffin Snr. of the Diocese of Elphin.

ABBREVIATIONS

The following texts are cited throughout the book; all references to them will be abbreviated as follows:

AN   Goldsmith, Oliver. *An History of the Earth, and Animated Nature*, 8 vols. London: Printed for John Nourse, 1774.

CH   *Goldsmith: The Critical Heritage*, edited by G. S. Rousseau. London: Routledge & Kegan Paul, 1974.

HE   Goldsmith, Oliver. *The History of England, from the Earliest Times to the Death of George II*, 4 vols. London: Printed for T. Davies; Becket and De Hondt; and T. Cadell, 1771.

L   Goldsmith, Oliver. *The Collected Letters*, edited by Katherine C. Balderston. Cambridge: Cambridge University Press, 1928.

W   Goldsmith, Oliver. *The Collected Works*, edited by Arthur Friedman, 5 vols. Oxford: The Clarendon Press, 1966.

CHRONOLOGY OF GOLDSMITH'S LIFE AND CAREER

1728 Goldsmith is born, probably at Pallas, Co. Westmeath, Ireland, second son of the Rev. Charles Goldsmith, an Anglican minister. Shortly after Oliver's birth, Rev. Goldsmith becomes curate in Kilkenny West. The family moves to Lissoy, where Goldsmith spends much of his childhood.

1735–45 Between the mid-1730s and 1745, Goldsmith receives his education from various diocesan schools in the Longford/Roscommon region.

1745–50 Goldsmith studies as a sizar at Trinity College, Dublin, graduating with a BA in February of 1750.

1750–52 Works as a tutor to the Flinn family in Roscommon. Abortive attempts are made to emigrate to America and to London.

1752–54 Studies medicine at the University of Edinburgh with financial assistance from relatives.

1754–55 Continues his medical studies at Leyden University in Holland.

1755–56 Travels through Europe, primarily on foot. His journey takes him through Flanders, France, Germany, Switzerland, and Italy.

1756–57 Works at various jobs: as an assistant to an apothecary, as a physician in Southwark, and as an usher at a boys' school in Peckham in Surrey. He may also have been a proofreader in Samuel Richardson's printing house. In 1757 he works as a reviewer for Ralph Griffiths, editor of the *Monthly Review*.

1758 Attempts unsuccessfully—he is not accepted as hospital mate for a ship—to travel, this time to Coromandel as a physician with the East India Company.

1759 Contributes to Tobias Smollett's *Critical Review*. French victories in India deter him definitively from traveling there. Following the publication of *An Enquiry into the Present State of Polite Learning in Europe* in April, Goldsmith's literary acquaintance comes to include Thomas Percy, Edmund Burke, and Samuel Johnson. Goldsmith writes the *Bee*, his own periodical, between October and November.

1759–61 Contributes essays to a number of magazines: the *Busy Body*, the *Weekly Magazine*, the *Royal Magazine*, and the *Lady's Magazine*. In January of 1760 he begins his "Chinese Letters" series in John Newbery's *Public Ledger*. The series continues until August of 1761. Goldsmith composes his novel *The Vicar of Wakefield* between 1760 and 1762.

1762 Contributes essays to *Lloyd's Evening Post*. On May 1, his "Chinese Letters" are collected and published as *The Citizen of the World*. In this year Goldsmith is contracted by Newbery to write what would become *A Survey of Experimental Philosophy*, eventually published after the author's death. His career as journalistic essayist effectively ends at this point; his career as a compiler and author of popular science and history begins. In October he publishes *The Life of Richard Nash*. While in financial difficulty, the rights of his novel in progress, *The Vicar of Wakefield*, are sold, at Johnson's instigation, to Newbery, who sells a third share of the rights to Salisbury bookseller Benjamin Collins, and another third to William Strahan.

1764 Is a founder member, with Johnson, David Garrick, and others, of The Club. He publishes *An History of England, in a Series of Letters from a Nobleman to His Son*, and an oratorio libretto entitled *The Captivity* is performed. In December, his major poem *The Traveller; Or, a Prospect of Society*, dedicated to his brother Henry, is published.

1766 *The Vicar of Wakefield* is published in March.

1768 His comedy, *The Good Natured Man*, is performed at Covent Garden in January. His brother Henry dies in May.

1769 Is contracted (by William Griffin) to write a natural history compendium. His *Roman History* is published in May; he is appointed professor of ancient history at the Royal Academy.

1770 His second major poem, *The Deserted Village*, is published in May.

1771 His *History of England, from the Earliest Times to the Death of George II* is published in August.

1772 Writes *Threnodia Augustalis*, a poem to honor the memory of Augusta, princess dowager, which is performed in February.

1773 Contributes to the *Westminster Magazine* between January and March, the month in which his second comedy, *She Stoops to Conquer*, is performed.

1774 Dies on April 4, having suffered renal infection and fever. His poem *Retaliation*, written in response to a satiric epitaph of Garrick's read at a meeting of The Club early that year, is published a fortnight after his death. His *History of the Earth, and Animated Nature*, is published on July 1. His *Grecian History* is published a fortnight later.

1776 A monument to Goldsmith is erected in Westminster Abbey. His *Survey of Experimental Philosophy*, a two-volume compendium of science, is published.

INTRODUCTION

O N DECEMBER 21, 1772, an as yet obscure excise officer by the name of Thomas Paine sent to the famed Irish poet, playwright, novelist and historian Oliver Goldsmith a copy of his twenty-one-page pamphlet, *The Case of the Officers of Excise*. Paine requested Goldsmith's "company for an hour or two, to partake of a bottle of wine, or any thing else," adding that he would "take the liberty of waiting on you in a day or two."[1] The pamphlet which was to be the occasion of their meeting was an expression of Paine's egalitarianism and reflected his simmering conviction that the prevailing social and economic system was one which exacerbated the plight of the poor.

Paine's job as an excise-man was a hard one, underpaid and unpopular. One of his workaday tasks involved measuring for tax purposes the beer-barrels of the common tavern. Those who brewed their own ale—the rich—were exempt from the taxes which Paine calculated. As one might expect, neither the publicans nor their hard-bitten customers had any great love or understanding for Paine or his fellow officers. For one with Paine's sympathies, the work was demoralizing. Nonetheless, he would persevere in solidarity with his colleagues, and his pamphlet would demand better conditions and pay. Paine wrote to Goldsmith because the latter was a celebrity with considerable public presence who two years earlier had published *The Deserted Village*, a poem which mixed nostalgic pastoral with pointed political complaint about the destructive negligence of the rich. That poem had ensured that Goldsmith was seen as a champion of the plight of the underclass. Anecdotes about his generous, eccentric, and hospitable personality were commonly known, and Paine clearly saw a potential ally, or at least a figure

[1]

with the public profile to bring his plight, and the plight of his fellow workers, to the attention of the greater public.

In other respects, however, Goldsmith—a Tory, a monarchist, and a Jacobite—was an odd figure for Paine to contact, especially given the latter's later career as an outspoken republican. Goldsmith was deeply skeptical of any move away from traditional, centralized governance, while Paine saw monarchy as an obstacle which stood between the people and their liberty. Paine declared himself "a citizen of the world," a cosmopolitan catch-phrase repeatedly deployed by Goldsmith and used as a title for his collected faux-Chinese letters of 1762; with this allusion, Paine invoked what he understood to be the spirit of Goldsmith's cosmopolitanism against muddled traditionalists. However, Paine failed to understand that Goldsmith saw himself as both cosmopolitan *and* traditionalist. Both men were of the enlightenment; but while Paine has come to represent the century's most revolutionary propensities, Goldsmith, wary of an enlightenment which rhetorically proclaimed the possibility of liberty for all, embodied that same enlightenment's more cautious tenor. Whatever brought about Paine's sense of Goldsmith's potential amenability to his cause, theirs was, given their divergent politics, an unlikely partnership. For their potential points of sympathy, there existed between the two men and their intellectual characters a central kink of incomprehension. For Paine, the concept of liberty was ideal, expansive, and transferable; for Goldsmith, it was nominal, expansive, and nontransferable, and for those very reasons potentially ruinous.

More than Paine could perhaps have appreciated, all of Goldsmith's major poetic and fictional works play, in tragic and comic registers, on those ironies of liberty and cosmopolitanism which emerge in moments of cultural encounter. Liberty was for him a vague and highly subjective concept, susceptible to political manipulation, while cosmopolitanism, the great boast of the enlightened commentator, was fraught with narcissism. This is not to say that Goldsmith was a counter-enlightenment figure; quite the contrary: his histories, natural and political, participate in the enlightenment's information revolution. And while his financial situation demanded that he reproduce some of the more imperialistic and ethnocentric strains of the enlightenment, his politics were equally influenced by anti-imperial and culturally sensitive strains of enlightenment thinking. His body of work is marked by a tension between poetic and professional imperatives, and between cultural and scientific spheres. For all of these reasons, he can be difficult to locate and has been characterized in various ways by critical posterity: as a passive purveyor of enlightenment thought, as a hackish translator and a purveyor of the French enlightenment for a generalist English audience, or an only nominally Irish author slavishly consolidating facetious English notions of national character. He is in prose an ideological lackey, or he is a subtle ironist; in poetry, he is a weak generic pastoralist or an engaged social critic. His career is as complex, and sometimes as contradictory, as the intellectual currents across which he wrote. For all that, there is a consistent set of ideas operating in Goldsmith's oeuvre which can be isolated and addressed as a manifestation of his Irishness. More than that, his politics find their source in that nationality, which has hitherto been ignored as largely incidental to his career. Goldsmith was opposed to the new imperialism, and thought contemporary English notions of liberty, overextended and corrupted in Ireland and beyond, pernicious. In holding these views he was, politically, a product of the cultural Jacobitism of the Irish midlands and the Swiftian patriotism which he would have shared with his fellow Trinity College students in Dublin in the 1740s.

In proposing such a characterization of Goldsmith, this book recuperates the critical potential of his pastoral poetry, and reevaluates his geographies—imaginative, poetic, scientific, and pseudo-scientific—by studying their oblique relation to the emerging discourses in which he wrote. It also partakes of a move, elaborated in this introduction, to multiply characterizations of the enlightenment, and to further question the too-singular view of the enlightenment's Eurocentric, expansive collusion with the imperial project. Goldsmith is a representative author in enlightenment, not because he holds views which in some way encapsulate enlightenment thought, but because his poetry and prose are immersed in, and grapple dialectically with, enlightenment modernity.

This study seeks to nuance the critical reception of Goldsmith by placing him in two contexts which are problematically related to each other. One context is that of the intellectual and political culture in which he worked as a professional author living in London. The other is that of his nationality and his politics. In the former, he is often seen as a derivative thinker; in the latter, however, he inflects conventions with pessimistic and dissident commentary. In reproducing contemporary geographical wisdoms, he is no more or less derivative than the majority of professional authors working in London in the 1760s; however, his oeuvre, considered more broadly, editorializes on his hackwork in politically intriguing ways. In appreciating both of these dynamics, and their interaction, his importance as an Irish author, and the importance of his Irishness to our understanding of his work and the milieu in which it was produced, is retrieved.

INTRODUCTION

Enlightenment Geographies

Geography and chronology, wrote Patrick Gordon in his 1693 reference work, *Geography Anatomized: Or, A Compleat Geographical Grammar*, "may be deservedly termed the Eyes and Feet of History."[2] Together, chronology and geography would demonstrate to contemporary readers how society had arrived at its current position. Histories and political geographies were, in the enlightenment, often biased in favor of the prevailing regimes of the countries in which they were composed. As a synthesizer of historical and geographical compendia operating in an English literary marketplace, Goldsmith appreciated that his endeavors were at least *meant* to be present-centered, or Whiggishly prompted to justify that society to which history was itself a coherently plotted preface.

Contemporary geography was history's spatial partner, its "eyes." It surveyed other races, nations, towns and cities, often in order to demonstrate, synchronically, that other countries were at a different stage of development, or organized, socially and culturally, in ways which were not so much different, but inferior. Modern geography began with the enlightenment; so too did the idea of progress, "and the tenets of that stadial or stage-by-stage theory" on which the very idea of progress was based.[3] Emerging geographies thus played an important role, not just in the constitution of enlightenment discourses, but also in constituting and conceptualizing notions of national character and imperial prowess.[4] There was, then, such a thing as a specifically Whiggish geography, according to which the past was, very definitely, another country.

Goldsmith's authorial career took place at an accelerating phase in the history of geography, where, it seemed, enlightenment and imperialism colluded to ink in the map. The rise of geography as a science coincided with a new empiricism engendered by unprecedented imperial expansion. With the paralysis of Portuguese and Spanish expansion in the eighteenth century, the Dutch, French, and English inaugurated a new period of colonialism. The Dutch and the English prosecuted entrepreneurial expansion in the East. The French had put the best portion of their energies into the New World, especially North America. The area under British rule in that theater also expanded from the New England colonies to take in New York, Georgia, the two Floridas, Nova Scotia, and Quebec. The project of completing the world's map gained new momentum; but there was still, as Edward Heawood explains, a thin line dividing "actual discovery and conjectural geography" in the seventeenth and eighteenth centuries.[5] The literature of the age paid attention to the objective side of that line, while writers such as Swift and Goldsmith indulged conjectural geography in political or satirical modes which illustrated the impossibility of strict objectivity in cultural survey and travel. Geographical literature of the eighteenth century, writes Colin Smethurst, tells us more about "the preoccupations of the literary or artistic geographer than about the physical and human geography of a given community, country or region of the globe."[6] Objectivity was thus perverted, or distorted, by the subject position of the geographer. Goldsmith understood this; he reproduced geographies in his professional prose, but he could also deploy his geographical knowledge, such as it was, in satire and allegory.

To define geography on the eighteenth-century's own terms, the obvious source is Samuel Johnson's *Dictionary*. "In a strict sense," geography is a matter of cartography, chorography, and location; in a slightly broader sense, it includes the study of the seas, but "in the largest sense of all, it extends to the various customs, habits, and governments of nations."[7] When the definition of geography extended to involve an understanding of climatology, anthropology, and natural history, encyclopedic publications proliferated.[8] Though he used the word "geography" itself rarely (as did the era generally—the Enlightenment was the period which produced the discipline's modern forms), Goldsmith's writing engaged with the various sub-disciplines which gathered under geography's broad remit. Geography was a term of natural science which covered physical and *human* dispensations: "Eighteenth-century thinkers," writes Christopher Fox, "sought to cap [the science of nature] with a science of human nature."[9] Thus it was that natural history took into its sights the comparative study of race and national character. Accounts of travel and scientific expeditions would study and classify plants and people in the same scientific swoop. Moreover, the objects of physical geography and anthropology were largely categorized according to a European way of seeing.[10] Claims to objectivity regarding the variety of the human species and human cultures could therefore be undone by imperialist motives. Edward Said's famous and influential application of Michel Foucault's critique of discourse identifies imperial power imperatives behind the ostensibly disinterested construction of the Orient as a monolithic object of knowledge from the eighteenth century on.[11] Enlightenment geographies were thus accused of Eurocentric and imperialist modes and motivations.

For some observers, however, the influence of Foucault in Said has been uncomfortably totalizing, thereby running the risk of an ahistorical Occidentalism, and of doing to western intellectual culture what the imperialist west had done to the east for centuries.[12] This charge has, however, been rebutted by Said himself, in his "Afterword" to the 1995 edition of *Orientalism*. Bill Ashcroft and Pal

INTRODUCTION

Ahluwalia have since argued that Said modified Foucault's method to allow for the critical agency of Westerners writing about the East.[13] Extending this possibility, Joseph Lennon has usefully applied a looser notion of discourse to Irish writing specifically, in which there exists an "agency within and outside of the discourse of Orientalism."[14] In this possibility it can be allowed that imaginative geographies of enlightenment are not necessarily or completely in league with imperialism; in particular, Goldsmith demonstrates that discourses contain within them the possibility of their own parody and critique.

This possibility also allows for a revisiting of the critical capabilities which the enlightenment, for all of its imperialist and oppressive flaws, enabled. As Max Horkheimer and Theodor Adorno have put it, an unreflective enlightenment contains within it the germ of ruin, of regression and repression—implicitly proposing that the prospect of ruin itself might prompt the very reflection which enlightenment discourses require in order to self-invigilate. What has been neglected, thus, since the publication of *The Dialectic of Enlightenment*, is Horkheimer and Adorno's equalizing conviction "that freedom in society is inseparable from enlightenment thinking."[15] In general, the multivalent critical potential of the enlightenment needs, after what Roy Porter has referred to as the "wilfully lopsided" Foucaultian and postmodern moment, to be properly acknowledged and studied.[16]

Such study has been undertaken in the history of political thought. Sankar Muthu has argued in his innovative *Enlightenment Against Empire* that virtually every prominent European thinker in the three centuries before the enlightenment and in the full century after it, was "either agnostic toward or enthusiastically in favour of imperialism." The enlightenment itself was more complex, and Muthu argues against essentializing or caricaturing its collusion in empire. Our understanding of that period needs to be more fully attuned, he proposes, to the period's "nuanced and intriguingly counter-intuitive arguments about human nature, cultural diversity, cross-cultural moral judgements, and political obligations." Such an interrogation has the effect of pluralizing the intellectual history of the period, and enables the exploration of a more complex and argumentative array of dispositions that, as Muthu has it, "reorient contemporary assumptions about the relationship between human unity and human diversity." Postmodern distinctions between universalism and relativism, or essential and constructed identities, are unable, according to Muthu, "to do justice to the arguments made by enlightenment anti-imperialists, who often treat such supposed opposites as interrelated features of the human condition."

Writers such as Goldsmith can be better understood in the contexts delineated by Muthu. Writing professionally in the enlightenment information industry, and at the same time producing poetic, satirical, and critical works which constantly played universalities against local specificities, Goldsmith refused, critiqued, and parodied exoticisms, cults of noble savagery, and moral relativisms, understanding these intellectual tendencies to provide, ultimately, the means of justifying all manner of abuse, including imperialism itself. He was of a piece with those enlightenment anti-imperialists, described by Muthu, who rejected expansion as

> unworkable, dangerous, or immoral—for economic reasons of free trade, as a result of principles of self-determination or cultural integrity, due to concerns about the effects of imperial politics upon domestic political institutions and practices, or out of contempt over the ironic spectacle of ostensibly civilised nations engaging in despotism, corruption, and lawlessness abroad.[17]

Muthu's central example of enlightenment anti-imperialism is the Abbé Raynal's *Histoire des Deux Indes* (1770), and he numbers it among the most sustained indictments of expansion and exploitation in the eighteenth-century pantheon. Raynal's text, to which Denis Diderot made substantial contributions, demonstrates a complex concern with unity and diversity, with (geographically inflected) cyclical optima, and with the moral quandaries of empire. Goldsmith shares with Raynal (or Diderot) and Charles de Secondat, Baron Montesquieu, a sense of the potentially disastrous consequences of empire for the European colonizing powers themselves. As Usbek writes to Rhedi in Montesquieu's *Persian Letters* (1721), "Colonies usually have the effect of weakening the mother-country without adding to the population of the country in which they are established."[18] And in Raynal—himself, like Goldsmith, an enlightenment author deeply suspicious of *libertarian* excess—it is ethical as well as economic degeneracy which empire engenders. The English, Raynal argues, have become corrupt in their displacement. They have become oppressive, abusive, unprincipled; and for this fall from grace there are predictable, even natural causes:

> Being now become absolute rulers in an empire where they were but traders, it was very difficult for the English not to make a bad use of their power. At a distance from home, men are no longer restrained by the fear of being ashamed to see their countrymen. In a warm climate where the body loses its vigour, the mind must lose some of its strength.

INTRODUCTION

> In a country where nature and custom lead to indulgence, men are apt to be seduced. In countries where they come for the purpose of growing rich, they easily forget to be just.[19]

There is, it is suggested, such a thing as a cultural climate to which nations are native, and in which they can best sustain their national characteristics, their moral as well as physical strength. There is also a Hobbesian sense in Raynal that people set adrift from their domestic, and domesticating, mode of governance will behave in brutalizing ways which ultimately betray the venality of acquisitive "freedoms" exercised in imperialism itself. The more efficiently European powers develop their colonies, and the greater the distance from home they travel, the more the colonist's mask of civility slips to reveal vicious capabilities. These are the vices which are more often ascribed, according to a European image of the Other's murderous savagery, to colonized peoples; confounding both of these images, Raynal sees the mask of civility slipping from the face of the *colonist*.

The enlightenment, as one encounters it in Raynal, and indeed in Goldsmith, is not a monolithic entity propagating a myth of normative European civilization against which non-European people might be judged as inferior or, according to the myth of noble savagery, superior. Rather, there are versions of enlightenment which understand a more broadly conceived unity in which all peoples are understood to live and work within environmentally determined advantages and disadvantages; human environments produce, through adaptation, geographically various manifestations of a shared cultural agency. This universalizing tendency, disdained in the Foucaultian moment, had a moral force. There is in Raynal a universal sense of ethical propriety at odds with the relativity which empires themselves incubate—a relativity Edmund Burke would describe as "geographical morality."[20] Raynal's ethical universalism, it is important to add, does not preclude cultural diversity. Rather, his dialectic of the universal and the relative provides an ethical basis for an enlightenment in which cultures can exist independently, on their own terms.

There have been several contributions to this reassessment of the enlightenment. In addition to Muthu's reappraisal, Daniel Carey and Lynn Festa's recent collection of essays on the postcolonial enlightenment seeks "to acknowledge the tensions within Enlightenment thought in order to reorientate the relation between eighteenth-century studies and postcolonial theories."[21] Clement Hawes' provocative 2005 study of the eighteenth-century's capacity for "global critique" announced itself as a counterweight to clichés about modernity and enlightenment inspired by the writings of Michel Foucault and Francois

Lyotard, peddled in recent decades as some sort of critical consensus about a very singularly defined, undifferentiated (and under-researched) enlightenment. Indeed what Hawes argues for, quite compellingly, is that the eighteenth century includes—instigates, even—"precisely what postmodern theory assumes to be absent: the basis for *modernity's self-critique*." So, it is not simply a question of applying postcolonial theory to eighteenth-century texts and authors and finding in them the sorts of imperialist and hegemonic prejudices one wishes to find, but instead to find an inchoate postcolonial critique forming in the texts themselves. Close historical study of eighteenth-century writing nuances postcolonial theory, inflecting it with historical contingency and an awareness of the conflicted experiences of hard-pressed authors operating amidst an emerging, incipiently globalizing modernity. This was a transitional period in philosophical modernity: not a closed or inert historical category, but one in critical flux. This flux, in Hawes' work, is the animating tension in the writings of Jonathan Swift and Samuel Johnson. Hawes sees in Swift's critique of colonial modernity "the potential for alternative modernities—roads not taken—that haunts the writings of the eighteenth century more generally." In repudiating "the colonial hijacking of modernity," Swift "looks forward to a decolonizing modernity yet to come." Johnson's critique, on the other hand, recuperates the "emancipatory energies of enlightenment thought," and this critique is effective "precisely because it arises from within the British Enlightenment."[22]

Equally, Goldsmith's famous cosmopolitanism, his expressed citizenship of the world, was one which appreciated, as did Swift and Johnson, the ironic possibilities of cultural encounter, and included a pronounced commitment to cultural respect and reciprocity. However, such tendencies problematically coincided with the scientific and categorical imperatives of his adventures in natural history. As James Watt has proposed, there is in Goldsmith's writing "the coexistence of seemingly contradictory languages." On one level, Goldsmith proposes the idea of a universal humanity; upon this base of universality, he could argue for an ethical anti-imperialism, and yet he was, in his natural history, "drawn to the apparent authority inherent in new and inflexible means of distinguishing between the peoples of the world."[23] These contradictory languages must be understood less as contradictions in Goldsmith's own outlook, but as reflecting the various strands which run through enlightenment discourses of race, national character, and natural history, discourses to which figures such as Goldsmith, Burke, Johnson, and Raynal were subject, and which these authors themselves made problematic in their political prescriptions.

INTRODUCTION

Thus, there are, broadly speaking, two geographical discourses jostling in Goldsmith's oeuvre. One is realized in his more creative work; this discourse surveys with sensitivity the differences between societies. The other discourse is ostensibly objective and categorical in character. It aspires to a system which can be called upon to verify the superiority of certain cultures and races. Goldsmith wrote across both discourses, but ultimately, he was, in his best work, less concerned with "objective" geography—mixing as he did plagiarism with factual error—as he was with the *perception* of other places and countries, and the political imperatives which informed those perceptions. John McVeagh has suggested that Goldsmith's deviations from more prejudicial geographical perspectives are due to his Irishness.[24] Similarly, R. W. Seitz believed that it was his Irish background which led Goldsmith to oppose "the encroachments of commerce and the new imperialism of his time."[25] Goldsmith's self-description as "half a patriot" is appropriate for Dustin Griffin primarily because of the author's ambiguities of "national identity and local attachment."[26] Prompted by these studies, the present study treats of geography in several of its enlightenment dimensions and connects them to the issue of Goldsmith's nationality; additionally, his Jacobitism, elaborated below, provides a coherent background to his political geography, and to his repeated denigrations of commercial oligarchy and imperialism. "Expansion," writes Rachel Crawford, "was underscored by an intensifying national belief in a uniquely British form of liberty conducive to productivity in all areas."[27] It was this expansion, and this "uniquely British form of liberty," that Goldsmith repeatedly questioned.

Of Oliver Goldsmith

There has, in recent years, been a movement in Irish studies to revisit the Irish origins of authors—particularly pre-1800 authors—whose careers have hitherto been narrowly conceived of in purely British, and more usually, English terms. Foregrounding the "'Irished" or "Re-Irished" author, or "the Irish version of the author we thought we knew," has, as James Chandler writes, "recently acquired the status of a quasi-disciplinary procedure." This has not been a chauvinist pursuit; rather it has prompted rewarding explorations of "how to locate an "Irish author" on a larger cultural map."[28] This is particularly true of Irish studies' intersection with postcolonial studies, and the two fields' mutually enabling reassessment of the careers of Swift and Burke, exemplified in the writings of Carole Fabricant, Luke Gibbons, and Seamus Deane.[29] Goldsmith has largely been left out of this revaluation exercise. Either invoked mawkishly as a gentle minstrel drawing nostalgically on his Irish childhood to please an English audience, or dismissed due to the mawkishness of such an invocation, Goldsmith has not aged gracefully in Irish studies, largely because he is seen, simply, as too English, in his preoccupations and in his sentiment. If Irish at all, he is seen as politically quiescent. Whether tweely played up, or critically played down, rarely does his Irishness play *well*.

Much of Goldsmith's latter-day reputation in Irish studies is filtered through W. B. Yeats' perceptions of him, early and late, neither of which is historically nuanced. His changing perception of Goldsmith, however, needs itself to be understood in the context of Yeats' romantic nationalism, and that nationalism's sectarian waning. Initially rejecting Goldsmith for being too immersed in English matters and manners, Yeats subsequently adapted and adopted him to an Irish Protestant literary lineage, turning him into a bardic chronicler of peaceful eighteenth-century Irish rural life. In "The Seven Sages" (1932), Goldsmith is characterized as sharing with Swift, Burke, and Berkeley an aversion to the glibly progressive temperament:

> Whether they knew or not,
> Goldsmith and Burke, Swift and the Bishop of Cloyne
> All hated Whiggery; but what is Whiggery?
> A levelling, rancorous, rational sort of mind
> That never looked out of the eye of a saint
> Or out of drunkard's eye.

Goldsmith takes on, by contrast with Whiggery, and alongside his Anglican brethren, a beatified aura, a knowingness born of his not holding with the efficiencies of modernity or commerce. Yeats' point on Goldsmith's attitude to Whiggery, though impressionistic, is correct. Goldsmith *did* despise Whiggery. He despised the self-satisfaction of its tone, and was dismayed by its uncritical celebration of the commercial spirit, which for Goldsmith, as for Yeats, implied social and cultural disaster. Greater liberty for Goldsmith meant, simply, greater liberty to expand the empire of trade, and to break the affective ties which held more traditional social forms together. Accordingly, when the second sage condenses, inexactly, the stock images of Goldsmith's poetry, he romanticizes him further by situating him in a pastoral scene poignantly untouched by violent nationalist agitation:

> Oliver Goldsmith sang what he had seen,
> Roads full of beggars, cattle in the fields,
> But never saw the trefoil stained with blood,
> The avenging leaf those fields raised up against it.

INTRODUCTION

Not only is Goldsmith situated by Yeats in the pastoral scene; he is active within it as a recorder of that scene's people and topography. He has turned into verse what he has observed, and that includes poverty; but the image of beggary is curiously neutralized by the inert description of cattle simply *being* in the fields, and that neutralization is taken further in the lines following which imply regret that things have taken a more revolutionary turn since Goldsmith's time. Yeats is projecting onto Goldsmith a conservative resignation in the face of poverty. The seventh sage concludes that these great Irish eighteenth-century figures "walked the roads/ Mimicking what they heard, as children mimic;/ They understood that wisdom comes of beggary."[30] The beggary which Goldsmith observed, however, was not that out of which wisdom, in Yeats' phrase, comes, but the real beggary which haunts *The Deserted Village*—that of the starving Irish peasantry in the famines of 1740 and 1741. The reality of Goldsmith's historical situation, and the anger which infuses his best-known poem, is not acknowledged by Yeats.

All four of Yeats' great eighteenth-century figures are invoked as Anglo-Irish figures particularly attuned to the rhythms of Irish life, high and low, political and cultural. They form a cultured, and potentially cultivating, phalanx against the empowered mob. The Ireland which Goldsmith had seen was rural and virtuous, largely because it was hierarchical. There were beggars, yes, but the social fabric was such that beggars were, in theory, protected. This was the benevolent social system which prevailed before the struggles of the later eighteenth and nineteenth centuries drove a factional, and fractious, wedge between the social classes. If Yeats and his image of Goldsmith are to be believed, this would mean that Goldsmith did, in his own time, see Ireland as a peaceful place, untroubled by political strife or poverty. However, there is much in Goldsmith, as in Burke, that Yeats' images must leave out in order that those images might cohere. Yeats' image of Goldsmith is complicated by a more precise intellectual and political historicization of the latter's career.

It is complicated too by a historically informed interpretation of "The Seven Sages." Goldsmith was included in Yeats' tradition because he suited a more harmonious, utopian vision of the Irish nation, and Anglican nationalism, a vision which could be deployed against what the later poet saw as the misshapen body politic of the new Irish state as it was beginning to emerge in the 1920s and 1930s. The new state, to Yeats' alarmed view, was Catholic in nature and materialistic, increasingly characterized by a prehensile, instrumental cast of mind—by an even duller shade of whiggery, in short, two centuries on. The invocation of Goldsmith against this emerging political reality was more problematic than Yeats could have known. Goldsmith, like Burke, was of Catholic stock himself.

Whenever Goldsmith is related to Ireland, as in Yeats' poem, his own output seems in itself less important than the manner in which it compliments our appreciation of his eighteenth-century Irish peers. Goldsmith's Irish reputation has waned as Swift's and Burke's have waxed. Not as incisive as one, or rhetorically as resonant as the other, he is not deemed quite as Irish as either. But Goldsmith has much in common with Swift; their political convergences have merely been obscured by the stylistic differences that exist between them. Swift was a severe and incisive satirist; Goldsmith, a gentler ironist. However, their basic convictions, especially in the area of social justice, were the same. To compare Swift with Goldsmith is in certain formal and historical senses not to compare like with like. Properly periodized, however, there is revealed a critical and thematic continuity between Swift and Goldsmith which direct comparisons, stylistic or tonal, cannot fully comprehend. Both authors manipulate imaginative geographies to subversive ends: Swift does so through keen-edged satire; Goldsmith, through less severe forms of geographical satire or through plaintive, poetic appeal.

Goldsmith echoes Swift, but the echo is distorted. Styles and forms had changed by the middle of the eighteenth century. The Tory comic intellect found itself working within a different set of conventions, writing to a middle-class audience less enamored with the robust bawdy and Hobbesian cynicism of the later seventeenth and earlier eighteenth centuries. Goldsmith was alive to the change that had occurred, and he was obliged, as one who wrote for survival, to pay practical heed; thus, there is much in the oeuvre which is both generically knowing, and knowingly generic. Appreciating Goldsmith's irony, and situating it more precisely in a midcentury milieu, Ricardo Quintana suggests that there is more commonality between *The Vicar of Wakefield* and Swift's *Gulliver's Travels* than first meets the modern eye. "It is fair to say," adds Quintana, "that, of the midcentury Georgians, it was Goldsmith who probably understood Swift best."[31] If, as Quintana argues, Georgian irony is not the same as Augustan irony, the critical and satirical registers of Swift and Goldsmith are inevitably different. Nonetheless, their *arguments* are similar, and not just in their two most famous prose fictions. *A Modest Proposal*, with its powerful critique of absenteeism and colonial neglect, can be compared with *The Deserted Village*, in which satire has been replaced with "argument by pathos." Goldsmith could not have written *A Modest Proposal*, acknowledges Quintana, any more than Swift could have composed *The Deserted*

Village; "yet Goldsmith understood Swift and Swift, surely, would have acclaimed as only he knew how to do Goldsmith's appeal for social justice."[32]

In much recent criticism in Irish studies, however, Goldsmith's views on Ireland have been denigrated as irretrievably compromised by his more conventional utterances, whether they be in discourses of national character or in pastoral literary modes. Seamus Deane's introduction to Goldsmith's writing in *The Field Day Anthology of Irish Writing* is particularly dismissive. Certainly, there are reasons to be suspicious of Goldsmith's professional writings on issues of national character and imperial politics. Deane writes that Goldsmith was aware "that the contrast between England and Ireland was one of the most painful examples of the discrepancy between rich and poor which modern Europe had to offer." Goldsmith, for Deane, was inclined to see the inequality of the two countries "as deriving from the different national characteristics of the two races, never for a moment envisaging them as conceivably distinct political entities." Taken in isolation, certain journalistic essays give this impression; however, Goldsmith's views of national characteristics are, when the body of work is taken as a whole, I argue, more complex and conflicted than this view allows. The oeuvre moves intriguingly between derivative climatic and political explanations of national character and critical commentaries thereon; added to this, many of his *prose* writings on national characteristics were submitted as anonymous hackwork, pieced together for British magazines and audiences. Thus, the first half of this book delineates, separates and analyses the various registers of Goldsmith's writings on race and nation with a view to problematizing any ready continuity between his more derivative utterances on issues of national character and his perceived quiescence on iniquities in Ireland's relationship with England. Indeed, the second half of this book demonstrates that Goldsmith did conceive of a stark difference between English and Irish political dispensations, a difference reflected in the degraded physical and political landscapes of his major works.

Rather than situating Goldsmith in a tradition of banal Anglocentric sentimentalism, therefore, I argue that he be viewed as a late Jacobite ironist writing for bread in the midst of a Grub Street environment where his oppositional politics are often obscured by professional requirements. Thus resituated, the occasional obsequiousness of his prose writings can be thought anew as merely one part of an historical complex. Deane argues that Goldsmith saw England as "especially fortunate in its historical fate and [. . .] therefore in many ways an exemplary country." This first part of this characterization is very true; the second, I argue here, is problematic. Goldsmith's benign journalistic take on England's good fortune is perpetually inflected by his persistent critique of England's not leaving well enough alone, of taking its good fortune for granted and going beyond a sustainable self-sufficiency into the new imperialist trade, for which "luxury," the quintessential neo-classical watchword, was the abiding euphemism. Deane writes, moreover, that "Goldsmith was anxious to support the idea that the form of liberty gained in England in 1688 was a commodity that had been exported to Ireland."[33] Contrary to this, I argue that Goldsmith distrusted both the legacy of 1688 and the ideology of liberty. This distrust is most evident in *The Traveller; or, a Prospect of Society* (1764) and *The Deserted Village* (1770).

Carole Fabricant has argued, in ways which rhyme with Deane's suspicion of Goldsmith, that those poems are undone by the poet's nostalgia and his seemingly liberal tendency to sentimentalize the plight of the poor. Such dismissals of Goldsmith are here reassessed and reversed in his favor. His complaints are not so much blunted by his pastoralism; rather, his pastoralism is deliberately undone by his complaints: he works within certain generic expectations in order to subvert them. Following on the observations of John Barrell, Goldsmith might best be thought of less as complicitly pastoral, but as radically pastoral, or pastoral in a genuinely critical sense. For Barrell, *The Deserted Village* "seems to offer a pastoral vision that has been radicalised, and so may easily answer the charge often levelled against it—and based on the assumption that the more actualised an image is, the more humane it will be—that Goldsmith's nostalgia is for a conventional literary ideal, and not for a rural community which could, at any time, have existed."[34]

Though this work disagrees with Deane and Fabricant on the particular case of Goldsmith, their politicized criticism, their insights on Swift, Burke, and the plight of eighteenth-century Ireland exert an indelible influence over its method and emphases. I wish to extend rather than to deny certain of those insights to Goldsmith; thus, what is questioned here is the implied comparative scheme which sets Goldsmith up as the sentimental foil to Swift's more severe genius, or to Burke's more ornate, sustained critiques of colonial abuse. In fact, Goldsmith should be relocated, alongside Swift and Burke, as a sometimes compromised, but often insightful commentator on Irish and imperial affairs—there is, I would suggest, as much Swift in Goldsmith as there is Goldsmith in Burke. With this reassessment allowed, the Irish provenance of Goldsmith's poetics and politics comes more clearly into view. Just as Carole Fabricant has remarked that "we cannot speak intelligently about Swift's landscape whether physical, aesthetic, mental, or ideological, without speaking of a specifically *Irish* landscape," so too must the Irish landscape be understood as the landscape which produced

INTRODUCTION

Goldsmith.[35] As an Irish outsider writing in London, however, his exilic sensibilities are, in some key senses, Swift's in reverse. The quandary of displacement provided both authors, and Burke, with the comparative framework within which they could pointedly question whether the liberties produced in 1688 were extended across the Irish Sea.[36]

John Lucas, sympathetic to Goldsmith's professional and exilic positioning, cautiously shores up this sense of continuity between Swift and Goldsmith, and questions the critical consensus on Goldsmith in Irish studies:

> Goldsmith has been misread by commentators. Irish critics more or less dismiss him as a Tom Moore before his time, a time-server who was content to supply sweet songs for his English paymasters. English critics tend to confirm this. They happily endorse Thackeray's praise of him as the "most beloved of English writers." Beneath such praise one detects a sigh of relief. Goldsmith is not going to disturb English complacencies in the manner of Swift. Nor does he. But he is a good deal more cunning, and cunningly subversive, than has been habitually recognised. This is not to deny that he can go through the routine drill of "disinterested" commentator, speaking to and from a set of culturally orthodox values. But he also, crucially, deflates the idea of a responsible commonwealth as being dependent on the monarchy. And he understands, better than Gray and Collins did, the cant of "liberty." In Goldsmith's best work liberty is a contested term rather than an agreed one.[37]

As Lucas suggests, Goldsmith does not disturb English complacencies in the *manner* of Swift; but he does disturb them in less obvious ways. On the face of it, he seems to participate placidly in the literary traditions—the pastoral, prospect, and travel poem—such as overlay ideologies of cultural superiority, of liberty, and of the new imperialism. Within those traditions, however, he inserts cutting analyses. In *The Traveller*, to take a signal instance, he stands aside from the conventional prospect poem to assess the fraught interconnectedness of liberty and empire:

> When I behold a factious band agree
> To call it freedom, when themselves are free;
> Each wanton judge new penal statutes draw,
> Laws grind the poor, and rich men rule the law;
> The wealth of climes, where savage nations roam,
> Pillaged from slaves to purchase slaves at home;
> Fear, pity, justice, indignation start,

> Tear off reserve, and bear my swelling heart;
> 'Till half a patriot, half a coward grown,
> I fly from petty tyrants to the throne. (W4: 265–6)

In this passage, Goldsmith's anti-imperialism explains his monarchism (and his Jacobitism) and vice-versa. The traveler views askance the upper-class Whig culture of chauvinism; this position allows him to behold the absurd factiousness of party which has, in his view, taken hold in England since the Glorious Revolution. The "factious band" agrees, irrespective of other differences, on one thing: the arrogation of freedom unto its own class, while remaining willfully ignorant of the un-freedom of others, at home in the lower orders, or abroad, among the colonized. Freedom for the factious benefits only the oligarchical few. As such that destructive freedom is, in the new political dispensation, guaranteed by the legal culture over which the oligarchs themselves preside. Commercial modernity is here characterized as a global and globalizing phenomenon enslaving the domestic working classes as well as those peoples outside of Britain caught up in inequitable systems of trade. Goldsmith argued that "liberty" was historically the preserve of one group; as such, it was inherently paradoxical and socially destructive. The ethical self-dramatization of the indignant "swelling heart" is offset by the poet's ironic admission of cowardice. This cowardice is no more that the emergence of a dissident bent in Goldsmith which is inclined to seek refuge in the institution of monarchy; thus, he inclines away from Whiggish patriotism toward its subversive Jacobite Irish counterpart. Like Swift, Goldsmith was temperamentally averse to forms of innovation—political and intellectual—which were, at best, nominal. He viewed the increasingly complicated political forms introduced since the Glorious Revolution as obscurantisms which had been particularly detrimental to Ireland.

Goldsmith's problem with the concept of British liberty was similar to Swift's, and indeed Burke's, and it was related to oligarchical and colonial dynamics: "When British liberty went abroad," writes Deane, "even that short distance across the Irish Sea, it remained the exclusive preserve of the colonists."[38] Liberty for one group, therefore, was especially problematic whenever it was geographically transplanted; what was to be commended in one jurisdiction could be denied in others, *to* others. Garishly flaunted in the colonial encounter, "liberty" could be construed by those to whom political rights were denied as a hollow concept. For Goldsmith, British liberty preserved, and was the preserve of, a partial opulence which demonstrated the interconnectedness of increased trade and increased poverty. Hence, his poetic geographies convey his abiding suspicion that "liberty" did little more than bolster chauvinism while exacerbating social problems.

INTRODUCTION

The insinuation that Goldsmith was a Jacobite is not new; the implications of such politics in his writings, however, have never quite been assessed or debated in the way that they have been in the writings of others. The attribution of pro-Stuart sympathies to key influences on Goldsmith—Jonathan Swift and Samuel Johnson—has been the controversial pursuit of scholars in the field over the last two decades; in the case of both "outed" authors, the imputation has been very vigorously questioned. For Ian Higgins' interpretive disclosure of Swift's Jacobite tendencies, there is the counterargument of J. A. Downie.[39] Samuel Johnson's Jacobitism, to take another contentious example, was indeed emotional rather than instrumental—a euphemism for a broader Toryism. Johnson did, after all, accept a pension from George III.[40] Goldsmith too had some regard for the more robust monarchy of George III; and as the '45 receded from real politics, his Jacobitism, never blindly wedded to the notion of the Stuarts' divine right to govern, turned to an advocacy for the return of strong, central government as a potential bulwark against commercial opportunism. Indeed, the proposition that Goldsmith was a Jacobite may seem to be too baldly or impressionistically made; however, closer inspection of his background, and indeed key moments in his biography, makes his Jacobitism difficult to refute or ignore.

While the Goldsmiths' family history in Ireland is patchy at best—largely due to misleading information provided by Goldsmith himself—those pieces which can be assembled provide an insight into his politics. At the Duke of Northumberland's house, on 28 April 1773, Goldsmith met with Thomas Percy in order to convey to him details of his life which were to be collected for a biography. Goldsmith dictated to Percy that he was descended from a Spaniard named Romeiro or Romero, who had come to England during the reign of Philip and Mary, and that a marriage to a Miss Goldsmith had altered the family name. In his more recent family history, Goldsmith related that his father was a native of Durham who had moved to Ireland to study at Trinity College, Dublin, before gaining a small living in England, and then returning to Ireland to become the rector of Kilkenny West.

Percy found much of this information dubious; Goldsmith had a tendency to lie about himself, and about his family. And so Percy looked to Goldsmith's brother Maurice for verification; Maurice, unfortunately, was not much more reliable. Juan Romero, maintained Maurice, was Oliver's great-grandfather: he had come to Ireland, not England, in the seventeenth century, as a private tutor to a touring Spanish nobleman. To compound the genealogical confusion, Maurice

INTRODUCTION

also described their father as a native of the diocese of Elphin, from Ballyoughter in County Roscommon, and not of Durham, as his brother had claimed.

The first obscure ancestor located by early Goldsmith biographer James Prior is one John Goldsmith, searcher in the Port of Galway in 1541. A more clearly drawn ancestor is an early seventeenth-century John Goldsmith, who was Vicar of Burrishoole in Mayo: Oliver's great-great-grandfather. In the Mayo book of survey and distribution commissioned by Thomas Wentworth, Earl of Strafford, John Goldsmith is noted in 1641 as an owner of twenty acres of profitable land. In that year, he was examined on oath by the commissioners assigned to measure the damage done to Protestants during the rebellion of that year. John reports a warning conveyed to him before 1641 by his brother Francis, a Catholic priest in Antwerp, that he should take his family out of Ireland. John, it seems, was himself formerly a Catholic priest, and as a convert would have been most despised by the rebelling Catholics. He reports that at one point he was deserted by his servants, threatened and robbed by rebels, but eventually fled to the house of Viscount Mayo. "Nearly all the verifiable information that exists in written form about Goldsmith's first clearly identifiable ancestor can be found in his 1643 Deposition," writes Patrick Murray; but "Where the written word stops, oral tradition and folklore take over."[41] The oral tradition and local lore in question is that recorded by John O'Donovan in Roscommon for the Ordnance Survey in 1837:

> There is a tradition here that the Goldsmiths are descended from a foreign friar who came to Ireland about a couple of centuries ago, and who, seeing every inducement to embrace the religion of the State, broke his vows of chastity, poverty, etc., and became Minister Legens. And hence the family were called by the Old Irish in their own language Sliocht Mhagarlaidhe an tSean Bhráthar, which I avoid translating for the sake of decency. This may or may not be true, but it is worthy of remark that the family are remarkable for their lasciviousness and that almost all the Goldsmiths now living here are illegitimate.[42]

O'Donovan himself believed that the friar was the Vicar of Burrishoole, who was, as the Deposition shows, once a Catholic. On his travels as inspector of schools in Mayo and Westmeath, Seamus Fenton gleaned from local lore that, in changing his religion, John Goldsmith may also have changed his name. Fr Sean MacGabhann, once Dominican friar of the Abbey of Burrishoole, converted to Protestantism in the Elizabethan wars, during which the abbey was attacked several times. Local Catholics called the family the Smiths. To quote Thomas Moran, one of Fenton's local sources who had heard his grandparents in West Mayo talk about the infamous unfrocked friar: "Och sure, they were not Goldsmiths at all; they were all descended from the jumper MacGuvane."[43] The Irish for Smith is MacGowan; the "Gold"-prefix was, perhaps, a matter of "gilding the lily" to camouflage the fact of conversion. Pragmatic "jumping" from Catholicism to Protestantism in the seventeenth and eighteenth centuries has, according to L. M. Cullen, been obscured by "the reckless modern use of the term Anglo-Irish."[44] Goldsmith's Ireland is rather different to that of the so-called Anglo-Irish gentry: his is, as W. J. McCormack phrases it, a "colonial Ireland as experienced by lower Protestant clergy descended from persecuted Catholic priests."[45] McCormack argues that Goldsmith's Catholic ancestry greatly complicates his status in Yeats' "Anglo-Irish" pantheon.

Having begun his biography, wrongly, by asserting that Goldsmith was "one of the most pleasing English writers of the eighteenth century," of a "Protestant and Saxon family" living in Ireland who had been "in troubled times, harassed and put in fear by the native population," Thomas Babington Macaulay enters an intriguing qualification, that Goldsmith, "though by birth one of the Englishry," and an Anglican to boot, "never showed the least sign of that contemptuous antipathy with which, in his days, the ruling minority in Ireland too generally regarded the subject majority." More than that, Goldsmith disavowed the Glorious Revolution, and "even when George the Third was on the throne, maintained that nothing but the restoration of the banished dynasty could save the country."[46] With similar certainty, Seamus Fenton wrote that Goldsmith hated subserviency; thus, "in politics he was an outspoken Jacobite, a dangerous political creed in those days."[47] No other biography of Goldsmith since Macaulay's has been so brazen in declaring Goldsmith a Jacobite; and few have been so brisk in supposing Goldsmith's interaction with the Catholic majority to have been more substantial than many Irish Anglicans at the time. The basis of Macaulay's assertions is unclear; he was, however, writing in 1856, when vivid accounts of Goldsmith's political character would still have circulated. But the political substance of the claim is verified in Boswell's *Life of Johnson*, where on April 15, 1773, the following remarks are recorded:

> GOLDSMITH. "Yes; all our *happy* revolutions. They have hurt our constitution, and will hurt it, till we mend it by another HAPPY REVOLUTION."—I never before discovered that my friend Goldsmith had so much of the old prejudice in him.

And on April 30, 1773, Johnson reported to Boswell:

> JOHNSON. "I remember once being with Goldsmith in Westminster-abbey. While we surveyed the Poets' Corner, I said to him,
> "*Forsitan et nostrum nomen miscebitur istis.*"
>
> When we got to Temple-bar he stopped me, pointed to the heads upon it, and slily whispered me,
> "*Forsitan et nostrum nomen miscebitur* ISTIS."

The Latin phrase translates as "perhaps even our name will be mixed with those." The heads in Temple-bar were those of Jacobite rebels executed in 1746, left there until 1772 to warn grimly of the consequences of sedition. Boswell's footnote remarks that the whispered phrase refers to the "supposed political principles" of Johnson and Goldsmith.[48]

In an Irish context, Goldsmith's was a Jacobitism of a rural, lower-class, high-church strand described by Eamonn O'Ciardha.[49] The Goldsmith family's Protestantism was less than a century old; and theirs was an Anglicanism not supercilious to, or separate from, the Jacobite, Gaelic, or Catholic culture which surrounded them in the Irish midlands. Goldsmith would, in 1760, pen for the *British Magazine* a journalistic account of Turlough O'Carolan (1670–1738), the blind harpist and composer who would come to embody the bardic ingenuity of the Gaelic Irish. His beloved uncle Thomas Contarine was friendly with Charles O'Conor, the historian of Gaelic Ireland, at whose house a very young Goldsmith may have met the harper. Contarine's relationship with O'Conor was convivial:

> But insulted nature resumes her own rights and Mr. OConor was too well acquainted with some of the Protestant nobility of this kingdom not to foresee that they would do signal services as soon as an opportunity presented itself for the exertion of their bright talents, manly patriotism and christian benevolence; happening one day to dine with Mr. Contarine,, "Mr. OConor," said the Parson, "I am glad to see that you like my beef—I hope it is <u>orthodox</u>." "Sir," said the other "every thing that is Irish is orthodox" = The reply was so unstudied and so much to the good Parson's taste that filling out a bumper, well then said he OConor here is "Everything that is Irish is orthodox. The two gentlemen then unbosomed themselves, the Magic influence of good cheer brightened up new horizons for futurity, fancy revelled in new combinations, the <u>Saturnian</u> reign with all its golden harvest and innocent pleasures was anticipated,

> the hearts of the two neighbours were expanded by a consciousness that tho' they differed in Religious opinions they differed not thro' worldly but thro' honest motives, and this rendered their convivial happiness more exquisite, it was a feast with fellowship that gave free course to the genial current of the soul.[50]

David Dickson has characterized a similar milieu in Munster as an ecumenical Jacobite "cultural ambience" in which rural Anglicans, particularly the clergy, would have patronized the "old" culture, "where harping was appreciated amid the Rabelasian feasting."[51]

There are also instances in which Goldsmith's journalism demonstrates a clear familiarity with Irish Jacobite culture. The authorial persona of "A Description of the Manners and Customs of the Native Irish. In a Letter from an English Gentleman," published in the *Weekly Magazine* in December 1759, is that of a mildly pompous English gentleman who has ventured out from Dublin and into the Irish "interior," where he meets in a hovel a poor Irish family. Goldsmith ventriloquizes the disaffection of Jacobite Ireland through the voice of the patriarch:

> Lord my dear Soul, says my landlord. Taking Quebec, burning the French fleet, ruining what d'ye call him, Tierconneldrago, what signifies all that, where is the wonder there [. . .] between ourselves my dear soul, I hate the double hearted French, for they have always deceived the Irish, but for all that my dear I love king James in my heart, and God knows I have a good right for my father lost a very good estate by him. (W3: 28)

The family, the weary father, and the ragged poverty in which they live are objects of sympathy. The patriarch is indifferent to celebrations of imperial success in the Seven Years' War. He is only vaguely aware of the Battle of Ticonderoga, a turning point in the Year of Victories (1759), confusing the name with that of an Irish county and the title of James II's Irish viceroy. His indifference is telling; what seems like an Irish bull is really a pointed confusion of, and connection between, colonial predicaments in Ireland and America. Aside from his indifference toward both of the protagonists across the Atlantic, all that this "native" Irishman knows for sure is that the situation has worsened for his family, as it has for his nation, since the Glorious Revolution. The tactic of impersonation allows the *Weekly Magazine* reader to trust the author-as-traveler; the Jacobite views of the lowly patriarch are not necessarily those of the *Magazine*, or of the essay's author.

This screen of persona is linked to a broader difficulty in locating Goldsmith. Throughout his work, and in the different genres and registers of professional, narrative, satirical and historical writing, Goldsmith necessarily deploys several authorial tones. This diversity of voice gives rise to the problem that, while his poetry can express clearly his political disaffection, his professional, historical writings betray, with good historical cause, little enough in the way of explicitly pro-Irish or indeed Jacobite sentiment. In his histories, his native country is often represented, as it was by many British and French observers in the period, as a benighted and quasi-barbaric place. And Goldsmith seems, on the face of it, to have had no pronounced love for the exiled house of Stuart. In his *History of England, from the Earliest Times to the Death of George II* (1771), James II is described in unfavorable terms. The description of William III is initially and predictably positive, though this positivity is more problematic than first appears. The people of England were, it is claimed, initially unanimous in favor of the Williamite settlement, even in spite of party-political affiliation: the Whigs despised James II on the point of liberty; the Tories on Protestant principle. James had encroached on both ideals, and his efforts at Derry and the Boyne are thus characterized as onslaughts against beleaguered Irish Protestants. In spite of all that, Goldsmith's description of James in decline is moving. As his power dissipated, James' affability allegedly increased; and he died, commendably, "with great marks of devotion" (HE4: 75).

William's ambitions abroad, meanwhile, led to neglect at home. His preoccupation with "the schemes of contending kings and nations" in Europe led to his neglect of domestic policy, creating a vacuum filled in turn by factional clamor. "Patriotism began to be ridiculed as an ideal virtue," and the "vulgar" took notions above their stations. "Decency" waned, talents were squandered; "and the ignorant and profligate were received into favour" (HE4: 77). The initially Whiggish account of his accession gets shorter shrift as William increasingly takes liberties with England's liberty. Goldsmith blankly praises William's general achievement; in most domestic and social respects, however, his reign is represented as a disaster.

Queen Anne, by comparison, "governed with glory, and left her people happy" (HE4: 91). During her reign, the people began to change. They came to favor "strict hereditary succession, divine right, and non-resistance to regal power" (HE4: 122). The Whigs had facilitated a glorious reign for Queen Anne, and that same glory had turned the people Tory. The Tories "pretended"—Goldsmith's cool detachment from his own opinion is characteristic of the *History*—"that while England was exhausting her strength in foreign conquests for the benefit of other nations, she was losing her liberty at home." As if to confirm the author's neutrality, it is added that "A part of these complaints was true, and a part exaggerated"

INTRODUCTION

(HE4: 155–6). War, at any rate, was more suited to the Whig than the Tory temperament: the latter were "submissive, temperate, and weak," and their weakness led them to "more willingly cultivate the arts of peace" (HE4: 168), and to be happy with mere prosperity. Though managing a delicate bipartisanship in the history, it is clear from his major poems which temperament Goldsmith favored.

As with William III, George I's neglect facilitated oppression at home: "The Whigs governed the senate and the court; whom they would, they oppressed; bound the lower orders of people with severe laws, and kept them at a distance by vile distinctions; and then taught them to call this—Liberty" (HE4: 197). The primary method in the oppression of the people was the attribution of Jacobitism to the disaffected, a governmental "artifice" (HE4: 202) deployed throughout the reigns of George I and II. Robert Walpole's 1738 remarks to convince doubters of the need to retain a strong army stress this concern:

> No man of common prudence will profess himself openly a Jacobite; by so doing he not only may injure his private fortune, but he must render himself less able to do any effectual service to the cause he has embraced; therefore, there are but few such men in the kingdon. Your right Jacobite, Sir, disguises his true sentiments, he roars out for revolution principles; he pretends to be a great friend to liberty, and a great admirer of our ancient constitution, and under this pretence there are numbers who every day endeavour to show discontents among the people, by persuading them that the constitution is in danger and that they are unnecessarily loaded with many and heavy taxes [. . .] these are the men we have most reason to be afraid of: they are, I am afraid, more numerous than most gentlemen imagine.[52]

The people were, writes Goldsmith in his *History*, "awed by fears of imputed Jacobitism, were afraid to murmur, and were content to give up their freedom for safety"—which is not to say that Goldsmith reckoned all to be innocent of this association. Tories, he concedes, even Protestant Tories, became Jacobite plotters, and the Scottish example took them into action. At the end of the rebellion of 1715, he writes, "we generally find little to applaud on either side" (HE4: 229, 228).

In his account of the years between 1715 and 1745, Goldsmith negotiates a treacherous, ostensibly neutral path through contentious recent history. He concedes in relation to such navigations in "the present reign," that it is "very difficult to steer between the partialities of mankind. To praise some, will be considered as a tacit reproach upon others; to cease entirely from censure, will be construed into paltry adulation." Goldsmith's neutrality leads him to condemn Whigs for oppressiveness; Jacobites, for delusion. But his antipathy is transparently, to borrow Linda Colley's title, defiant of oligarchy—in both Britain and Ireland. For all that, his privately expressed view of the *History* itself seems to disown the politics of the work, or at least to be baffled by its reception:

> I have published or Davis has published for me an Abridgment of the History of England for which I have been a good deal abused in the newspapers for betraying the liberties of the people. God knows I had no thoughts for or against liberty in my head. My whole aim being to make up a book of a decent size that [. . .] would do no harm to nobody. However they set me down as an arrant Tory and consequently no honest man. When you come to look at any part of it you'l say that I am a soure Whig. (L: 105–6)

Goldsmith is being disingenuous here, for whatever about the borrowed Whiggery that informs much of the history, its overture is all but unequivocally Tory. Added to his complaints about "Liberty," he glosses his use of David Hume as a source with a prefatory disclaimer upon Hume's political philosophy:

> In his opinions respecting government, perhaps, also, he may be sometimes reprehensible; but in a country like ours, where mutual contention contributes to the security of the constitution, it will be impossible for an historian, who attempts to have any opinion, to satisfy all parties. It is not yet decided in politics, whether the diminution of kingly power in England tends to encrease the happiness, or the freedom of the people. For my own part, from seeing the bad effects of the tyranny of the great in those republican states that pretend to be free, I cannot help wishing that our monarchs may still be allowed to enjoy the power of controlling the encroachments of the great at home. A king may easily be restrained from doing wrong, as he is but one man; but if a number of the great are permitted to divide all authority, who can punish them if they abuse it? Upon this principle, therefore, and not from any notion of divine or hereditary right, some may think I have leaned towards monarchy. (HE1: vii–viii)

Goldsmith's point about monarchy is an iteration of his abiding political thesis: that monarchy is better than republican oligarchy because as an institution it is singularly answerable.

Such explicit expressions of the author's own opinion, however, are few enough and far between in his professional writing; more often than not, the

INTRODUCTION

histories simply reproduce the political and/or prejudicial stances of the authors from whom they derive. Therefore, the hack histories cannot always be taken at face value, or read as though they consistently reflected Goldsmith's own political views, though such readings are sometimes attempted. Graham Gargett, for instance, argues that Goldsmith's reproduction of Hume's anti-Irish sentiment in his *History of England* "indicates that any nationalist, Catholic, genes in his character were singularly inactive."[53] Samuel Johnson's view, however, is more to the point. Thinking him an excellent compiler, he found the idea of Goldsmith doing the type of reading which could empirically nuance his recapitulation of Hume faintly absurd. He remarked in 1778 that Goldsmith was "at no pains to fill his mind with knowledge. He transplanted it from one place to another; and it did not settle in his mind; so he could not tell what was in his own books."[54] Though he took from the histories of others the examples which he needed to make certain points, he actually knew very little, historically speaking, and did no primary research of his own. This fact was acknowledged by his contemporaries. In his biography of Goldsmith, Thomas Percy writes that the *History of England*, "though elegantly written, and highly calculated to attract and interest young readers, enters into no critical discussion of disputed points, and is often superficial and inaccurate."[55] It is potboiler history, meant for the general entertainment and education of a target (primarily English) audience. A drudge in the production of information and amusement, Goldsmith's historical abilities resided in synthesizing and writing in an accessible style—for this reason, his histories were often used as school texts throughout the later eighteenth century. Jane Austen, who as a schoolgirl was a committed if very belated Jacobite, annotated her edition of Goldsmith's *History of England* in alternating tones of pointed agreement and hurt indignation, according to the vacillating politics of its compiler's editorial commentary.[56] The difficulty with Goldsmith, for Austen as for the modern reader, lies in separating the derivative hackwork and the "transplanted" facts from the discernibly Goldsmithian.

To understand large tracts of Goldsmith's output, therefore, is to understand the milieu to which he wrote. And to understand that milieu it is also useful to understand the category of popular writing as it might have been understood in the eighteenth century's exploding print culture industry, in which magazines and miscellanies proliferated and competed. In this scene, those organs of general interest and edification which survived were those which best appealed to the audience's (sometimes narcissistic) sense of itself. Popular culture "survives by flattering its audience," as Robert Bataille writes in his study of Goldsmith's fellow Irishman and Grub-street worker Hugh Kelly. For Bataille, the term "popular culture" serves as a broad category of writerly activity, one which includes journalism and popular history. Its defining characteristic is that it is "user centered. It cannot be successful employing the creator-centered bias of high art but must serve the needs and purposes of its audiences."[57] The required use-value of Goldsmith's historical and geographical texts, therefore, and their intended status as popular and readable histories, necessarily renders their author's politics unclear. Goldsmith did not have the expertise or the breadth of reference to emplot his histories in such a way as to consolidate his political argument. To locate a political stance in the histories, therefore, the reader must isolate those (infrequent) editorial digressions which rhyme with the repeatedly expressed political sentiments of the other works.

In this context, and amid the distortions of professional prose-work, the two major poems—*The Traveller* and *The Deserted Village*—are the key to Goldsmith's politics. They are the works which are consistent with each other and explore best his abiding concerns with social and political decline. "Biographically," writes Roger Lonsdale, these works, "both written with painstaking care and with no immediate motive, almost certainly represent what he himself considered the only true manifestations of his literary integrity and talent."[58] Both poems, one a poetic exercise in comparative cultural geography within Europe, the other a survey of ruined and ruinous landscapes in Ireland and America, yoke together Goldsmith's own political perspective and his extensive, though hurriedly absorbed, readings in contemporary geographical thought. Goldsmith's absorption of geographical sources, literary and scientific, informed his poetry and satire; his poetry and satire, however, could just as often contradict and critique the facetiousness of his geographical sources. This dialectic, by turns playful and politically serious, is at the heart of Goldsmith's writerly enigma.

All roads in these chapters lead, in one way or another, to *The Deserted Village*, and to the tragic ironies of commerce and empire which this poem describes. There is, as Roger Lonsdale suggests, a hierarchy of forms in Goldsmith's writing; and the long poem encapsulates Goldsmith's political argument best. His prose writings—his popular science, his journalism, *The Citizen of the World* and *The Vicar of Wakefield*—are thus studied here in relation to *The Traveller* and *The Deserted Village*. The prose writings clarify the politics of the poems, both by contrast *and* continuity. The plays, intriguing entertainments both, are touched upon intermittently: their commentaries on contemporary discourses of sentiment, benevolence, and cosmetic culture cast useful sidelights on Goldsmith's milieu and his politics, and the genres and fashions across which he operated.

INTRODUCTION

The structure of this study, therefore, is neither chronological nor strictly generic. Both approaches have been quite thoroughly taken.[59] Rather, this work takes the form of four thematic essays. Its division and trajectory reflect a movement from the general to the particular. The first two chapters deal with Goldsmith's surveys of humankind, in global and in European spheres, and address contemporary enlightenment theories of climatic influence, national character and race. In the first chapter, natural history and climatic extrapolations of national character are addressed. Scientific, or pseudo-scientific, notions of racial difference are then measured against Goldsmith's fraught cosmopolitanism and his sense of universal adaptability in human nature. Developing the comparative framework across genres traditionally understood as more "literary," chapter 2 studies Goldsmith's jaundiced take on the Whig politics and prejudices engendered in travel, and in travel writing. His repeated disavowals of "liberty" are traced through *The Traveller* and *The Vicar of Wakefield*—with the latter studied in terms of its political digressions and its commentary on travel.

The second part of this book deals in political landscapes, and in so doing addresses Irish themes and concerns more directly and substantively. Shifting the focus from the wandering, observing exile of *The Traveller* to Lien Chi Altangi, the Chinese philosopher residing in London through whom Goldsmith ventroliquizes *The Citizen of the World*, the third chapter examines Goldsmith's parody of an emerging orientalism and his deployment of oriental garden allegory to Jacobite ends. His impersonation of a Chinese philosopher is the occasion of an ironic commentary on modernity in London, one which encompasses an incisive critique of imperial commerce, consumer faddishness, and Anglo-centrism. This chapter narrows to a study of landscape design in later eighteenth-century London, and the political contest between oriental and "native" English modes, in the midst of which Goldsmith, through allegory, reveals his political allegiance. This allegiance explains the imagery of a key verse paragraph of *The Deserted Village*, imagery which allegorizes the forlorn Irish body politic by representing the land as woman. His immersion in debates about land and landscape anticipates the concerns of the fourth and final chapter, which places that poem in new interpretive frameworks. The final chapter's reassessment of *The Deserted Village* accumulates the previous chapters' studies in climate, travel, and landscape, and adds to these dimensions a historicizing, in Irish and Atlantic contexts, of Goldsmith's most explicitly anti-imperialist poem. Emigration and the long absentee debate in Ireland are the real contexts for Goldsmith's famous critique of luxury and a liberty ruinously understood only in commercial terms.

Part I

COMPARATIVE VIEWS OF RACES AND NATIONS

1

THE CULTURAL CLIMATE: NATURAL HISTORIES OF NATIONAL CHARACTER

> To begin with Ireland, the most western part of the continent, the natives are particularly remarkable for the gaiety and levity of their dispositions: the English, transplanted there, in time lose their melancholy serious air, and become gay and thoughtless, more fond of pleasure, and less addicted to reasoning. The difference of disposition cannot properly be said to arise from climate or soil, which is in general the same as in England; but merely from the nature of their government. They live in a fruitful country, sequestered from the rest of mankind, protected by a powerful nation from foreign insult; and regardless of neighbouring greatness, they have no important national concerns to make them anxious, or cloud their tempers with the solemnity of pride. In such circumstances they are contented with indolence and pleasure, take every happiness as it presents, are easily excited to resent, and as easily induced to submission.
>
> —"A Comparative View of Races and Nations" (W3: 84).[1]

EVER THE MAINSTAYS of casual conversation, weather and government represented two contending schools of thought on one of the enlightenment's crucial puzzles. Precisely what were the strongest causal factors in the forging of national characteristics? In France, Montesquieu's *L'Esprit de Loix* (1748, translated into English two years later as *The Spirit of Laws*) and the *Histoire Naturelle* (1749) of Georges-Louis LeClerc, Comte de Buffon, both deriving their opinions from the "hard" evidence of natural-historical observation, argued that climate was the source of national character. Key thinkers in

CHAPTER 1

the Scottish enlightenment, meanwhile, and most noticeably David Hume, proposed the mode of government. Both explanations were given credence in Goldsmith's professional writing; in his natural history, climatic influence was foregrounded; in his anonymous political journalism, a greater emphasis was placed on political culture. Climate as a cause was scientific and absolute; political cultures were relative. Goldsmith's discourses of national character borrowed from climatology *and* political theory: for him, the matter was not necessarily a zero-sum conundrum. The emphases of Goldsmith's writing on such subjects vacillated, in a characteristic enlightenment exchange, between the universal and the local; in his "Comparative View," accordingly, Ireland's national character was explained by government and politics. Climatic conditions in Ireland and England were equal; thus, the differences between the countries were not environmentally determined. Nor were they attributed to any metaphysical or mysterious first cause. Rather, the English watched over the Irish so that they had become passive and pliable; English rule in Ireland provided a protective regime under which the Irish had become modest, content, and good-natured. Goldsmith's essay, therefore, exonerates English governance as benignly paternalistic, and portrays the Irish nation as characteristically yielding.

These explanations read like wishful thinking, proffered as they are at the beginning of a decade which sees an upsurge in violent agitation in Ireland against an iniquitous land ownership regime. The "Comparative View," however, must be understood as an anonymous and paid piece of journalism geared toward a metropolitan English audience, an audience which, in the political climate of the Seven Years' War, and particularly after 1759's "Year of Victories" against the French, might in the Whig mainstream be given to bouts of cultural and political self-congratulation. Published in 1760 by the *Royal Magazine*, this piece was just one instance of Goldsmith's compromised entry into the world of professional writing in the metropolitan center. "In order to rise in his adopted republic of letters," writes Laurence Goldstein, "he had to assume English attitudes, and to some extent—depending on the periodical—he had to praise imperial policies whose effect on Ireland was devastating."[2] In his assessment of the compromises in Goldsmith's writings on national character, Wolfgang Zach, similarly, argues that "under the pressure of 'writing for bread' in England he could not possibly make the political grievances of Ireland against England his own as Swift did," and this explains how he could describe Ireland, in an ostensibly scientific work, as being in some sense under the protection of England. Drawing upon the various theories of Buffon, Hume, Montesquieu and others, Goldsmith attempts to explain national character, but he is unsure of his bases. He reproduces prevalent ideas over the course of his career and across these writings without necessarily knowing how to tally or reconcile them. Nor would he, as an aspiring poet caught among the mess of professional writers producing miscellaneous knowledge in eighteenth-century London, have any grounds for making an original contribution to a discourse still largely wallowing in the pseudo-scientific. Thus, Goldsmith contradicts himself specifically on the causes of the Irish national character.[3] The authorial voice, then, cannot be too readily associated with Goldsmith; rather, it is the voice of the anonymous magazine writer masquerading as polymath. It is Goldsmith cast in the role of the "man of science," doing the "science of man."[4]

Goldsmith's reproduction of classical, renaissance and contemporary enlightenment natural histories of man is the subject of this chapter. As hired prosateur, he composed and compiled much on the subjects of climate and national character, and on differences in manners and systems of governments. Toward a survey of contemporary opinions on such matters, his prose writings are a pretty barometer. Essays such as "A Comparative View of Races and Nations" and "The Effects which Climates have upon Men, and Other Animals" (1760) indicate the extent of the demand for such speculation among the reading public of the day. That demand is reflected in the fact that Goldsmith was to receive his largest payment for any of his works from the bookseller John Nourse for an exhaustive eight-volume work that recapitulated many of the arguments, sources, and evidences of his earlier essays. Published in the last year of the author's life, *An History of the Earth, and Animated Nature* (1774) was the culmination of his exercises in the realm of natural history.

The tone of his natural history, however, does not always sit well with his poetry or his fiction. His incarnation as a professional writer complicates his professed cosmopolitanism, his frequently iterated desire to be a "citizen of the world," in ways that evince conflicting themes, tendencies and tensions in eighteenth-century geographical thought.[5] Goldsmith alternates between celebrating, on the one hand, the cultural potential of allegedly less-developed societies and, on the other, disdaining their endemic and brutish lack of refinement. In his poetry Goldsmith would confound the categorical impulse which is the borrowed tenor of his natural history, reflecting his own suspicions of the chauvinist ends to which natural-historical discourses of race were put. This contrast between scientific and poetic registers is analyzed over the first two chapters here. The purpose of the first chapter, therefore, is to profile the influences on and works of Goldsmith the agile hack scientist. Thus, he is first situated in the intellectual context of contemporary

CHAPTER 1

ideas of climate and culture. His engagements with scientific and natural-historical concepts of race and nationality are then surveyed.

Spirited Nations

According to David Bell, writings on national difference and national character ranged, in the eighteenth century,

> from learned treatises to the crude propaganda of the Seven Years' War. The authors wrote for different purposes and in wildly varying styles. Nonetheless, they generally saw national character determined by three broad factors: climate, political action, and historical evolution. *Moeurs*, manners, and religion, all of which they also frequently invoked, generally depended in their schemes on politics or evolution, while the phrase "moral causes," which appears frequently in their works usually amounted to a conflation of the two.[6]

Goldsmith wrote in the thick of the milieu which Bell describes. In respect of national character, he was immersed in contemporary French, English and Scottish theories. His longer histories, natural and political, though hurriedly composed, could be said to have attained the status of "learned treatises," even though they were, in the main, patched together from the researches of others. His magazine essays on topics of national character, however, necessarily tended toward the propagandistic, and need to be understood as such. Depending upon audience and context, different factors in the designation of national character, as outlined by Bell, might be emphasized. At different times, and depending, it should be said, upon the author to whose research Goldsmith was most indebted for any given piece, causal priority in the designation of national character could be switched from climate to political culture.

The fundamental tenets of eighteenth-century scientific or pseudo-scientific geographical discourse were by no means new; climatic and racial theories had not evolved very far from the classical worldview, the theoretical rudiments of which were bequeathed from Plato, Aristotle, Vitruvius, Vegetius, and, most substantially, Hippocrates and Pliny. Even in the eighteenth century, the basic biological paradigms were almost of a piece with the thesis of Hippocrates' *Airs, Waters' and Places*, composed in the fourth century BC:

> Asia differs very much from Europe in the nature of everything that grows there, vegetable or human. Everything grows much bigger and

finer in Asia, and the nature of the land is tamer, while the character of the inhabitants is milder and less passionate. The reason for this is the equable blending of the climate, for it lies in the midst of the sunrise facing the dawn [. . .] The small variations of climate to which the Asiatics are subject, extremes of heat and cold being avoided, account for their mental flabbiness and cowardice as well. They are less warlike and tamer of spirit, for they are not subject to those physical changes and the mental stimulation which sharpen tempers and induce recklessness and hotheadedness. Instead they live under unvarying conditions. Where there are always changes, men's minds are roused so that they cannot stagnate.[7]

For Goldsmith, as for many other eighteenth-century observers, Hippocrates was a still-legitimate intellectual predecessor.[8] The latter's claim that uniformity of climate caused Asiatic feebleness was augmented in Goldsmith's writing with the notion that traditions of monarchical rule in Asia induced laziness: those who did not govern themselves, it was argued, would feel no inclination to organize their lives according to an individual sense of duty. Conversely, the European is courageous because he has greater self-determination. The cultural implications of differences in mode of government between Europe and Asia are strikingly analogous to the differences of national character between England and Ireland drawn by Goldsmith in his "Comparative View." Neither the common Irishman or the common Asian has cause to assert himself, for they both have paternal entities—England and the Asian tyrant, respectively—asserting things for them, thus determining, as much as climate, their supposedly docile national characters.

In England itself, meanwhile, climate was first noticeably conceived as an influence on literary culture and national character toward the end of the seventeenth century. It figured as an explanatory factor in the burgeoning debate, of which Swift's *Battle of the Books* (1697) was the apotheosis, regarding the relative merits of modern and ancient writing, a debate which, in turn, produced questions as to whether "rude" or even "barbarous" societies were more amenable to the forging of energized literatures. It was symptomatic of new enlightenment materialist discourses that investigations of the hard sources of culture should arise; thus, the attempt to explain the proper conditions for such an energized literature eventually turned to environment. Geography, climatology, and anthropology interacted to produce a new understanding of cultural life, and in the literary sphere these developments prompted a new exploration of the specific conditions which yielded "genius." Such conditions were described with reference to a range of factors such as liberty, social stability, soil and climate.

CHAPTER 1

The first noteworthy English investigator of the influence of climate and government together was Swift's early mentor Sir William Temple. In "An Essay upon the Ancient and Modern Learning" (1690) Temple listed racial temper, pureness of air, equanimity of climate, and peaceful government as the incubators of knowledge and of learning.[9] His essay "Of Poetry" (1690) measured the various influences that imbue a nationality with poetic, musical and comedic genius. For "The more true and natural Source of Poetry," Temple proposed, we must look to the ancients, who deemed Apollo, the sun, to be the inspiration for poetry and music. A "certain Noble and Vital Heat of Temper [. . .] especially of the Brain" was conducive to art, though Temple believed that a consistently warm climate was bad for comedy.[10] Thus, the moderate English climate was understood to provide the best environment for a vigorous artistic culture. Temple's nationalistic thesis gained literary currency up to and into the early eighteenth century. In 1695 William Congreve professed that there was more humor in English comic writers than those of any other nation. Humor was, he claimed, "almost of English Growth," attributable to "the greater Freedom, Privilege, and Liberty which the common People of England enjoy."[11] George Farquhar recalled both Temple and Congreve when he claimed that the English "have the most unaccountable Medley of Humours among us of any Nation upon Earth."[12] Swift himself, while suspicious of the chauvinism of his predecessors, was nonetheless intrigued by the issue of climatic influence, deeming it a "Question fit for Philosophers to Discuss."[13]

And discuss it they did. With David Hume, the debate over climate and the moral and cultural attributes of peoples was central to the cultural self-definition of Europe and, more importantly, of Britain.[14] For Hume, as for Goldsmith's "man of science," the influence of climate on the cultural potential of nations was a crucial issue—although Hume was not convinced that it was the main determinant. In his writings, climate was situated in euphemistic coincidence with, rather than as a strict cause of, the presence or the lack of liberty and self-sufficiency. In his essay "Of the Rise and Progress of the Arts and Sciences," the highest point of Greek civilization was explained by rational commercial and cultural interaction between the principalities. "There concurred," he added, "a happy climate, a soil not unfertile, and a most harmonious and comprehensive language."[15] He questioned purely environmental causes further in his essay "Of National Characters." There, he argued that men did not owe "any thing of their temper or genius to the air, food, or climate." Further historical investigation would "discover everywhere signs of a sympathy or contagion of manners, none of the influence of air or climate." The only climatically induced difference was that northern peoples "have a greater inclination to strong liquors," while southerners were inclined toward the pleasures of "love and women."[16] As climate was thus relegated, the primary determinant became the mode of government.

Hume knew his mind on this subject; Goldsmith's own views were contingent upon his sources and are as a consequence more difficult to pin down. Hume was also, perhaps, writing a little more thoughtfully; Goldsmith was translating, compiling, and editing contemporary writings together so that he would have material for inclusion in his natural history. As a result, Goldsmith's writings on national character derived mostly from those eighteenth-century French authorities he would translate and condense for Anglophone consumption: writers who were, comparatively speaking, fixated on climatic causation. Thus, in his first major work, *An Enquiry into the Present State of Polite Learning in Europe* (1759), Goldsmith writes:

> For a state to attain literary excellence, besides, it is requisite, that the soil and climate should, as much as possible, conduce to happiness. The earth must supply man with the necessaries of life, before he has leisure, or inclination, to pursue its more refined enjoyments. The climate also must be equally indulgent, for, in too warm a region, the mind is relaxed into languors, and by the opposite excess, is chilled into torpid inactivity. (W1: 263)

The effect of climate on the life of the mind is explained more fully in his "Comparative View." That essay's medical exposition was influenced by Montesqiueu, for whom a cold climate was considered better than a warm: cold air, Montesquieu claimed, tensed the fibers and made the heart stronger, while warm air diminished the "force and elasticity" of the fibers. The inhabitants of warm countries were meek and febrile; those resident in colder climates were, "like young men, brave."[17]

Goldsmith tends in some of his works to see both extremes as detrimental. Comparing the bodies of those living in temperate climates with those who live in the frigid or torrid zones, he explains that climatic extremities prevent the vigorous physical activities which slow the aging process and encourage intellectual assiduousness:

> That permanent vigour of the body is also the most proper to supply a fund of materials to supply the mind; as the soul often sympathizes with the decaying outward frame, before an inhabitant of the frigid or torid zone has an opportunity of growing learned, he is grown old: the season

CHAPTER 1

> for memory and invention is past; and he is, from the natural infirmities consequent upon age, more desirous of preserving the acquisitions of knowledge he has made, than of treasuring up new. On the contrary, the philosopher of the temperate climate, has a long period in which to collect his inductions; and as from the nature of the climate, a greater variety of objects offer instruction, so he has a longer period to enjoy the fruits of his acquisition. (W3: 82)

Temperate Europe thus enjoys a climatic-cultural advantage over non-European nations and races. But even within Europe there are differences in cultural potential; the colder, more northerly countries—and here the influence of Montesquieu is stronger—fare best. Goldsmith thus contributes to the view, fashionable amidst the gathering cults of Ossianic and Scandinavian literature, that less "polished" northern European peoples, with their "rude" language, their "jealous sense of liberty," and their "strength of thinking" (W1: 283), had greater potential for improvement into literary and cultural excellence. The extremes of heat and cold may be similarly inconvenienced; moderate northern nations, however, are climatically and topographically more enabled than are moderate southern nations.

In "The Effects Which Climates have upon Men, and Other Animals,"[18] Goldsmith expands on this theme as it affects modern Italy. His examples, however, are rather brazenly plagiarized from François-Ignace Espiard de la Borde's *The Spirit of Nations* (1753).[19] Originally published in 1743 in three volumes as *Essai sur la génie et le caratére des nations*, Espiard's treatise was reedited into two volumes in 1752 and retitled *L'Esprit des nations*, before being translated—anonymously, though possibly by Thomas Nugent, who had translated Montesquieu—into a one-volume edition in 1753. Goldsmith's account of Italy's decline is substantially if not syntactically identical to Espiard's:

> The climate of Italy has, for several ages, been different from what it was in the times of the ancient Romans. Those sharp winters of which the ancients complained, are felt there no longer: their rivers are now no where frozen over, as in the times of Horace, the fens of Ostia and Otranto being dried up: and the appearance of volcanoes and mines of arsenic serve to evince, that the country now is warmer than it was about two thousand years ago. Need we then be at such a loss to account for the different manners of ancient Romans and modern Italians? a warm country ever producing an effeminacy of manners among the inhabitants. (W3: 112)

Espiard's *Essai* was arguably the first book on the concept of nations; and while its importance to eighteenth-century thinking on race and climate has not been studied in any great detail, there is good cause to suppose that it was a major influence, not just on Goldsmith, but on the more famous work of Montesquieu. An obscure Dijon magistrate, Espiard's work has, according to David Bell, been "remarkably and unjustly ignored" — though Bell adds that this is possibly due to the author's "muddy style."[20] Style aside, *L'Esprit Des Nations* is an innovative account of the nature of nationality, treating, before Montesquieu, of the substantial influence of climate on the character of nations and the extent to which national character can be modulated or altered by political action transforming the state. The *Essai*, and subsequently *L'Esprit des Nations* were, both in the former's influence on Montesquieu and in their own right, compelling contemporary examples of the midcentury's preoccupation with the geographically variable nature of the human animal and human society. Espiard did not treat climate as *fully* determinant: laws and political action also played a central role. The character of the nation could be modified through a significant political shift which would in turn have a pronounced effect on legal culture.

It is significant that Goldsmith should have adapted *The Spirit of Nations*, the work's English-language translation, for the purposes of filling out a journalistic essay on climate and comparative national character. Espiard complains that the topic had not been treated systematically enough; all that has been achieved to that point, he maintains, were "detached Sentences and vague Definitions; no general system of Man has been attempted, where the Choice of Facts, the Quality and Order of Principles, accounted for the moral Phenomena, and assigned to every Thing its sure and distinct Character." He proposes a judicious synthesis of a variety of materials to elucidate the topic of national character, necessarily "collecting into a few Ideas, the different Parts of universal History and the Relations of Travellers. The Multitude of Views, of Relations and Connections is such, that the most exact Attention is required not to lose the Clew of this Labyrinth of Reflections." He distinguishes between his own task and that of naturalists, who "rationally" reserve judgments, awaiting further proofs of cause and effect. Espiard's scheme is, he declares, more extensive, and necessarily insouciant on specifics. The hard science, it seems, is ongoing; "but for a System of Man, the Time is now come."

Goldsmith deals, throughout his oeuvre, with the key opposition posited by Espiard: that which existed, in theory, between occidental liberty and oriental despotism. The description of the broadly oriental system of governance in *The Spirit*

CHAPTER 1

of Nations is damning from the outset. Liberty being the natural state of mankind, the orientals, "without excepting the *Chinese* themselves," and notwithstanding the naïve admiration of European missionaries, are bereft of these natural/national qualities which produce a free and open society. The orientals have been, and remain, "absolute Slaves." Misogyny, especially the confinement of women, is "the most unjust and unphilosophical of any thing in the whole World," and is attributed to eastern culture as a whole. Given to patriarchal despotism, they also want the liberality which would be engendered by more extensive cultural contact with foreigners; and they have no military virtues. In every social respect, the oriental "has violated the general Principles of Society; it has counteracted the simple Ideas" of a rational society.[21]

In Goldsmith's corresponding essay, the gradual degeneration of sturdy liberty from West to East is repeated, as is the notion of a sort of antievolution in national character. In describing the historical process of decline, Goldsmith uses the example of the inhabitants of northern Siberia. Even though situated in the same country, the ancient Scythians are "superior" to modern Siberian Tartars. Their superiority is due to their more temperate weather. Modern Siberians are "dwarfish, cowardly, and insolent to the last degree: extreme cold producing the same inconveniences with extremity of heat."[22] Goldsmith documents the changes in behavior which occur with peoples who have been transplanted. The Turks have degenerated when compared to their Scythian ancestors: their ferocity and valor have dwindled. The Dutch colonists at Batavia have surrendered their frugality for Asiatic luxuriousness—an observation which anticipates Raynal's comment on the same colony: "The force and example of an European government struggle in vain against the laws and manners of the climate of Asia."[23] The Galatians have done likewise in Lesser Asia.[24] Even the "pensive, modest, and frugal" English colonists have become "vindictive, hasty, and profuse" in their displacement (W3: 113).

These comments on colonial decline are instances of a slyly instrumental critique of imperialism which echoes Montesquieu: "Men ought to stay where they are. There are illnesses which come from changing a good climate for a bad one, and others which are due simply to the change of climate itself"; so writes Usbek to Rhedi in the *Persian Letters*.[25] In *The Deserted Village* too, trade and empire ruin the villagers—ostensibly English, actually Irish—who have been forced abroad into a strange, debilitating climate. Goldsmith rarely offers a sustained plea on the behalf of the colonized; so doing in the London hack economy upon which he depended for survival would be deemed too shrilly antagonistic toward imperial interests. More subtly, his critique takes the form of demonstrating the negative consequences of empire for the colonists themselves. Their robust national characters will wither in the foreign climate, which is really a euphemism for the climate and culture of empire. In Goldsmith, the ironic effect of colonial prowess is a weakening of the national character. Nations lose their vital strength by extending themselves colonially into environments—political and natural—to which they are not native; the vigor which brought them there in the first instance is that which is lost in the colonizing process. Thus, imperialism and the geographical and climatic displacement which it requires are subject to a law of sharply diminishing marginal returns.

That threat of decline is particularly true in the case of the Briton, whose home climate makes for a supposedly sturdier creature. It is climate alone, Goldsmith claims, "that makes the Italians effeminate, and the Briton brave" (W3: 113–4). Goldsmith's Chinese philosopher, in *The Citizen of the World*, concedes the bravery of the English, and allows an environmental explanation for that courage:

> I know of no country where the influence of climate and soil is more visible than in England, the same hidden cause which gives courage to their dogs and cocks, gives also fierceness to their men. But chiefly this ferocity appears among the vulgar. The polite of every country pretty nearly resemble each other. But as in simpleing, it is among the uncultivated productions of nature, we are to examine the characteristic differences of climate and soil, so in an estimate of the genius of the people, we must look among the sons of unpolished rusticity. The vulgar English therefore may be easily distinguished from all the rest of the world, by superior pride, impatience, and a peculiar hardiness of soul. (W2: 368–9)

Goldsmith is gently parodying here what he is peddling in his scientific writing: the prevalent belief that human beings are affected, not merely by the same environmental factors, but in much the same *manner* as animals: they develop, under the same sun—or lack of sun—similar characteristics. This point derives from Goldsmith's most trusted sources in natural history; and it is within the parameters of natural history, especially as exemplified in the work of Linnaeus and Buffon that humans come to be "simpled"—categorized and differentiated—in the same genre of geographical array as other plants and species.

Animated Natures

"Of all the studies which have employed the industrious or amused the idle," writes Goldsmith in his preface to Richard Brookes compendium of 1763,

CHAPTER 1

"perhaps Natural History deserves the preference; other sciences generally terminate in doubt, or rest in bare speculation, but here every step is marked with certainty" (W5: 229–30). Published just over a decade later, *An History of the Earth, and Animated Nature* (1774) is a more complete gauge of the author's "learning"—it took Goldsmith five years to prepare. Described by one biographer as his "most substantial literary legacy"[26]—an enigmatic description that might describe either quality or quantity—*Animated Nature* was originally commissioned by the bookseller William Griffin in 1769. The rights eventually fell to John Nourse, who was to pay Goldsmith £840, the largest payment the author had received for any of his works.[27] While much of the material is derived from Buffon, Goldsmith's writing often shadows Buffon's schema with his own editorializing; and his digressions are as floridly literary as they are scientific. Johnson's remark to Boswell, anticipating the publication of *Animated Nature*, acknowledged that Goldsmith "had the art of compiling, and of saying every thing he has to say in a pleasing manner. He is now writing a Natural History and will make it as entertaining as a Persian Tale." It was also Johnson, however, who stated: "Goldsmith, Sir, will give us a very fine book upon the subject; but if he can distinguish a cow from a horse, that, I believe, may be the extent of his knowledge of natural history." Following another of Goldsmith's rather absurd contentions—that horses go mad if a tub of blood is put into their stable—Johnson remarked:

> If he is content to take his information from others, he may get through his book with little trouble, and without much endangering his reputation. But if he makes experiments for so comprehensive a book as his, there would be no end to them; his erroneous assertions would then fall upon himself; and he might be blamed for not having made experiments as to every particular.[28]

The work was certainly, at various stages and according to fluctuating degrees of necessity, a work of compilation: an exercise in selection, translation, and mild editorializing rather than a display of wide learning. However, Goldsmith is more explicit about his sources in *Animated Nature*; and while the charge of plagiarism may be leveled at the essays, it is more difficult to be churlish with his natural history.

Animated Nature is foremost an encyclopedia of living creatures. In order to construct it, Goldsmith had to educate himself quickly by thinly reading through the history of natural history. However much, or little, of the substance of natural history he absorbed, he was always especially sensitive to differences in method and register. This sensitivity, and his ability to turn information into stylistically memorable prose, was what earned him such commissions in the first instance. In the course of its compilation, he had noticed a trend toward a more immediate categorical impulse; his synopses of later moderns, accordingly, reflected his dismay at the way natural history had developed. Ray, Klein, Brisson, and Linnaeus, have, for their part, given the "dry and disgusting air of a dictionary to their systems" (AN1: viii).[29] Linnaeus in particular, though renowned for his scientific prowess, earns for his minute exactness Goldsmith's bemused disdain. He wrote satirically to John Bindley, MP for Dover, in 1766:

> You tell me the wood is clear'd away from the ox park, that I believe, and that the fields looks as green as grass, that I deny. How could you assert a thing of this kind, Ill make an oration against it in the true style of the arts and sciences. Mr. Chairman Sir. I entirely agree with the gentleman that his fields are very green, but when he asserts that they are as green as grass there I humble think he wants precision. There are several kinds of grasses Mr Chairman, Linnæus gives us a catalogue of twenty five kinds, and all these kinds are green, but then Sir on the other hand there are several kinds of herbs that are not green at least in the flower. There is the crowfoot for instance there are several kinds of crowfoot, one of them is called geranium Roberti and this has a yellow blossom, and great quantities of this grows in the fields in question so that it gives them a yellowish greenish sort of a look so that they are not quite as green as grass. I therefore move sir for the greater precision that before the word fields, the words *grass of* be inserted, and then the whole paragraph will run elegantly thus, All the wood is removed from the ox park, and the grass of the fields looks as green as grass. Which is very true. All this is lost upon you if you have never attended the arts and sciences.[30]

Natural history, thus, has the effect of undoing the immediate effect of poetic observation. Reading Linnaeus may be useful for his purposes, but to copy his style will ultimately make his work less appealing to a general audience. Though still an acknowledged source of information for Goldsmith's natural history, Linnaeus also embodies the stultifying scientific tone.

Buffon's *Histoire Naturelle* was a more important and pleasing source. Credited in contrast to Linnaeus with a good deal more eloquence and poetry, Buffon was for Goldsmith the one modern whose work had brought the discipline to life. Goldsmith suggests that Buffon's lack of method—he lists his subjects "almost in

CHAPTER 1

the order they happen to come before him"—lends itself to criticism diametrically opposite to that which might be leveled at Linnaeus; he can, however, "lose little by a criticism which every dull man can make, or by an error in arrangement, from which the dullest are most usually free." Buffon's (lack of) method, for all of its incongruities, is most amenable to Goldsmith's approach. Commending "The warmth of his style, and the brilliancy of his imagination" (AN1: x-xi), Goldsmith freely admits to taking the Frenchman as his guide. His reasoning on Buffon's influence is plain enough: he borrows from him because he is the most literary of natural historians.

His sources acknowledged, the substance of Goldsmith's natural history is begun. The first chapter offers a perfunctory sketch of the universe, while the second consists of "A Short Survey of the Globe, from the Light of Astronomy and Geography." Differences in physical geography are explained in terms of the sun's providence. "Man alone seems the child of every climate, and capable of existing in all," claims Goldsmith in his nineteenth chapter, "An Essay Towards a Natural History of the Air," before sharply disclaiming that "this peculiar privilege does not exempt him from the influences of the air; he is as much subject to its malignity, as the meanest insect or vegetable" (AN1: 315). Racial diversity, thus deterministically explained, is the central concern of the second volume of *Animated Nature*; and Goldsmith's contentions on this front are much indebted to Buffon's expansive treatment of the subject in his *Histoire Naturelle*.[31]

The terms "race" and "nation" were in the process of separation during this period, and Buffon was writing on the cusp of a more categorical language of geographical and cultural comparison. Nicholas Hudson has proposed that this dynamic was engendered by the accelerating development of geographical anthropology in the eighteenth century. Nation, for Buffon and Linnaeus, was a subdivision of race; it came to denote, within races, differences in political systems, languages, and temperaments. Race, for its part, grew to be defined in biological and environmental terms. Hudson proposes that the evolution of the term "is marked particularly by the use of the term "race" to describe ever larger populations."[32] The racial system of Buffon specifically is seen by Hudson as dealing in rather large brushstrokes. As in Buffon, Goldsmith's catalogue of racial variations is based upon a declension of countries and regions of the globe according to degrees of barbarity or otherwise, with gender relations and sexual conventions deemed to be reliable cultural indicators. In "savage" nations—the natives of Madagascar and of the Congo are given as examples—men think nothing of prostituting their wives or their daughters to strangers for the smallest advantages. "Mahometans" differ in that they keep their wives faithful by confining them with the threat of execution upon suspicion of adultery. Differences within Europe, so important in the micro-discourse of nations, are in the macro-sense of *race* subsumed under the assumption that all Europeans are predisposed to the "passion of love, which may be considered as the nice conduct of ruder desire." In terms of sexual relations, we learn that "what other nations guard as their right, the more delicate European is contented to ask as a favour" (AN2: 75). Europe is thus figured as a single cultural entity—although often it seems as though Goldsmith is substituting, according to what Felicity Nussbaum has deemed the "conventional sentiments" of Anglophone racial discourse, the European for the specifically English.[33]

As the racial typography unfolds, by way of empire and empiricism, Europe becomes, comparatively speaking, more familiar and more homogenous; non-European peoples, meanwhile, are broadly, that is to say, racially, inferior, and in their more particular national characteristics, perverse. The characteristics of the European blend into a benign, almost poetic generality; the study of distant nations grows ever more squarely anthropological. This is noticeably true when Goldsmith writes of racial attitudes to female beauty. With Europeans, it is only implied that a woman's "good sense alone can preserve what she has gained by her beauty," whereas:

> The Persians admire large eye-brows, joining in the middle; the edges and corners of the eyes are tinctured with black, and the size of the head is encreased by a great variety of bandages, formed into a turban. In some parts of India, black teeth and white hair, are desired with ardour; and one of the principal employments of the women of Thibet, is to redden the teeth with herbs, and to make their hair white by a certain preparation. The passion for coloured teeth obtains also in China, and Japan; where, to complete their idea of beauty, the object of beauty must have little eyes, nearly closed, feet extremely small, and a waist far from being shapely. There are some nations of the American Indians, that flatten the heads of their children, by keeping them, while young, squeezed between two boards, so as to make the visage much larger than it would naturally be. Others flatten the head at top; and others still make it as round as they possibly can. The inhabitants along the western coasts of Africa, have a very extraordinary taste for beauty. A flat nose, thick lips, and a jet black complexion, are there the most indulgent gifts of nature. (AN2: 76–7)

CHAPTER 1

While this cluster of observations is blandly anecdotal, the net effect of Goldsmith's tone is to suggest that foreign cultural standards for beauty are absurd. In other respects, however, and in other formats, Goldsmith satirically reverses the cultural telescope, as when his Chinese philosopher, with Swiftian/Gulliverian pseudo-naiveté, ruminates on an innocent encounter with London prostitutes:

> In spite of taste, in spite of prejudice, I now begin to think their women tolerable; I can now look on a languishing blue eye without disgust, and pardon a set of teeth, even though whiter than ivory. I now begin to fancy there is no universal standard for beauty. The truth is, the manners of the ladies in this city are so very open, and so vastly engaging, that I am inclined to pass over the more glaring defects of their persons, since compensated by the more solid, yet latent beauties of the mind; what tho' they want black teeth, or are deprived of the allurements of feet no bigger than their thumbs, yet still they have souls, my friend, such souls, so free, so pressing, so hospitable, and so engaging: I have received more invitations in the streets of London from the sex in one night, than I have met with at Pekin in twelve revolutions of the moon. (W2: 42)[34]

What Goldsmith purveys in racial thought, he also usefully satirizes; what he satirizes, however, he also purveys. The ethnographic observations and categories developed in Goldsmith's career-spanning adventures in natural history are, as subsequent chapters will demonstrate, manipulated and modulated across the genres of his writing.

In *Animated Nature* itself, however, the typologies are bluntly and severely delineated. The system which Goldsmith devises for categorizing mankind racially is sixfold. Four varieties are derived from Linnaeus; two (the Laplanders and the Tartars), from Buffon.[35] Goldsmith's scheme situates the first distinct race of men in the polar regions. "The Laplanders, the Esquimaux Indians, the Samoeid Tartars, the inhabitants of Nova Zembla, the Borandians, the Greenlanders, and the natives of Kamskatka": these peoples are deemed to be the constituent nations of one particular race of people, similar in stature, complexion, customs, and ignorance. Their environment is harsh, and their physical appearance evidence of nature's improvidence. They are dwarfish, "rude," "superstitious," "stupid," and "cowardly" (AN2: 213–14). All of these traits are linked, directly and indirectly, to climate.

The second race is the Tartars, a collective name given to several nations which inhabit the largest portion of Asia, a race consisting "of various forms and complexions." As unalike as these nations are to one another, they are collectively "unlike the people of any other country whatsoever" (AN2: 219). Their geographical and racial "integrity" so established, their culture is described as bereft of religion, morality, decency. Included in and descending from the Tartar race are the Chinese and the Japanese. Differing from their "brutal progenitors," these two nations owe their relative civilization "to the mildness of the climate in which they reside, and to the peculiar fertility of the soil" (AN2: 223).

Distinguishable from the Tartars by the form of their features and their persons are the third race: the Asiatics. They inhabit the peninsula of India, with their stock having spread also to the islands of the Indian Ocean. Slender, with straight black hair and Roman noses, they are not unlike the Europeans in stature, although their olive-and-black complexions set them apart. Their inability to ward off invaders is a function of the usual climatic and cultural causes:

> The Indians have long been remarkable for their cowardice and effeminacy; every conqueror that has but attempted the invasion of their country, having succeeded. The warmth of their climate entirely influences their manners; they are slothful, submissive and luxurious: satisfied with sensual happiness alone, they find no pleasure in thinking; and contented with slavery, they are ready to obey any master [. . .] Upon the whole, therefore, they may be considered as a feeble race of sensualists, too dull to find rapture in any pleasures, and too indolent to turn their gravity into wisdom. (AN2: 225–26)

The description is no more intricate or forgiving than was Hippocrates treatment. Nonetheless, this facetiously orientalist view is one which Goldsmith could invert elsewhere; it is clear too that, while they are presented as detrimental oriental characteristics here, Goldsmith elsewhere expresses a temperamental preference, if not for indolence, then certainly for peaceability, over tendencies to ambition, industry and war.

The treatment of "the Negroes of Africa," the fourth variety of humankind, however, is if anything even harsher and more generalizing than the dismissal of the Asiatics. "This gloomy race," we read, "is found to blacken all the southern parts of Africa, from eighteen degrees north of the line, to its extreme termination, at the Cape of Good Hope." At one point, Goldsmith indulges the "pendulous breast" motif, a recurring image in early modern colonial and imaginative travelwriting: "The women's breasts, after bearing one child, hang down below the navel; and it is customary, with them, to suckle the child at their backs, by throwing the breast over the shoulder." (AN2: 228) Although there are numerous examples of this sort of description, Goldsmith may well have derived his image from a passage in Daniel Beeckman's 1718 account of his voyage to Borneo which describes the native women in Table Bay at the Cape of Good Hope: as ugly, it seems, as their menfolk, they have "long flabby Breasts, odiously dangling down to their Waste; which they can toss over their Shoulders for their Children to suck, whom they generally carry on their Backs."[36] Such tropes of colonial grotesquerie were satirised in Swift's descriptions of the yahoos in part 4 of *Gulliver's Travels*, where the physically alien allegorizes a general intellectual ugliness. But these images had been deployed in specifically Irish contexts too; Scottish pilgrim William Lithgow had, in his Irish travels of the early seventeenth century, remarked on the sight of

> women travelling the way, or toyling at home, carry their infants about their necks, and laying the Dugges over their shoulders, would give sucke to the Babes behinde their backes, without taking them in their armes: Such kind of breasts, me thinketh, were very fit to bee made money-bags for East or West-*Indian* Merchants, being more than halfe a yard long, and as well wrought as any Tanner in the like charge, could ever mollifie such Leather.[37]

This image is remarkably resilient and transferable, and is obviously keyed to amuse and/or horrify a domestic audience keen in the mainstream to feel themselves more advanced, physically and morally, than others, whether in Africa or Ireland. In Goldsmith's natural history, the physical aspects of race are taken—with no evident satirical intention—to signify a related degeneracy. Their bodies are deformed "at least to our imaginations," an external signal that "their minds are equally incapable of strong exertions. The climate relaxes their mental powers still more than those of the body; they are, therefore, in general, found to be stupid, indolent, and mischievous." (AN2: 228)

Stupidity extends to the fifth race: the inhabitants of America. Copper-colored, black-haired, flat-nosed, with high cheekbones and small eyes, they are weak and cowardly, have a serious, though seriously unthinking air. In this instance Goldsmith merely reproduces condescending European attitudes to the supposed characteristics, physical and intellectual, of the native American.[38] Such thinking, however, was in its own time increasingly at odds with the primitivist celebration of native American culture which was, according to Benjamin Bissell's influential study, a "singular product of the purely literary imagination" in the eighteenth century; this sensibility saw "the transformation of the sinister and forbidding savage into the idealized embodiments of picturesqueness, pathos, fortitude, and heroic sentiment."[39] In the natural-historical mode, however, Goldsmith has no inclination or obligation to dwell on the plausibly positive characteristics of the American Indian; nor would he in *The Deserted Village*.

In sum, the customs of savage nations "in every country are almost the same" (AN2: 230). All such nations have their virtues and vices: patience, hospitality, content, sincerity, indolence, stupidity, and rapacity. Virtues might be emphasized by the poetic primitivist; more instrumentally, as far as imperialist ambitions are concerned, vices are constructed, categorized, and exaggerated before being deployed for the purposes of comparative self-congratulation. Against such vices, the moral and physical virtues of the European race, the sixth and final variety of the human species, are starkly contrasted.

There are considerable cultural differences between the European nations—differences as pronounced as those which exist between other races; all share, however, the same physical attributes. Blunt in his other descriptions, Goldsmith waxes lyrical on the charm of the white European:

> Of all the colours by which mankind is diversified, it is easy to perceive, that ours is not only the most beautiful to the eye, but the most advantageous. The fair complexion seems, if I may so express it, as a transparent covering to the soul; all the variations of the passions, every expression of joy or sorrow flows to the cheek, and, without language, marks the mind. (AN2: 232)

This flourish is both poetic and unusually racist in the context of Goldsmith's oeuvre. But it is very much of a piece with much of his reading in natural history. Following Buffon's theory of racial degeneracy, and rejecting Linnaeus claim that man is a native of tropical climates and only "a sojourner in the north" (AN2: 240), Goldsmith reproduces a racial theory whereby non-Europeans have atrophied, culturally and physically, due to the extreme effects of exposure to the sun, the wind, and the extreme cold; added to these disadvantages are the hard labor and the sparse nourishment which result from geographical and climatological improvidence. Moving toward a conclusion on the subject, it is claimed that the deformities and the inadequacies of the African, the Asiatic and American are accidental; they are inconveniences which "a kinder climate, better nourishment, or more civilized manners, would, in a course of centuries, very probably remove" (AN2: 242). In his treatment of the varieties in the human race, then, nature and environment are the original sources of distinction and national character, but

CHAPTER 1

they are not entirely immutable. Manners and customs are determined by the climatic history of a people; as such, they are malleable according to movements from one climate to another. Hence it is plausible that, by degrees, people can assimilate to the cultures of their near neighbors.

א

In "A Comparative View of Races and Nations," to return to this chapter's point of departure, the English, if transplanted, partake of the Irish national character, becoming less serious, and more genial. Benevolent English dominion in Ireland allows the natives to be infectiously lighthearted. This is soft primitivism of the sort which reemerges in the pastoral reminiscences of *The Deserted Village*; as with the poem, however, the felicitous view is interrupted: soft primitivism and the discourse of national character are the media through which Goldsmith suggests the long-term incongruity of imperialism. The free-and-easy national character of the native Irish is supposedly a product of protective colonial government. In the very act of "going native," however, the English lose those national characteristics, martial and sternly reasoning, which are needed to govern the Irish; in short, the English lose their ability to govern well in Ireland, simply by governing it. Some *have* gone native; others, the colonial class, made up of negligent, time-serving administrators and absentee landlords—those figures who haunt Goldsmith's long poems—remain supercilious, disconnected from, and intermittently seeking to extirpate what they perceive to be an inferior culture while refusing to reinvest anything back into the economy which has produced their wealth and influence. Having flattered his London audience by praising the culture and ideal climate of England, Goldsmith's cultural observer seeks to temper English patriotism with a greater awareness of the achievements of other cultures. In an unexpected piece of editorializing, he takes the English national character, such as it has been established, to task. Though blessed by so many environmental advantages, he claims, the English lack the "temper" to enjoy them. He wishes to "teach the English to allow strangers to have their excellencies," and to "mend that country in which I reside, by improvements from those which I have left behind" (W3: 67–8). The author has developed this more sensitive view in his extensive European travels, in which cultures and political systems have been observed from the point of view of the poor, wandering exile improvising his way across the continent. Of those countries which the author has left behind, that which most deeply imbues his worldview is England's nearest colony.

2

THE LIE OF THE LAND: LIBERTY AND TRAVEL

Though patriots flatter, still shall wisdom find
An equal portion dealt to all mankind,
As different good, by Art or Nature given,
To different nations makes their blessings even. (W4: 251)

WHILE NATURAL HISTORICAL discourses sought out the hard explanations for the nature of nations, another, less deterministic literary perspective saw peoples intelligently adapting to their climatic worlds, and becoming, in their own "primitive" ways, cultural agents. Science, in the ideological form which characterized it throughout to the early modern period, was still condescending to non-European peoples, and would remain so for a long time after. Poetry and fiction, however, offered alternatives, in which condescending views could be counteracted by a new sensibility, sometimes in the same thoughtful and dialectically complex work. Goldsmith's *The Traveller; or, A Prospect of Society*, is a work produced out of this conflicted, but ultimately more generous perspective. Almost as a designing question, the poet wonders where the world's "happiest spot" might be found, before rhetorically challenging the imperious and the imperial by asking: "Who can direct, when all pretend to know?" Everyone, Goldsmith seems to suggest, has some theory of cultural causation; most theories, however, are grounded on the arrogation to the culture of the theorist a superiority which permits the attribution of some lack to others. This is especially true wherever the concept of "liberty" is introduced. On their own terms, Goldsmith-as-poet proposes, all cultures are valid. It is only the supercilious observer, blinded to the cyclical vulnerability of his own culture and society, who would disagree. Thus, Goldsmith describes sympathetically "The shudd'ring tenant of the frigid zone," who "Boldly proclaims that happiest spot his own." In the equatorial regions, he describes "The naked Negro, panting at the line," who "Boasts of his golden sands and palmy wine." All patriots, whether refined or "primitive," proclaim their native country to be best. Those primitive countries may lack the English virtue of liberty, but whatever mode of government was enjoyed was legitimate for as long as the people consented to it. As against Montesquieu's more rigid climatic causality, Goldsmith, though facetious toward southern and eastern peoples, celebrated the ability of the human animal to adapt to conditions. A degree of determinism did not necessarily preclude a generous perspective; what Montesquieu offered Goldsmith, and what Goldsmith developed in verse and in fiction, was a sense of the agency of people in making their own culture in the climate given them by providence.

In their various works, Montesquieu and Goldsmith negotiated the exchange between literary cosmopolitanism and comparative ethnography. Montesquieu's career embodied that balance in the difference between his *Persian Letters* and his *Spirit of Laws*. The cosmopolitanism of the former work facilitated a sympathetic allusion to the contemporary plight of the Irish nation. "A whole nation," wrote Montesquieu through the character of Usbek "expelled from its country, was observed to cross the seas and settle in France, without anything to assist in providing the necessities of life except a redoubtable talent for debate."[1] Montesquieu narrates here the fleeing of Irish Catholics to European convents and colleges in order to avoid the consequences of the post-1688 Williamite settlement at home.

Goldsmith knew these exiled communities well. He traveled about the continent of Europe between 1755 and 1756, assisted financially whenever the need arose by his uncle, Thomas Contarine. When Contarine died, Goldsmith was at Padua in Italy. Forced then to make and pay his own way back though Switzerland, France, and Holland, he traveled on foot, "lodging at Convents chiefly of the Irish Nation,"[2] earning his keep as he went by debating, in the manner described above by Montesquieu. This was the travel-mode of Goldsmith's fictional alterego George Primrose in *The Vicar of Wakefield*. Though published in 1766, *The Vicar* was effectively composed contemporaneously with *The Traveller*. Both texts comment incisively on the rhetoric of liberty; and both inflect contemporary sensibilities and stock notions of national character with critical perspectives earned in their author's experience of travel. *The Traveller* is a "prospect poem" which follows some of the strictures of convention implied in its subtitle; but there is within it a palpable tone of dejection which derives from Goldsmith's own experiences and observations. It is, as Katherine Turner writes, "a more subjective dramatization of the Traveller as melancholic exile," one which would provide a new template for travel writers of "dissident inclinations." Appreciating the poem's highly charged ambivalence toward English patriotism, Turner emphasizes the difficulties which would have been encountered in the negotiation of personal and national identity by a travel writer of Goldsmith's background. The poem's survey of nations "might be expected to make way for a climatic celebration of English liberty—as indeed is the case with Goldsmith's own, earlier essay, "A Comparative View of Races and Nations." But such a celebration is conspicuous by its absence."[3] Celebratory constructions of English national identity are addressed, therefore, from the point of view of the wandering Irish Jacobite; literary conventions provide the medium through which the poet can address and contradict cultural narcissisms. Goldsmith's traveler-persona is less that of the aristocratic surveyor of nations than that of a pensive exile among exiles.

The value of travel in the eighteenth century resided especially in its contribution to the delineation of national identities. But the project was thoroughly fraught, not least because one's parameters for cultural criticism were usually bequeathed from preexisting literatures and prejudices. Hume and Montesquieu were limited in their insights into notions of national character because, as John G. Hayman writes, both writers relied "largely on travel accounts and common knowledge for the support of their general attitudes, and neither observes freshly or closely the character of any specific countries."[4] Up to a point, the same is true of *The Traveller*; the poem is mediated, and its geography partially preordained, by the examples of others. Its shape and dynamic derive from the influence of Joseph Addison, of Sir Richard Blackmore's *The Nature of Man* (1711) and James Thomson's *Liberty* (1736). The central political and philosophical point of the poem, however, diverges substantially from the views of those authors. Goldsmith reproduces some of the views and tropes shared by Grand Tourists and aristocratic prospect poets; but the poem's defining inflection is its rejection of the chauvinism and complacency which went with England's self-identification as a land of liberty. This achievement might be called discursive inveigling, a subversive adventure in prospect poetry which performs Goldsmith's negative reaction to the post-1688 dispensation.

This chapter, like the last, deals with generic and geographical conventions and with Goldsmith's by turns compliant and critical activities within them. Two texts, and their social and political perspectives on liberty and travel, are substantially addressed: *The Traveller* and *The Vicar of Wakefield*, works in which the author's politics jostle with the imperatives of, respectively, prospect poetry and

CHAPTER 2

sentimental fiction. In relation to the latter, Goldsmith's soft sentimentalism is reassessed; too easily characterized in the critical heritage as a politically naive tale of rural virtue in distress, *The Vicar of Wakefield* is here reread as a partially disaffected work, thus, sequences in that novel which demonstrate Goldsmith's wary political stance are foregrounded. Earned in travel, the political views of George Primrose, the novel's exiled conscience, echo those of his father, its eponymous comic protagonist. They also echo *The Traveller*. Both *The Traveller* and *The Vicar of Wakefield* were composed in the closing years of the Seven Years' War; and in both, the beleaguered and melancholy circumstances of the poorer traveler produce a worldview which sets Goldsmith's traveler-persona and political stance apart from the Whig mainstream. As a coda, and toward a conclusion, the domestic geographies of the dramatic work *She Stoops to Conquer* demonstrate, in miniature, Goldsmith's critique of liberty as understood by the upper-class traveler.

North and South

The Traveller deals in the well-worn subjects of early eighteenth-century prospect poetry: the theme of liberty and the climatic and cultural differences, within Europe, between north and south.[5] The central and the most influential figure in this poetic tradition was Joseph Addison. His *Letter from Italy* (1701) and his *Remarks upon Several Parts of Italy* (1705) were the models that many eighteenth-century travelers sought to emulate: Boswell took a copy of Addison's *Remarks on Italy* with him on his tour of the continent, and was always ready to consult it whenever he crossed Addison's path. Addison himself was criticized in *A Table of All the Accurate Remarks and Surprising Discoveries, of the Most Learned and Ingenious Mr. ADDISON, in his Book of Travels thro' Several Parts of Italy* (1706) for transcribing passages from the classics. Horace Walpole remarked that "Mr Addison travelled through the poets, and not through Italy: for all his ideas are borrowed from the descriptions, and not from the reality."[6] Ultimately, eighteenth-century travel writings were answerable to generic obligations; Addison himself was no exception, although for many he would come to provide the rule. As the body of English travel writing consolidated itself, portrayals of certain other cultures became standardized; but, as John Hayman observes, "while it is possible that such agreement results on occasion from precise observation, it is more probably the result of one commentator copying another."[7] Enlightenment literatures of travel and cultural comparison generated, not a greater wealth of detail, but a larger intertextual constellation from which future travelers could draw.

While eighteenth-century travel writing participated in an enlightenment culture of cosmopolitanism, its genres often betray little which is discernibly enlightened, or indeed cosmopolitan. Indeed, Heinz-Joachim Müllenbrock has usefully identified what he sees as the *counter*-enlightenment provincialism of English travel writing. Chauvinistic self-representation, for Müllenbrock, depended upon the dramatization of the oppressive nature of government in other countries, especially where this oppression involved nationally characteristic inclinations toward popery and arbitrary power. This political ideology was most concentrated in more stylized travel writing—stylized in this sense often denoting a marked indebtedness to the Addisonian tradition—which was characterized by its aristocratic, patriotic self-assurance. Among the best examples of this sort of literature were the verse epistles of Lord Lyttelton and the Earl of Cork and Orrery's *Letters from Italy in the Years 1754 and 1755*. Addison's views were recapitulated at length by James Thomson in *Ancient and Modern Italy Compared*, the first of the five constituent parts of *Liberty* (1735). For Müllenbrock, *The Traveller*, by comparison with these other works, partakes of a more genuine cosmopolitanism.[8] It is an enlightenment poem, but it undoes the prejudicial tenor of those poems such as Addison's and Thomson's which, while influential in terms of poetic construction, were symptomatic of some enlightenment tendencies to ethnocentrism.

Alongside its classicism, therefore, was also a generic element to the *politics* of Addison's poem: everything that he saw on the continent, Ciaran Murray has remarked, "he saw as a convinced Whig should."[9] The obligation of travel poetry was to weigh up the positives and negatives of countries; this tallying process was always preloaded, however—not necessarily toward an outright celebration or dismissal of another country, but toward a negative comparison of that country with the traveler's own. Responding to Samuel Sharp's *Letters from Italy* (1766), Joseph Baretti observed that most English observers did not even speak the native languages of the countries which they facetiously described. Baretti finds it remarkable that any observer should venture a description of the domestic lives and manners of a country without understanding their language. A traveler who is at least aware that he cannot enact some quick cultural diagnosis on the natives would display a less imperious, more capacious appreciation of the variety of the species: "A judicious man travels," writes Baretti, "in order to profit himself by observing the varieties that the wide world affords, and not to make himself uneasy because men are not to be found wise according to his model in every part of the globe. The variety of the world, is, on the whole, beautiful; and to a well disposed mind will be pleasing." On these principles, Baretti could critique the stereotyping of Addison and Sharp by attributing ethnic calumny to "the disordered imagination of a good-natured protestant traveller."[10]

Goldsmith admired the ambition, if not the ethnography, of Addison's *Letter from Italy*; and whereas for Baretti misinformation and prejudice sullied contemporary depictions of his native country, Goldsmith felt that Addison's attempt at political philosophy compensated for his poem's trundling rhythm: "There is in it," writes Goldsmith, "a strain of political thinking that was, at that time, new in our poetry" (W5: 321). Thus, Goldsmith commends the *aim* of the poem. In Addison, the vistas open to the poet inspire high-flown thoughts on the historical and geographical habitat of the Muse. Addison's eyes are "ravisht"; the fields are "Poetick"; the ground is "Classic"; and yet the people, the progeny of the ancient Romans, are "degenerate." The languorous climate sponsors popular subjection to "proud Oppression" and "Tyrannie."[11] Attempting balance by describing both the natural scene and the political demeanor of the country, Addison offers a primary example of what a travel writer, and specifically a travel *poet*, should compose. However, he fails to examine his own prejudice by observing anything other than the landscape. Without commenting upon any specific people or communities, he paints a sprawling political canvas; his imaginative geography lacked, as Baretti observed, ground-level empirical nuance.

In its breadth and in its patterning, *The Traveller* also follows Sir Richard Blackmore's *The Nature of Man* (1711). The design of Blackmore's poem was "to show what Advantages those receive, who are born in a mild Air and temperate Climate; and what Disadvantages, in respect of Understanding, Reason and moral Improvements, those Nations lye under, who suffer the extream of Cold or Heat." The second book of Blackmore's work narrows this panorama to particular instances, "by giving the distinct Characters of many European Nations." The third book is evaluative: it is written "in Honour and Praise of Liberty, as it was found in the ancient Republicks of Greece *and* Rome, and is maintain'd in the Present Government of the United Netherlands."[12] Predictably, Blackmore, a staunch Whig, prefers the British constitutional monarchy—and therefore reserves some admiration for whichever countries adhere to something like such an arrangement—to the arbitrary power structures of other nations. Goldsmith himself follows this argument, up to a point; more than the argument itself, he follows the sequencing in which the argument is made. Blackmore's work includes a strict climatological determinism, while Goldsmith's analysis is a good deal more flexible; he observes that countries have a cultural potential for a particular type and level of liberty which accords to national aptitudes. As opposed to complete, *a priori* dispositioning, Goldsmith argues the case for a verifiable law of comparative cultural advantage.

The politics of *The Traveller* are clearly linked to events in England following the accession of George III in 1760; as Leo Storm has described it, the poem participates in the contemporary "search for a via media between monarchical tyranny on one side and organized faction on the other." It responds to the consolidation of the Hanoverian regime by interrogating the contrast between contemporary Italian tyranny and British liberty, and extends to encompass a comparative study of the characteristics of five European nations: Italy, Switzerland, France, the Netherlands, and England. The qualities which nations display in these writings are, according to Storm, "little more than implications of conventionalized didactic discourse endemic in eighteenth-century thought."[13] This point, though overstated, is given extra heft by Rodney Stenning Edgecombe, who has grouped Johnson and Goldsmith together as "ideologues" of a nationally inflected universality of moral life: "Even though he has taken pains to stress his own detachment and lack of national feeling," writes Edgecombe, "the writer has none the less spent the greater part of *The Traveller* observing distinct national characters, and connecting these to geographic circumstance." Though Edgecombe sees a discrepancy between the poem's delineation of national character and its cosmopolitan pluralism, there is in the poem an increased awareness that differences between nations stem from geographical adaptations rather than essential ethnic divisions. Thus, the poem moves away from the strict neoclassical imperatives of such as Addison and Blackmore toward the more pluralistic regionalism which underwrites later romantic poetry. And so, for Edgecombe, this symbiosis between setting and national character in *The Traveller* "represents a milestone in the growth of regional consciousness [. . .] a (no doubt unconscious) shift away from the established neo-classical position."[14] In spite of the points where Goldsmith's travels correspond with the Grand Tour, Goldsmith does not emphasize, as classically educated Grand Tourists often did, the continuity of high European cultures; nor did he display any great aristocratic hauteur in his treatment of culture generally.[15] Grand Tourists regularly sought out only what was "high" in European culture. They were rarely in a position to examine mankind "more closely"—from the point of vantage which Goldsmith recommended. If, as Goldsmith suggested, countries wear different appearances to travelers of different circumstances, there were definite *philosophical* benefits to be gained by making the journey on foot.

The Traveller is prefaced with a dedicatory letter to the poet's brother, the Reverend Henry Goldsmith, still residing in Ireland. In that letter, Goldsmith

CHAPTER 2

states: "a part of this Poem was formerly written to you from Switzerland" (W4: 245). Oliver sent Henry about two hundred lines.¹⁶ It has been suggested, with good cause, that the fragment consisted of the descriptive bones onto which would eventually be grafted the philosophical flesh of the completed poem.¹⁷ The dedication would "throw a light upon many parts of it, when the reader understands that it is addressed to a man, who, despising Fame and Fortune, has retired early to Happiness and Obscurity, with an income of forty pounds a year" (W4: 245). Henry's human example simply serves to imbue with affective humanity his brother's ruminations on ambition, party, and monarchy in Britain. The dedication's consideration of ambition includes an assessment of the state of poetry. "Unpolished" nations are juxtaposed with "refined" nations to demonstrate the more pedantic—and counterproductive—efforts of critics in the latter to improve poetry and restore it to preeminence among the arts.¹⁸ More dangerous to poetry than the critics is party, or faction, which "entirely distorts the judgement, and destroys the taste" (W4: 246). For Goldsmith, party is a disease which militates against poetic endeavor; he seeks to illustrate that there are, irrespective of factional politics, cultural truths alongside which party is a paltry abstraction. These cultural truths dictate that an excess of any quality beyond certain optima results in inevitable decline: "Without espousing the cause of any party, I have attempted to moderate the rage of all. I have endeavoured to shew, that there may be equal happiness in states, that are differently governed from our own; that every state has a particular principle of happiness, and that this principle in each may be carried to a mischievous excess" (W4: 247).

The familial sensibility of the poem's dedication is renewed in the opening of the poem itself. Goldsmith addresses his brother in claiming that his "heart untravell'd fondly turns" to him, while the distance between them drags "a lengthening chain" (W4: 249). The apostrophe recalls the third Chinese letter, wherein Altangi writes: "those ties that bind me to my native country, and you are still unbroken. By every remove, I only drag a greater length of chain" (W2: 21). Henry and Ireland are touchstones in the midst of the poet's travels. The patriot's boast is that "His first best country ever is at home"; but this particular type of patriotism is one of a pained, immanent experience of displacement. Thus the poem develops still further a mainstay in Goldsmith's autobiography: his "pangs of separation" from the home place, the Lissoy fireside, described in a letter to his brother-in-law Daniel Hodson as an "Unaccountable [fond]ness for country, this maladie du Pays" (L: 28). The traveler is not destined to share that homeliness, set adrift as he is to spend his prime in wandering and worry.

His destiny is to "traverse realms alone," separated from scenes of familial affection, his sense of place discommoded (W4: 249–50).[19] That these realms are traversed alone, thus leading the poet to reflect on his alienation, signifies the poem's strong autobiographical, exilic resonance.

Goldsmith's traveler writes initially from a slightly clichéd scene of expansive view, which imitates the opening of Johnson's *The Vanity of Human Wishes* (1748).[20] Situated "on high above the storm's career," Goldsmith surveys "an hundred realms" and observes the social scene from "The pomp of kings" to "the shepherd's humbler pride." The poet asks of the reader whether the human scene should be condescended to from that height: "Say, should the philosophic mind disdain/That good, which makes each humbler bosome vain?" Rather than accommodating any anthropological elitism or superciliousness, the elevation is a poetic device; before descending, an introductory statement can be made from a metaphorical platform. This Alpine view does not preclude the more intimate and involved application of the "sympathetic mind," which "Exults in all the good of all mankind" (W4: 250).[21]

A general approval is, initially at least, bestowed upon trade and nature together: upon "glittering towns, with wealth and spendour crown'd," "fields, where summer spreads profusion round," "lakes, whose vessels catch the busy gale," and happily "bending swains," whose labor prettifies the vale (W4: 250). The poet is pleased with every benefit of providence; however, he is anxiously aware that material gifts cannot bestow bliss upon the recipients. To find, "amidst the scene" (W4: 251), one locus of true happiness is the imaginative quest of the poem's geography; the river image with which the poem commences is analogous to the poem's method. The poem must travel through realms of experience and literary convention to demonstrate that both categories are always limited unless fastened into a broader geographical dialectic.[22]

The splenetic—"Remote, unfriended, melancholy, slow"—traveler reports at the outset to his brother from an unspecified place which might be by the Scheld or by the Po—or any European river, northern or southern, to which the poet's nearness might signal exilic abjection. Following quickly on from the obvious autobiographical import of the address to Henry, there is the more clichéd reference to the Roman Campania, or Campagna, a region described, with some political import, in Addison's *Remarks on Several Parts of Italy* (1705), and in Thomson's *Liberty*. For the Whiggish observer, the desertion of the Campania was an indicator of the destruction wrought by arbitrary power, linked to the religious credulity of the Italian nation. It was a scene much depicted in the visual art of

CHAPTER 2

the period. Contemporaneous also with Goldsmith's travels were the Italian travels of the Welsh painter Richard Wilson. His *Pastoral Scene in the Campagna*, painted between 1752 and 1757, depicts a prospect which corroborates the image of the forsaken plain. The painting foregrounds three human figures playing musical instruments. Further in the distant background there is a vague and anonymous urban entity. In between there is an expanse of empty landscape that rises to a foreground breached by a ruined and overgrown gazebo.[23]

Until the later twentieth century, the Italian landscape drawings of the Irish artist James Barry were mistakenly attributed to Wilson. Barry's sketches seem almost as though they might have been the adumbrations upon which Wilson proceeded to paint images such as his *Pastoral Scene*. Both artists exhibit an early Romantic appreciation of the rustic; unwilling to patronize the Italian peasant, Barry commented in his correspondence with friend and patron Edmund Burke on the "unfavourable, virulent, and scandalous" literary misrepresentations of Italy in the writings of Samuel Sharp. While he was more admiring of Addison's work, he disdained the manner in which Addison and Sharp together blamed Italy's decline on the credulity of the Italian Catholic peasant; his landscape sketches, such as that of *The Palatine Hill from San Gregorio* (1769), thus demonstrate his sympathy for the predicament of the figures in his landscapes, tinily set against a backdrop of faded glory. Their poverty, he reflects, "has kept it out of their power to flaunt about after the deliriums and new fangled whims of fashionable people in great cities."[24] Barry thus imples that it was not the Catholicism of the peasantry

James Barry, *Part of the Palatine Hill from the steps of San Gregorio* (1769) © The Fitzwilliam Museum, Cambridge.

but the imperial luxury of contiguous Rome which had created the forlorn scenes of his sketches. The ruin in wider European treatments of modern Italy was thus a pointed emblem; in England it was a symbolic counterpoint to the material wealth generated by British freedoms in trade and government. For Barry, it was the future which plausibly lay ahead of that wealth; equally, when Goldsmith brought ruination closer to home in *The Deserted Village*, he reversed the English norm to associate denudation with those very freedoms.

When Goldsmith writes of the "Arno's shelvy side," he evokes another standard. The Italian river, with its lush vale, was the subject of much eulogy in the eighteenth century. James Thomson referred in 1735 to the rich vines of "Arno's fertile plain"; in equally lush language, John Dyer wrote in *The Ruins of Rome* (1740) of "The Vale of Arno, purpled with the vine."[25] When Goldsmith refers to the Arno, he visualizes the shelflike terraces on which the vines are grown, and reflects on their significance. The image bespeaks the productive pliability of nature wherever labor and art are applied. As with the foreboding cliffs of Idra, the Arno's banks can, "by custom, turn to beds of down." Human geography imposes upon physical geography to produce the means of happiness; physical geography imposes upon human geography to determine those means: this is a fundamental tenet of existence in societies, whether "rude" or "refined." Wherever arts become more various, there emerges a potential conflict: wealth, commerce, and liberty only serve to disrupt the potential for contentment and honor amongst men. Spurning contentment, man is thus prone to exaggerate his needs and to augment his wants, "'Till, carried to excess in each domain,/ This favourite good begets peculiar pain." These are the truths which Goldsmith proposes to try "with closer eyes" (W4: 252).

The Italian section of the poem—as with Thomson's *Liberty*, the first section—is, at its outset, picturesque and felicitous: Italy extends, "Bright as the summer," with its landscape, its woods and mouldering temples bestowing a "venerable grandeur" upon the physical scene. If nature's bounty alone were enough, Italy would be a sensuous utopia. Whatever fruits are found in different climes, whether torrid or varied, are found here to spring, as if unfarmed, from the ground (W4: 253). In describing the threatened fecundity of the Italian landscape, Goldsmith echoes Addison; like Addison again, Goldsmith sets up this bucolic vision only to dislodge it. "Sensual bliss," such as derives from the Italian soil and climate, is small bliss, and small bliss is all that Italy knows. The only thing that can grow in this landscape is man. The Italians are, according to the contemporary prejudice, typically Catholic: though poor, they manage to be luxurious; though submissive,

CHAPTER 2

they are also vain. Seemingly grave, they are "trifling"; seemingly zealous in their faith, they are untrue, plotting, as papists apparently do, new sins even as they are confessing the old. These are the "contrasted faults" which the poet sees residing in the national character. "All evils here contaminate the mind," which is why the profligate Italians have lost their national strength. Where Goldsmith the natural historian borrowed from continental writers the thesis that the climate of Italy had changed to such a degree that its people were no longer as militarily vigorous, Goldsmith the Traveler, or prospect poet, reproduces Samuel Sharp's prejudices: those of the "good-natured protestant."

Italy's decline, explained elsewhere in climatic terms, is further evidenced by a displacement of present happiness into a love of the past and a pallid imitation of past cultural glories. Arts are the "splendid wrecks of former pride" (W4: 254), a source of amusement and nostalgia rather than productions of a living culture or an inspiration for the future. Nobler aims have been "represt by long controul" (W4: 255). The clichéd implication is that, through the centuries, the state of Italy has declined into cultural flaccidity.[26] Symbolizing Italy's atrophy toward the end of Goldsmith's treatment is the ruin. The Italian ruin was especially significant for the English traveler in Europe; as Paul Langford writes, "a favourite cause of self-congratulation to Englishmen and women on the Grand Tour was the manifest decay of Italian city states and the resulting absurdity of their boasted laws and traditions."[27] In Goldsmith's less celebratory view, however, Italy's ruination is less a marker of degenerate national character than it is a sign of the fate of empire, of the logical outcome of imperial self-congratulation and luxury. In "A City Night-Piece," an earlier essay, a sense is conveyed that what has happened to Italy might happen to all cultures: "The sorrowful traveller wanders over the awful ruins of others, and as he beholds, he learns wisdom, and feels the transience of every sublunary passion" (W1: 431).

Participating in midcentury poetic trends toward masochistic pleasure-in-melancholy, *The Traveller* often drifts to a lyrical, elegiac mode which will find its way into the European mainstream in the decades following. Indeed, Arnd Bohm has measured the influence of Goldsmith's poem on Goethe's *Der Wandrer* (1774), the clearest indication of which is their shared account of ruins in the Italian landscape which have been reinhabited. For Goldsmith, according to Bohm, the ruins are a topographical-political metaphor; for Goethe, they are aesthetic emblems. Like *Der Wandrer*, *The Traveller* includes the Italian ruin as a reminder of ineluctable cycles of decay; unlike Goethe, Goldsmith is more pointedly using the image to complicate politically an otherwise picturesque panorama.[28] There is, in *The Traveller*, a figure in the landscape, just as there are small figures in Richard Wilson's ruin-paintings. Reoccupying the ruined dome is a "shelter-seeking peasant," building his shed and wondering why any man would desire the larger dome, when he might exist happily in a small cottage of his own (W4: 255). The peasant's contentment is Goldsmith's ideal; the fact that he is seeking shelter in a ruin, however, demonstrates that his will to frugality has been undone by the contiguous luxury of others.

Ruminating, in his *Memoirs of My Life* (1796), on the uses of foreign travel and the qualifications most essential to an inquisitive traveler, Edward Gibbon explains that it was the personal experience of Italy and the sight of the ruins of Rome which inspired his *History of the Decline and Fall of the Roman Empire* (1783–91).[29] The ruins are the inspirational markers of the decline of Italian culture for the British observer in the eighteenth century; they are the symptoms of luxurious degeneracy and loss of liberty. However, Gibbon wrote his *History* in Lausanne in Switzerland. These coordinates recall *The Traveller*'s direction, its juxtaposition of Italian degeneration and the liberty, however primitive, of the Swiss. Stephen Turner has argued that this British conception of Switzerland and its predisposition to liberty participate in a wider "enlightenment topography." "Enlightenment," writes Turner, "is precariously situated between a prejudiced nationalism and a nostalgic primitivism."[30] This too is the thought complex through which Goldsmith's poem moves.

Like his idol Voltaire, Goldsmith thought highly of Geneva, which is where he spent most of his Swiss sojourn, making regular excursions to the Alpine ranges.[31] Like Voltaire again, he would have admired Switzerland for its promotion of intellectual freedom.[32] Whereas the languorous climate of Italy engenders a degeneracy presided over by tyranny, the rougher, more various climate of Switzerland yields "a nobler race" (W4: 256), seemingly blessed by a degree of liberty. In writing of Switzerland, Goldsmith does not deal in specifics, topographical or political. His judgment on this nation is conventional: he is following a primitivist tradition up to a point beyond which he sees the disadvantages of primitive simplicity looming. Following in the tradition of Albrecht von Haller's *Die Alpen* (1732), Goldsmith sees in the Swiss peasantry worthy examples of the benefits accruing to a return to nature. Privation prompts simple virtue; hence, the barren yet picturesque landscapes of Switzerland produce a people of physical and moral sturdiness. As Cardinal Bentivoglio remarked in 1764: the Alps were made for the Swiss and the Swiss for the Alps.[33] At first glance Goldsmith seems to appreciate this scheme. Indeed what he admires in the Swiss peasant is precisely the

CHAPTER 2

contented frugality of the Italian peasant building his cottage in the ruined dome. His hut is poor, his food is plain, and his sphere of understanding is such that he understands his own existence to be the general existence of mankind. He sees "no contiguous palace" which might make him feel inadequate or stir resentment and ambition. He is calm; reared as he is "in ignorance and toil," his desires are limited, and he is invariably cheerful, whether fishing, ploughing, or bear-tracking. Contained in his cycle of labor, he is the proud "monarch" of his mean shed. His children are as ruddy as he is, and his wife is proud and contented with her domestic regime (W4: 256–57). When he describes the loyalty which the Swiss feel toward their homeland, Goldsmith reiterates another standard, exemplified in Thomson's *Liberty*: "It is reported of the Swiss, that, after having been long absent from their native Country, they are seized with such a violent Desire of seeing it again, as affects them with a languishing Indisposition, called the *Swiss Sickness*."[34] In Goldsmith's poem, equally, the "native wilds" of Switzerland "Imprints the patriot passion on his heart." The landscape and his attachment to it augment the happiness which he derives from his frugal store. His soul "conforms" to his shed; his character is ever analogous to his physical surroundings. Even the hillside upon which he lives is dear to him, though it might expose him to the worst of the Swiss weather. He is "as a child, when scaring sounds molest,/ Clings close and closer to the mother's breast"; the landscape's dangers "But bind him to his native mountains more" (W4: 257).

The poem is fuguelike, and for each celebration of the characteristics of a country there is a reversal. And so at this point the poet turns to critique the primitivist element in his own geography. Scientific progress, which might be maligned for its excesses in other contexts, is invoked here as an absence. The simplicity of the Swiss precludes their material advancement; hence, there is little enough that the Swiss can enjoy, in physical or in intellectual terms. If the peasant knows nothing beyond his narrow existence, he will want for nothing beyond his happy valley or mountainside; if he is aware of a lack, he will seek its pleasurable redress. Material progress "first excites desire, and then supplies." Up to a certain point, material progress is an engine of national refinement. Unknown to the peasant are "those powers that raise the soul to flame," those vague phenomena which "Catch every nerve and vibrate through the frame." Such qualities of frugality, which Goldsmith celebrates in *The Deserted Village*, come under scrutiny here. Unmotivated by want or desire, the Swiss are by default unfit for the refined joys or sorrows of urbane sensibility, their only extremes coming at yearly festivals where they might indulge in wild excess, "'Till, buried in debauch, the bliss expire" (W4: 257–8). Whatever enjoyments are mustered are prior to science, and hence crude; possessed of sterner virtues, the Swiss are lacking in those gentler morals "such as play/Through life's more cultur'd walks" (W4: 259).

Those more cultured walks reside under the "kinder skies" of France. After the primitivism of his Switzerland, Goldsmith's delineation of the French character again includes autobiographical traces, but they are mediated by generic imperatives, in this instance those of the picaresque. Imagining Goldsmith's appreciation of the difference between playing his music to the receptive, lower-class French audiences, and to the haughty, fashionable elite, Prior remarks that "No ordinary love of learning, of novelty, of acquaintance with men and manners, or of persevering determination to examine them all as far as circumstances permitted, could induce any one to subject himself to such a precarious existence."[35] There was some truth, as evidenced by *The Vicar of Wakefield*, in Goldsmith's having played a good deal of music to survive on his travels, and the "lower" mode of travel is that which he repeatedly advocates—making a political virtue of material necessity—for viewing mankind more closely. When Goldsmith asks rhetorically: "How often have I led thy sportive choir,/With tuneless pipe, beside the murmuring Loire?" (W4: 259), he is clearly playing up, even romanticizing the autobiographical element of the poem. One biographer doubts that Goldsmith's itinerary took him along the Loire; it is more likely, claims A. Lytton Sells, that Goldsmith made his way up the Marne before crossing the Vosges into Strasbourg. His exact route is not important; what matters are the political resonances of place. That Goldsmith should mention the Loire suggests "the literary and poetical associations" of that river. At any rate, it is argued, "Marne" does not rhyme with "choir."[36]

As was the case with luxurious, picturesque Italy and noble, primitive Switzerland, the positive attributes of France and the French are equally the beginnings of their profoundest flaws. The French "social temper" is produced and hampered by a false code of honor whereby all are eager to please and to be pleased. Praise "too dearly lov'd or warmly sought" (W4: 260) is the counterfeit currency in the French social economy; it weakens the soul, and produces hollow ostentation, or vanity. This has very little to do with France, perhaps, but it has a great deal to do with received versions of the French national character; very little has changed, in this version, since the affected Gallic fops of Restoration drama, susceptible to false praise and predisposed to self-congratulation. The upper-class English traveler almost invariably betrayed a prejudice toward the French which was unaffected by traveling itself.[37] Goldsmith does not seem to have deviated from these observations in *The Traveller*; in his *Enquiry into the Present State of Polite Learning in*

CHAPTER 2

Europe, however, he seeks, as might be of expected of a writer so immersed in French intellectual traditions, to look beyond the bounds of national prejudice toward a more generous description of French culture.[38]

Between France and Holland there is no cultural segue. The complimentary vision of the topography and the commercial prowess of Holland employs a panoramic vista.[39] The happy vista is quickly dispersed by an equally generalizing diagnosis of democratic atrophy brought on by love of gain:

> Thus, while around the wave-subjected soil
> Impels the native to repeated toil,
> Industrious habits in each bosom reign,
> And industry begets a love of gain.
> Hence all the good from opulence that springs,
> With all those ills superfluous treasure brings,
> Are here display'd. Their much-lov'd wealth imparts
> Convenience, plenty, elegance, and arts;
> But view them closer, craft and fraud appear,
> Even liberty itself is barter'd here.
> At gold's superior charms all freedom flies,
> The needy sell it, and the rich man buys (W4: 261).

The Dutch are industrious, but at the expense of social cohesion; the opulence generated by their industry is matched, in a degenerative dynamic, to their increasing fraudulence, in trade and in politics. Central to Goldsmith's disparagement is the view that the commodification of liberty has produced "A land of tyrants, and a den of slaves" (W4: 262). But this is not, nor could it ever be, a specifically Dutch complaint. This phrase appears in two other instances: in Goldsmith's descriptions of Venice and Genoa.[40] Thus, this crucial phrase in Goldsmith's treatment of Holland is an interchangeable and general social warning against a spurious republicanism. A. J. Barnouw claims that Goldsmith should have known better than to represent Holland as tyrannical, or its citizens as slaves, because "the philosophic vagabond speaks from his own experience."[41] He should, more than any observer, have appreciated the multivalence of Dutch political and cultural life. Having substantial experience of the Netherlands, he might not have equated its republicanism with oppression so readily. His acquaintance with, and borrowings from, the work of the Dutch essayist Justus Van Effen should have complicated further his description of the national character. On one level, Goldsmith's criticisms seem rather arbitrary; on another, they manifest his general antipathy toward the commercialism of the contemporary republic. This is the direction in which he sees Britain moving. In other poems of this sort—Blackmore's *The Nature of Man* again suggests itself—the trope of tyranny might be manipulated so that the liberty and productivity of Britain might be thrown into full and glorious relief. In *The Traveller*, however, the problems of the Dutch republic merely adumbrate the flaws from which Britain herself suffers.

The Dutch of old were "Rough, poor, content, ungovernably bold." Warlike and free, they were "unlike the sons of Britain now!" (W4: 262). This is an abrasive comparison, meant to demean the present, supposedly emasculated Dutch culture, and to compare it negatively with that of Britain, a country which, on the face of it, still demonstrates an optimal mixture of Spartan toughness and artistic prowess:

> Fir'd at the sound, my genius spreads her wing,
> And flies where Britain courts the western spring;
> Where lawns extend that scorn Arcadian pride,
> And brighter streams than fam'd Hydaspis glide,
> There all around the gentlest breezes stray,
> There gentle music melts on every spray;
> Creation's mildest charms are there combin'd,
> Extremes are only in the master's mind;
> Stern o'er each bosom reason holds her state,
> With daring aims, irregularly great,
> Pride in their port, defiance in their eye,
> I see the lords of human kind pass by
> Intent on high designs, a thoughtful band,
> By forms unfashion'd, fresh from Nature's hand;
> Fierce in their native hardiness of soul,
> True to imagin'd right above controul,
> While even the peasant boasts these rights to scan,
> And learns to venerate himself as man. (W4: 262–3)

As celebratory as these lines seem, they contain within them an ironic preface to what follows. Britain's physical beauties exceed, Goldsmith seems to say, the georgic scenes of Arcadia and the Hydaspes river in India; in so exceeding, however, those beauties are also scornful. This personification imputes to British landscapes a calculated artificiality—a willed, and therefore ultimately dubious, superiority. Creation has bestowed mildness on Britain; but Creation's gifts have been second-guessed by the powerful, who will seek to outdo nature. The hardiness and vigor

CHAPTER 2

which has given them the capacity to do so, will be undone by the application of art and the acquisition of luxury.

The "lords of human kind," initially seeming to signify national strength, are soon to be derided as avatars of national weakness. There is already a palpable sense, given what has gone before, that the poet is going through the motions of puffing up the Briton's vigor and climatic luck, before stripping away the façade of Freedom and Liberty to expose a fractured and fractious reality. On the cusp of a downturn which the Swiss have yet to approach, the Briton does not recognize that where the freedom to acquire wealth is known too well, wealth is inevitably desired to a self-destructive extent. The organic social ties which bind society are constantly threatened by overweening commercial ambition. Excessive personal and commercial freedom undermine freedom proper; the love of independence—hailed by James Thomson as "HEAVEN's next best Gift,/To that of Life and an immortal Soul!/The Life of Life!"[42]—is scorned by Goldsmith:

> That independence Britons prize too high,
> Keeps man from man, and breaks the social tie;
> The self-dependent lordlings stand alone,
> All claims that bind and sweeten life unknown;
> Here by the bonds of nature feebly held,
> Minds combat minds, repelling and repell'd;
> Ferments arise, imprison'd factions roar,
> Represt ambition struggles round her shore,
> Till over-wrought, the general system feels
> Its motions stopt, or phrenzy fire the wheels (W4: 263–4).

Taken to excess, liberty threatens an eruption of factional madness, of ambitions in the national mind-set best left repressed. These sentiments illustrate Goldsmith's abstracted sensitivity to imperial cycles which accommodate ambition and progress toward optima beyond which excess results in ruin. This cyclical sense might require fatalistic resignation in the face of a depressing inevitability; however, the warning is issued in the continuous present, intimating that the current moment is one in which the arc of commerce is at its precarious apex. The smooth running of the smaller wheel of contained and self-sustaining rural life is being replaced by the widening wheel of commercial and imperial expansion, a change which threatens either a violent juddering stop, or a manic acceleration in the revolutions of social life.

The Traveller winds its way home after a journey around Europe in which the traveler-observer himself finds that the same dynamics apply in countries differentiated—as much by climatic providence as by culture—by their respective temporal stages of development. The implication is that, even with cultural variations acknowledged, all countries will conceivably develop beyond capacity and, economically, culturally, and metaphorically, either hemorrhage or faint. Rome did in the past; Switzerland might in the future. But neither of these test-cases is as important to the present as the case of Britain, where excessive liberty is no more than a loss of social cohesion. Where Thomson might have celebrated the joys of production and the potential of an empire guided by the Goddess of Liberty, Goldsmith's vision is weighed down by a critical sensitivity to the merely sectional interests by which expansive and prejudiced nationalism are served.[43] For him, "Liberty" is a fiction of faction for as long as it involves the exploitation of the poor by the rich; it camouflages the violation of affective alignments, and destroys functioning communities:

> Yes, brother, curse with me that baleful hour
> When first ambition struck at regal power;
> And thus, polluting honour in its source,
> Gave wealth to sway the mind with double force. (W4: 266–7)

These lines are the most important in the poem, in that they call on familial, Irish support to lament the political state of Britain, and more specifically, the social state of the Ireland in which the poet's brother resides. The "baleful hour" to which Goldsmith refers, although it intimates a temporal specificity, is a general reference to those political upheavals begun in the 1640s which culminated in 1688.

The passage is important too in what it precedes; from it is extrapolated the poet's lament for the gradual commodification of human life in commerce and colonialism:

> Have we not seen, round Britain's peopled shore,
> Her useful sons exchang'd for useless ore?
> Seen all her triumphs but destruction haste,
> Like flaring tapers brightening as they waste;
> Seen opulence, her grandeur to maintain,
> Lead stern depopulation in her train,
> And over fields, where scatter'd hamlets rose,
> In barren solitary pomp repose?
> Have we not seen, at pleasure's lordly call,
> The smiling long-frequented village fall?

CHAPTER 2

> Beheld the duteous son, the sire decay'd,
> The modest matron, and the blushing maid,
> Forc'd from their homes, a melancholy train,
> To traverse climes beyond the western main;
> Where wild Oswego spreads her swamps around,
> And Niagara stuns with thund'ring sound? (W4: 267–8)

This passage is a comment, not just on Britain, but on Britain's relationship to Ireland. The opulence of one is the depopulation of the other; the splendor and pleasure of the absentee landowner is equally the source of his tenantry's woes. Prefiguring *The Deserted Village*, pastoral types are juxtaposed with threatening distant scenes; in this manner is the poem's denouement primed with one more expansive view, one which creates a panorama of suffering and painful exile in the American colonies, where the forlorn pilgrim strays among thick forests populated with wild beasts and murderous Indians.

The process is one of dehumanization; the worth of people and of communities has been subordinated to the imperatives of trade. This verse paragraph also proposes that expansion is the starting-point of national decline: the flaring of the commercial element in the national character is also the harbinger of the nation's burning out. There may in these works be no real sympathy for the American Indian, for the French, the Italians, the Swiss, or the Dutch; Goldsmith is writing, after all, to an English audience. Indeed, he mollifies his readership with his partial prejudices against, and partial stereotypes of, non-British peoples. He is speaking, knowingly, to their prejudices but more subtly to their fears for Britain itself, and to the anxiety, current in the popular classicism of the mid-eighteenth century, that Britain will share the fate of imperial Rome.

The Traveller was subtitled *A Prospect of Society*, and the latter was the poem's original title.[44] In Johnson's *Dictionary*, the word "prospect" has diverse definitions: it can describe the view of something distant, the place which affords an extended view, the many objects which are open to the eye, or the particular object of observation. Added to these meanings is the idea of a prospect as a view into futurity. In Goldsmith's poem, all of these definitions are relevant; most telling, however, is the fact that the poem's title switches from an emphasis on the possibilities of the prospect poem as genre to one which foregrounds the individual traveler, and the perspective of the individual to whom such prospects are available. The subjective, autobiographical register of the poem's beginning returns, after several literary maneuvers, to register melancholic disaffection. Goldsmith's marginal and less than aristocratic origins led him to question the genre's prevailing coincidence of individual and political self-satisfaction. Only structurally is *The Traveller* a regular prospect poem; its more conventional literary geographies are, ultimately, an extended prologue to its problematizing perspective on liberty, on the Glorious Revolution, and on British expansion. Its tones of displacement and complaint manifest the experience of a traveler depending for sustenance on his periodic involvement with the exiled Irish nation on the continent.

Fictions of Liberty

Goldsmith was concerned about how his own traveling days might be portrayed; though they were undertaken in penurious conditions, and dependent upon the employment opportunities offered by aristocrats and hosts, he wished to be seen as someone who traveled with a genuine and humane purpose. John Ginger, a latter-day biographer, claims that Goldsmith wanted his biographers, and posterity, "to see him, in his mid-twenties, as a latter-day troubadour seeking refuge among peasants whom he charmed with his flute and priests or academics whose interest he aroused with his scholarship and skill in debate."[45] The earliest and most important influence on the picaresque self-image which Goldsmith wished to cultivate in his travel and travel writing was Baron Lewis (Ludvig) Holberg. The trajectory and mode of his own European excursions were derived from the Danish author, about whom Goldsmith wrote:

> Without money, recommendations or friends, he undertook to set out upon his travels, and make the tour of Europe on foot. A good voice, and a trifling skill in musick, were the only finances he had to support an undertaking so extensive; so he travelled by day, and at night sung at the doors of peasants houses, to get himself a lodging. In this manner, young Holberg passed thro' France, Germany and Holland. (W1: 284).

James Prior claims that when Goldsmith set off for the continent in 1755, Holberg's "example was in his eye, and in fact became the model of his conduct."[46] The idea that someone could travel through Europe without money intrigued Goldsmith, and appealed to his sense of which dimensions of society were worth seeing. This mode of travel was advocated in *An Enquiry into the Present State of Polite Learning in Europe* (1759): "Countries wear very different appearances to travellers of different circumstances," wrote Goldsmith; "A man who is whirled through Europe in a post chaise, and the pilgrim who walks the grand tour on foot, will form very different conclusions" (W1: 331). Goldsmith's avowal of monarchism

CHAPTER 2

was attributed to the extensive view which traveling on foot afforded him; walking along from place to place, he could examine mankind more closely. Influenced by Holberg, he viewed the political life of Europe from an earthier vantage point.

In the case of Holberg, this ground-level travel took on, in one famous work, the allegorical caricature of a subterranean exploration. Translated in 1742 into English from its Latin original of 1740, *A Journey to the World Under-Ground*, Holberg's account of fantastic travel, was published under the pseudonym "Nicholas Klimius." In his survey of subterranean peoples, Klimius, the fictive narrator, relates that the Monarchs of the "Potuans" possess "rather a paternal than a regal Power." In a reversal of the libertarian ideals which were prevalent in contemporary England, the Potuans, though they are "Lovers of Justice, Power, and Liberty," subscribe to paternalistic authority. Concepts deemed incompatible in England, Klimius reports, "do here go Hand in Hand." Added to this, Potuan Princes "endeavour to preserve an Equality between the Subjects, that is, as far as the Nature of Government will admit. You see here no different Ranks and Titles of Honour." The problems associated with a libertarian politics are more clearly delineated in the Land of Liberty, where people are accountable to no authority whatsoever. Anticipating Goldsmith, Liberty in Klimius' account leads to fraught factionalism, bordering on civil war. Klimius flees the land of liberty in fear of his life. The Gulliverian satire of Klimius' journey uses the device of fantastic travel as an indirect means by which to comment on contemporary European society. Klimius visits societies which provide a caricature of European politics; he also encounters in his travels in the world underground *Tanian's Journey to the Super-terranean World, or a Description of the Kingdoms and Countries upon Earth*, a text expressing the perspective of a subterranean on his travels in Europe. It is easy, Tanian observes, to make the Europeans "swallow the greatest absurdities"; he diagnoses in the observed societies a blinkered self-regard: "they imagine that nobody has any Understanding but themselves; and being puff'd with this opinion, they look down with Contempt upon other Mortals, as if they were Barbarians in Comparison with them."[47]

Influenced by his biography, Goldsmith was equally influenced by Holberg's ideas; and if the latter's utopian/dystopian travel account provided a template within which Holberg/Klimius could warn against the emptier rhetoric of liberty, against chauvinism and cultural presumption, so too could Goldsmith's generic works, from the sentimental entertainments to the weightier poems, convey his own brand of subterranean disaffection. *The Vicar of Wakefield*, like Goldsmith's stage comedies, may be "lighter" than *The Traveller*; nonetheless, it repeatedly stabs at the venality of human action parading under the ideological banner of liberty.

Even in his most innocuous-seeming works, indeed, there is subtle incision; his need as a professional author to generate commercially viable works vies perennially with smart caveats, within the texts themselves, about the compromises necessitated by the provision of happy endings. These works convey, in spite of such compromises, the harsher social realities which in their generic imperatives they sometimes distort. As such, Goldsmith's popular narrative works, and *The Vicar of Wakefield* in particular—can be better and more sympathetically understood as something more than the sentimental entertainments characterized by latter-day readings.

One such reading was James Joyce's. *The Vicar of Wakefield* made Joyce briefly uncertain as to the negative direction the stories of *Dubliners* were taking, as he wrote to his brother Stanislaus in July of 1905:

> The preface of *The Vicar of Wakefield* which I read yesterday gave me a moment of doubt as to the excellence of my literary manners. It seems so improbable that Hardy, for example, will be spoken of in two hundred years. And yet when I arrived at page two of the narrative I saw the extreme putridity of the social system out of which Goldsmith had reared his flower. Is it possible that, after all, men of letters are no more than entertainers?[48]

An avowed devotee of *The Vicar of Wakefield*, Joyce's question about that novel perceptively goes to the quick of the Goldsmith enigma: how does the famous ease and facility of Goldsmith's style sit with the awfulness of the economic system in which it was produced and which, in many ways, produced it? Goldsmith's novel might be viewed as an ideological screen, but it is more than that: it is a satire on the futility of unworldly sentiment, while at the same time partially a vehicle for it. It is also a fictional model of rural virtue, and yet it represents a social order under threat. Though yielding to sentiment in the tenor and conclusion of his novel, Goldsmith also undercut such sentiment in exposing its fraught and untenable quality in the context of the new economy. Ultimately, the book is as much about the putridity of the emerging social system as it is a pretty pastoral tale with a happy ending.

The Vicar of Wakefield appealed to contemporary taste and its appeal lasted.[49] The nature of that appeal, however, changed over time. In the Sternean

CHAPTER 2

1760s, it had enough sentiment *and* enough satirical self-reflexivity to please. Through the nineteenth century, and into the early twentieth, it was increasingly received as unequivocally sentimental, a reception that was enhanced by its scenes being lushly illustrated, or rendered on canvas by, among others, Charles Ryley (1787), Thomas Stothard (1792), Thomas Unwins (1812), Thomas Rowlandson and John Martin (both in 1817), Gilbert Stuart Newton (1828), George Cruickshank (1830–1832), Daniel Maclise (1839–41), William Mulready (through the 1840s), William P. Frith (from the 1840s through to the 1860s) and Arthur Rackham (in 1929). Mulready's illustrations in particular add dramatic effect to the narrative, intensifying the arcadian, and subsequently the distressful, experiences of the displaced family.[50] Like Goldsmith, Mulready was an Irishman who pursued his career largely in London. The Ennis-born son of a private soldier in the Irish Volunteers, the surface Englishness of Mulready's style and subject matter, belied, as such characteristics did in Goldsmith's novel, the exilic origins of the artist's nostalgia. That he should have worked most extensively on *The Vicar* in the 1840s, the decade of Ireland's Great Famine, adds a poignancy to illustrations of the family's distress.

Other illustrations and illustrated editions, however, contributed to the book's gradual apotheosis as a sort of fairy tale of benevolence and familial comfort pitted against a cruel commercial and legal logic. Illustrators supplemented, even exaggerated, the bucolic nature of the text, encouraging the tendency of readers to view it, as Walter Scott did, as an exemplary idealization of "quiet labour and domestic happiness" (CH: 276). Arthur Rackham in particular added to the story an otherworldly ambience. His signatures—he famously illustrated *Gulliver's Travels, Aesop's Fables, Charles O'Malley, the Irish Dragoon, Rip Van Winkle, Hansel and Gretel*—included sinewy arboreal life and translucent young women, images, respectively, of resilience and vulnerability.[51]

Though obscured by subsequent presentations and readings, there is in *The Vicar of Wakefield* a complex blend of sentiment, irony and political dissidence. Goethe appreciated the interplay of the first two qualities; the influence of Goldsmith and Laurence Sterne's *Tristram Shandy* together taught him "high, benevolent irony, this just and comprehensive way of viewing things." But there were clear differences: "it is strange that Yorick should incline rather to that which has no Form, and that Goldsmith should be all Form" (CH: 278). In Goethe's understanding, the absurd density of plot in *The Vicar* partakes of a subtler irony. Goldsmith was involved in that culture of sentimentality which *The Vicar* and *Tristram Shandy* gently mock from different ends of a formal spectrum. *The Vicar*

William Mulready, Illustration of a scene from *The Vicar of Wakefield*.

is more satirical and reflexive than modern criticisms of Goldsmith might allow; at the same time, it is not experimental enough to warrant *formal* comparison with *Tristram Shandy*. In short, Goldsmith's novel is only partially satirical, and certainly less Menippean in its execution.[52] Absurdities of plot construction reveal themselves in the high intensity, the claustrophobic relentlessness of dramatic

Arthur Rackham, "A Favourite Song of Dryden's." Illustration of a scene from *The Vicar of Wakefield*.

events. An impacted and compacted narrative, *The Vicar* was hurriedly produced; accordingly, Goldsmith acknowledged the criticism that certain parts would have benefited from more work. Time, for the Grub Street prosateur, was money; the material comedy of professional authorship was indelibly projected into his ramshackle story, not least because it was unfinished, rushed into publication when Goldsmith was threatened with arrest for nonpayment of rent.[53]

The Vicar is a comedy which manipulates, and mediates between, those two opposing worlds which feature throughout Goldsmith's oeuvre. As Richard Helgerson has cogently put it, there is "the static world of the village home that he and many of his heroes left behind and the active urban world to which they were drawn. Each world has its own values and its own shortcomings." Goldsmith deliberately sets one scene, and one register, against the other—the rural against the urban, the sentimental against the satirical, the spiritual against the material; in so doing, argues Helgerson, he "finely tunes our response, relieving the sentimental regret for the lost village life with a comic perception of its innocent foolishness, and preventing an easy acceptance of the material necessity of urban life with an ironic perception of its spiritual insufficiency."[54] This is part of a larger dialectic which operates throughout his oeuvre: a geographical opposition of country and city, of home and away, where "away" can refer to either the corrupted city or the new world.

In Goldsmith's poetic and fictional works, the sphere of action is the smaller circle of provincial or rural life. His benevolent characters can only survive in the village environment; if to the city sped, their good-nature is equally their downfall. What was for Goethe Goldsmith's characteristic "high, benevolent irony" is also a highly ironic benevolence. Principled and unworldly, Primrose's benevolence threatens to destroy his family. Equally, the character of William Thornhill "carried benevolence to an excess when young"; like Henry Mackenzie's eponymous *Man of Feeling* (1771), Primrose and the young Thornhill are possessed of too much sensibility to function properly in a world of credit and commerce.

This foolishly benevolent male figure appears time and again throughout the oeuvre. In his 1762 biography, Goldsmith portrayed Richard "Beau" Nash, the famous Bath socialite, as someone who combined "an honest benevolent mind with the vices which spring from too much good nature. He had pity for every creature's distress, but wanted prudence in the application of his benefits" (W3: 295). Similarly, the Man in Black of *The Citizen of the World* resembles Goldsmith himself, in being the son of a clergyman who encouraged generosity at the expense of *nous*. And in *The Good Natur'd Man*, the character of Honeywood has been

CHAPTER 2

ruined by good nature and a desire to please others. Given Goldsmith's generic dexterity, benevolence can be either altered—in comic drama and fiction—into a more knowing equanimity, or it can figure, poetically, in the larger social tragedy of migration and rural ruin. The plot of *The Vicar*, indeed, is built around the idea of a Fall caused by commerce: Sir William Thornhill's becoming Mr. Burchell, and the descent of the Vicar's family to poverty, illustrate, for Samuel H. Woods, Goldsmith's general point about "the social disruption when the power of the monarchy was being eroded by the growing wealth of nabobs."[55] Their experiences, their fall from one scene to the other, are equally the experiences of the exiled villagers in both *The Traveller* and *The Deserted Village*.

The novel is narrated almost entirely from the perspective of the Vicar himself, and the narrative voice is gently and intermittently parodied. Primrose is self-assured in his piety and goodness, but in this self-assurance he is bumptious and blinkered. He portrays his family scene as one of cloyingly soft pastoral, and pastoral in the most technical sense, for he is every inch akin to the shepherd tending his flock. He is opposed to romantic embellishments, and his description of his children is a preposterous caricature of fey frugality: "My children, the offspring of temperance, as they were educated without softness, so they were at once well formed and healthy; my sons hardy and active, my daughters beautiful and blooming" (W4: 19).

At the outset, the Vicar's family lives happily in the middle range of society, in the midst of a kindly providence which sees them all healthy, ruddy, and satisfied. They visit with their rich neighbors without jealousy and they relieve the local or transient poor; there is in this world an organic connectedness between the social classes. This is an economy held together by charity and obligation, and as such it is a society which only needs to have one component subtracted in order for the protection which it provides to be undone. The essential goodness of the family at its center is only a thin buffer against the full scourge of the emerging economic system. The entire chain of misfortunes which befalls the Primrose family begins with Primrose's unbending stance on the question of whether Anglican priests can remarry after the deaths of their wives. Disastrously for his family, the Vicar's stance is directly opposed to that of the father of his son's intended. Their argument, added to the unexpected financial ruin of the family, causes the match to be broken off, where the successful marriage of his son George might have ameliorated the loss of the family savings. The cause of their ruin, then, is twofold: they suffer at the hands of mercantilism and philosophical systematizing, conjured here as the external and internal enemies of familial and pastoral safety.

Focusing Goldsmith's perspective, *The Vicar*'s nineteenth and twentieth chapters feature a concerted assault on the delusions of liberty. These chapters are, politically, at the novel's center; they suspend the narrative of the family's misfortunes in order to indict the commercialism which threatens to pollute the social scene from which they emerge.[56] Displaced by the forces of commerce, the Vicar has himself become an observant traveler, and with that a social commentator. In chapter 19, he arrives at the house of Mr. Arnold, whom he has met in an alehouse, and with whom he has discussed contemporary politics. Mr. Arnold, in the Vicar's eyes, seems at first "a Parliament-man at least." In their subsequent discussions "liberty," at once Mr. Arnold's "boast and his terror," is assessed. Arnold celebrates the liberty which is manifested in the freedom of speech in the magazines and reviews; "and though they hate each other, I love them all." Liberty, to which the cacophony of journalistic voices attests, is associated with the British national character: it is, singularly, "the Briton's boast." The Vicar interjects that Mr. Arnold should therefore reverence the king as liberty's guardian. Mr. Arnold claims that the king is only to be listened to when he is possessed of sound advice. The Vicar counters that all of the advice which is offered is only in the service of commercial interests. It is the duty of the honest, as he sees it, to shore up the "sacred power that has for some years been every day declining, and losing its due share of influence in the state. But these ignorants still continue the cry of liberty; and if they have any weight basely throw it into the subsiding scale." Mr. Arnold asks whether "there should be found at present advocates for slavery? And who are for meanly giving up the privileges of Britons." The Vicar responds:

> "No, Sir," replied I, "I am for liberty, that attribute of Gods! Glorious liberty! that theme of modern declamation. I would have all men kings. I would be a king myself. We have all naturally an equal right to the throne: we are all originally equal. This is my opinion, and was once the opinion of a set of honest men who were called Levellers.

The utopian intentions of the Levellers proved untenable, the Vicar concedes, because of the discrepancies in natural abilities between men. Some are born, he claims, to command, and some to obey; thus, even in ostensibly egalitarian systems, tyranny arises, masquerading as freedom. Worse than that, local tyrannies in republics proliferate and congeal into a broad oligarchical domination. Against that tendency, the Vicar maintains—as Goldsmith did repeatedly—that the institution of monarchy was the best guarantor of social justice. The "great," or those who would be tyrants, despise the raising of a higher authority; they seek therefore to diminish monarchy and deploy all of their political might against what is perceived as arbitrary power. If the circumstances of the state are such that the powerful can gather more wealth, the political ambition of the oligarchy is strengthened, but that wealth is not generated by domestic industry:

> An accumulation of wealth, however, must necessarily be the consequence when, at present, more riches flow in from external commerce than arise from internal industry; for external commerce can only be managed to advantage by the rich, and they have also, at the same time, all the emoluments arising from internal industry; so that the rich, with us, have two sources of wealth, whereas the poor have but one. For this reason, wealth, in all commercial states, is found to accumulate; and all such have hitherto in time become aristocratical.

The laws of the nation contribute to the accumulation of wealth, and laws are entwined with, and shaped by, the interests of the rich. The Vicar's, and Goldsmith's, attitudes resonate with Edmund Burke's: for the Vicar, the emerging order breaks "the natural ties that bind the rich and poor together." The learned, not being rich, have no say in governance, and this change in social emphasis infects the wise with material ambition. Those with wealth, once furnished with the necessities and niceties of life, use their surplus to enslave those without. They make dependants "by purchasing the liberty of the needy or the venal." Opulence then draws to itself a circle of poverty and exploited dependence. In such a system the polity "may be compared to a Cartesian system, each orb with a vortex of its own." The impoverished "rabble" is thus trapped in the opulent man's vortex of power and pomp.

Nonetheless, the Vicar maintains, there are people outside of these vortices. This beleaguered group is the middle order of mankind, the custodians of "all the arts, wisdom, and virtues of society," in whose orbit can be found a more workable conception of freedom. In the new capitalism, however, their influence is internally and externally threatened: they may seek influence through material ambition, or their voices may be "in a manner drowned in that of the rabble." The only way in which the middle order can preserve its influence is to seek protection in the institution of a single, regulating entity: monarchy "divides the power of the rich, and calls off the great from falling with tenfold weight on the middle order placed beneath them." If the rich diminish the power of monarchy, the positive, respectful, modest understanding of freedom which Goldsmith attributes to the middle orders will be replaced by a negative freedom from monarchical meddling in the imperial accumulation of wealth. The Vicar concludes:

> I am then for, and would die for, monarchy, sacred monarchy; for if there be anything sacred amongst men, it must be anointed Sovereign of his people, and every diminution of his power in war, or in peace, is an infringement upon the real liberties of the subject. The sounds of liberty, patriotism, and Britons, have already done *much*, it is to be hoped that the true sons of freedom will prevent their ever doing more. I have known many of those pretended champions for liberty in my time, yet do I not remember one that was not in his heart and in his family a tyrant.

Liberty, patriotism, Britons: the self-congratulatory conception of the national character as uniquely attuned to liberty was the object of Goldsmith's complaint; in chapter 19, therefore, the often ironic distance between the author and the Vicar's narrative voice is put into abeyance.

Toward the end of this chapter, the Vicar is reintroduced to Arabella Wilmot, his son George's erstwhile betrothed, lost to George due to his father's hubris and the family's sudden financial disaster. She asks the Vicar whether he has seen George. He responds that he has not seen him in three years; he relates with sadness that he does not know whether he will see him again. Recalling fondly the pleasing hours spent by the fireside in Wakefield—a clear echo of Goldsmith's own expressed nostalgia for his homeplace in the Irish midlands—the Vicar informs Arabella that his family is being dispersed due to poverty and infamy. "The good-natured girl let fall a tear at this account; but as I saw her possessed of too much sensibility, I forbore a more minute detail of our sufferings" (W4: 98–104). To the Vicar, Arabella's propensity for tears is at least a sign of her continuing affection for his son, which he finds gratifying.

That evening, they watch a group of strolling players perform Nicholas Rowe's *The Fair Penitent*. As it turns out, the lead actor is the returned George Primrose, who has since become the "Philosophical Vagabond." Chapter 20 of *The Vicar* is George's traveler's tale, in which the "Philosophical Vagabond" recounts the progress of an ultimately disappointed curiosity. After leaving his family, he had set off for London to make his way in the world. In the course of a failed literary career, he is exposed to the venality of Grub Street, in which his essays, like Goldsmith's own, "were buried among the essays upon liberty, Eastern tales, and cures for the bite of a mad dog" (W4: 111). After a subsequent encounter with Ned Thornhill, nephew of Sir William Thornhill, George is nearly sold into American slavery. Deflected from this fate by the offices of a ship's captain, he travels to Holland, where he falls into the company of an Irish student who in turn

CHAPTER 2

directs him to Louvain to teach Greek. In Louvain, he finds that there is no need for Greek; thus he resolves to go forward, using his knowledge of music to provide food and lodgings as he makes his way through Flanders to Paris. In Paris, he is recommended as a traveling tutor to a young English gentleman on the Grand Tour. Heir to a massive fortune earned in the West Indies, "avarice" was this young man's "prevailing passion: all his questions on the road were how money might be saved" (W4: 120). He is deserted by his young student at Leghorn, and is left to make his way back to England using his skill in debate:

> In all the foreign universities and convents, there are upon certain days philosophical theses maintained against every adventitious disputant; for which, if the champion opposes with any dexterity, he can claim a gratuity in money, a dinner, and a bed for one night. In this manner therefore I fought my way towards England, walked along from city to city, examined mankind more nearly, and, if I may so express it, saw both sides of the picture. My remarks, however, are but few: I found that monarchy was the best government for the poor to live in, and commonwealths for the rich. I found that riches in general were in every country another name for freedom; and that no man is so fond of liberty himself as not to be desirous of subjecting the will of some individuals in society to his own. (W4: 121)

George has dallied, then, as had Goldsmith, at places of Irish and Jacobite exile during his travels across the continent. Like Goldsmith again, George is the traveler-observer who has surveyed European society not from the privileged perspective of the English aristocrat, but from a lowly vantage point. In both cases, a monarchical social, political and economic outlook is produced out of the crossing of the lowly traveler's perspective with the enlightenment imperative of geo-cultural comparison.

George's hard-earned political views fall neatly into line with his father's; and from this confluence forward the story proceeds to plot the family's inevitable homeward course and ultimate salvation. Thus, *The Vicar of Wakefield* narrates the exile, redemption, and restoration of a flawed, mildly foolish but endearing paternal authority; the exile of the father figure is plainly analogous to the plight of a monarchy stoutly defended by father and son in the novel's central chapters. *The Vicar of Wakefield* is, thus, a Jacobite parable.[57] In its way a response to oligarchy, to imperialism, and to the Seven Years' War, its politics have been obscured to the extent that it has in some critical quarters become no more than a winsome tale in which rural Englishness is charmingly rendered. Its context and worldview have been obscured by an attention to the novel's more saccharine pastoral excesses; dehistoricized, or understood only in terms of its subsequent incarnations, the novel's central chapters lose their declamatory charge. This charge, when reactivated, situates the novel more usefully as a fictional companion piece to *The Traveller*, itself a poetic redaction of those chapters' political geography, and of the novel's politics in general.

א

The panoramic political geographies of *The Vicar of Wakefield* and *The Traveller* are, finally, miniaturized and domesticated in the dramatic writings. Kate Hardcastle remarks in *She Stoops to Conquer* that "in this hypocritical age there are few that do not condemn in public what they practice in private, and think they pay every debt to virtue when they praise it" (W5: 147). Like hollow "liberty," "virtue" is betrayed by real practices at a geographical or social remove from the scene in which such qualities are most glibly celebrated. Such a discrepancy explains the initially appalling behavior in the play of its central characters Marlow and Hastings, two travelers of ostensibly high sentiment, who, having been fooled by Tony Lumpkin into mistaking the Hardcastle home for a "lowly" inn, think themselves out of polite society. The mask of civility drops when Marlow thinks he is dealing with people of an "inferior" sort; when agents of polite civility are not looking, he is mouthy, louche, and rapacious. Marlow is well traveled, and supposedly sophisticated, but that does not stop him from behaving like a boor around those he presumes to be of a different social order. Mr. Hardcastle, who wishes for the betrothal of his daughter Kate to Marlow, encourages his visitors to be "under no constraint in this house. This is Liberty-Hall, gentlemen. You may do just as you please here" (W5: 132); when he sees their presumptuousness, he asks whether such behavior should be tolerated in one's own house. This discrepancy constitutes, in a more localized sphere of action, Burke's "geographical morality."

Though the central comic plot device of *She Stoops to Conquer* is generated by the unpleasantness of upper-class travelers, Goldsmith does not, in acceding to the imperative of a happy ending, follow through with his critique of their expectations. Instead, Marlow the would-be exploiter is gradually manipulated into a more meaningful romantic relationship by the wily Kate Hardcastle, whose subtle agency in continuing to play the role of bar-maid enables Marlow—anxious and timid in the company of upper-class women—to make his suit more successfully.

CHAPTER 2

His ultimate success, however, is also dependent on his acquiring a more profound respect for the "bar-maid." Indeed, toward the end—in love, but still thinking her beneath him—he agonizes about marrying her against his father's wishes. All such worries are, of course, put aside when her true identity is revealed. Marlow and Kate will, at the play's conclusion, live happily ever after.

The conclusion of *She Stoops to Conquer* is proclaimed by Kate's mother to be no more than "the whining end of a modern novel" (W5: 215). Her remarks clarify the ironic distance between the author and the contemporary genres of sentimentality in which his works operate. Goldsmith's plays *and* his novel resolve themselves in cloying endgames. And predictably so: cultures of sentiment and sensibility provided the author with a ready audience, one which he necessarily appeased, but with a germ of self-reflexive mischief which the same audience, still enthralled with the fiction of Laurence Sterne, also appreciated. In *She Stoops to Conquer*, betrothals and marriages channel potentially farcical energies into a relieving, but transparent resolution which is not nearly as compelling as the delusions and double standards which sustain the narrative. The conclusion belies the play's knowing political subtext: that those who travel with an air of entitlement and an exalted sense of their own liberty will, in their encounters with others, *take* liberties.

Marlow's chauvinism is, in the end, problematized by the realization that his supposed superiority is no more than a fiction of the scenario into which he has been fooled. Thus, he earns, through the mistakes of a night, a greater critical self-awareness, a quality which, cumulatively, Goldsmith's writings seek to instigate at the level of the nation. In the place of chauvinism, Goldsmith recommends that other societies be viewed, as far as possible, from below, so that a greater cultural empathy, and a better understanding of how societies function, or fail to function, might be made available. In the various characters of George Primrose and Altangi, the oriental visitor of *The Citizen of the World*, Goldsmith, influenced by Holberg, repeatedly claimed that a man who travels to inform himself and enlighten his home nation should be a mixture of philosopher and vagabond—experiencing other societies on the revealing level of closer cultural contact. These imperatives yielded the peculiarly beleaguered and dissident tones of what are, at first glance, generic works.

Part II

POLITICAL LANDSCAPES AND BODIES POLITIC

3

DELICATE ALLEGORIES: IRELAND AND THE EAST

As some fair female unadorned and plain,
Secure to please while youth confirms her reign,
Slights every borrowed charm that dress supplies,
Nor shares with art the triumph of her eyes.
But when those charms are past, for charms are frail,
When time advances, and when lovers fail,
She then shines forth sollicitous to bless,
In all the glaring impotence of dress.
Thus fares the land, by luxury betrayed,
In nature's simplest charms at first arrayed,
But verging to decline, its splendours rise,
Its vistas strike, its palaces surprize;
While scourged by famine from the smiling land,
The mournful peasant leads his humble band;
And while he sinks without one arm to save,
The country blooms—a garden, and a grave.

—*The Deserted Village* (W4: 298)

WHEREVER AND WHENEVER anyone is defined by appearance or dress alone in Goldsmith's writing, the assumption is that substance is lacking, or waning, in the definer and in the defined. In an epilogue to *She Stoops to Conquer*, accordingly, Kate Hardcastle congratulates herself on having "gain'd a husband without aid from dress" (W5: 103). By combining, in her persona of bar-maid, practical clothing with substantial and endearing good

CHAPTER 3

sense, she has won over, and improved, a man who would otherwise have obliged her to gratify him sexually before betraying and disowning her in "superior" company—a fate which has befallen, in *The Deserted Village* above, a "fair female unadorned and plain." Thus, in Goldsmith's poem, fares the land. In Goldsmith's use of the trope, the betrayed country dresses herself in imported finery to mask either her real poverty, or her anxiety about the substance of whatever prosperity she does possess. Either show tells of a lack of real wealth and, ultimately, of a lack of sovereignty and economic substance.

This discrepancy between anxious display and actual prosperity is captured too in the lesser of Goldsmith's two plays, *The Good Natur'd Man* (1768). In that play, Croaker aligns cosmetic culture with the decline of economic self-sufficiency: "The women in my time were good for something. I have seen a lady drest from top to toe in her own manufactures formerly. But now a-days the devil a thing of their own manufacture about them, except their faces" (W5: 25). Further on in the play, Mrs. Croaker remarks of Biddy Bundle her that "as her natural face decays, her skill improves in making an artificial one," leaving her "looking for all the world like one of the painted ruins of the place" (W5: 28). The analogy between the cosmetic and the ruined is also loaded—as in *The Deserted Village*—with a commentary on the state of the political landscape. In a tradition of eighteenth-century writing coming through from Swift and Alexander Pope, Goldsmith connects issues of the commercial, the imperial and the cosmetic, and suggests that all three are mutually stimulating.[1] For male authors especially, cosmetic and sartorial excess, seen as endemic weaknesses of women, were correlatives of the advance of capitalism and imperialism. These excesses were produced by the new consumer economy, and that new economy required their perpetuation. In Swift's "Proposal for the Universal Use of Irish Manufacture" (1720) and "A Proposal to the Ladies of Ireland" (1729), there is a repeated association of the female body, and its dress, with commerce, empire, and the loss of the nation's integrity. In the earlier pamphlet, thus, Swift had asked: "What if the Ladies would be content with *Irish* stuffs for the Furniture of their Houses, for Gowns and Petticoats to themselves and their Daughters?"[2] Croaker's complaint in Goldsmith's play alludes directly to Swift, and to the political complaints of Ireland.

The betrayed, forlorn woman had long been a symbol of the Irish nation. In that tradition, Swift and Goldsmith's political arguments shared their feminizing symbolism—the analogy between the dereliction of land and woman—with Irish Jacobite verse. Such symbolism locates Goldsmith's work especially in an Irish context. Robert Graves noted this connection when he credited Goldsmith with defying contemporary poetic insincerity with the indignant tone of *The Deserted Village*, which, though "disguised as an essay on the break-up of English village society" was actually "a lament for the ills of Ireland, modelled on contemporary Irish minstrel songs—walk, description, meditation, moral vision, invocation of the Goddess."[3] Especially suggestive is the link drawn by John Montague between the poem and the Gaelic *aisling* or Vision poems—exemplified in "An *Aisling*" by the eighteenth-century Munster poet Aogán Ó Rathaille (c. 1675–1729).[4] The *aisling*, for Joseph McMinn, is "an unusual combination of the political, the religious and the erotic," which includes, "religious allegory, in the form of a miraculous apparition of female beauty, and directs the longing towards the political hope of the Pretender's restoration." Like *The Deserted Village*, with its curious mixture of neoclassicism, political protest, and elegy, the *aisling* is "a ritualised form of anger and grief."[5] Swift was adapting the narrative element of the *aisling* mode when he composed *The Story of the Injured Lady* (1746), in which Ireland is represented, or represents herself, as a once-beautiful woman betrayed and left neglected, forlorn, and ragged by a fickle England. It is also plausible, probable indeed, that Goldsmith knew and understood the mode, with which the analogy of landscape and female figure is consistent.

This personification of landscape as woman is one instance of a frequently noted and much studied analogy in the history of literature generally.[6] Closer to the subject considered here are seminal essays by James G. Turner and Carole Fabricant on sexually inflected aspects of landscape description and design theory in the eighteenth century.[7] To augment such studies, and to develop connections made by Turner and Fabricant, Goldsmith's use of this traditional analogy of garden and woman is traced here in terms of a network of personal and intellectual friendships and influences. Prompted further by the argument of Fabricant's *Swift's Landscape*, it is proposed that Goldsmith's landscapes, political and poetical, are, like Swift's, implicitly Irish. Against Fabricant, however, it is argued here that Goldsmith's landscapes are not weakly nostalgic in their Irishness; rather, they are subtly and intriguingly allegorical. For Goldsmith, the Irish interior was, for all of its flaws and political neglect, home. For Swift, it was a place of compounded exile, a scene where English abuse had conspired with native indolence to produce misery and mess. Auburn as it was mirrors England now; as it has become, it is Ireland, betrayed and untidy. Goldsmith's modification of the *aisling* image in generating the poem's central simile derives from his involvement in English landscape debates of his time, specifically the debate over the merits, or otherwise, of the Chinese garden, a pretty allegorical vehicle for some, a garish import equivalent to a constitutional violation for others.

CHAPTER 3

Swift had attacked imported fashions; so did Goldsmith, in a similar vein, critique the fripperies and destructive follies which were prevalent in London through the 1760s. These fashions were not merely material, or sartorial. Intellectual fashions also stimulated, and were stimulated by, mercantile interest. Through the eighteenth century one such intellectual fashion was an emerging orientalism, a modish addition which would, for some, demonstrate just how hollow things had become in the metropolitan artistic scene. The new orientalism had, no matter what its pretensions, very little to do with the Far East, though claims to geographical and cultural accuracy were certainly made, and at times exaggerated. The fashion for the East was ridiculed in Goldsmith's writing; however, Goldsmith, through inversion, used in *The Citizen of the World* the hollowness of the pseudo-oriental as a satirical vehicle, just as Swift had used ludicrous travel to equally satirical ends in *Gulliver's Travels*.

Satirical and allegorical intentions, however, have been missed in some studies of Goldsmith's orientalism. In his postcolonial critique of *The Citizen of the World*, Tao Zhijian has criticized Goldsmith's Chinese letters for his complicit reproduction of the western imperialist view that "China, in particular, is a stagnant society; it hardly ever changes—at least for the better."[8] Goldsmith's imperial facetiousness is exemplified, for Zhijian, in a passage where Altangi writes to Fum Hoam, his correspondent in Peking:

> In every letter I expect accounts of some new revolutions in China, some strange occurrence in the state, or disaster among my private acquaintance. I open every pacquet with tremulous expectation, and am agreeably disappointed when I find my friends and my country continuing in felicity. I wander, but they are at rest; they suffer few changes but what pass in my own restless imagination; it is only the rapidity of my own motion gives an imaginary swiftness to objects which are in some measure immovable. (W2: 261)

This letter might indeed indict Goldsmith on the charges brought by Zhijian but for the fact that exactly the same sentiments are expressed with regard to friends and country in a letter sent by Goldsmith in 1757 to brother-in-law Daniel Hodson, still residing in the Irish midlands: "as my thoughts sometimes found refuge from severer studies among my friends in Ireland I fancied to myself strange revolutions at home, but I find it was the rapidity of my own motion that gave an immaginary [sic] one to objects really at rest" (L: 30). In *The Citizen of the World*, Goldsmith uses the Far East as a foil against which the foibles of London society can be demonstrated all the more pointedly. Like *The Traveller*, it also provides a vehicle for commentary on the condition of exile. *The Traveller* is not ultimately "about" Italy, Switzerland, France, or Holland; equally, Goldsmith's Chinese letters have very little to do with the East. Instead, the East figures, alternately, as an exotic geo-cultural opposite *and* analogy for societies closer to home. Christopher Brooks suggests that "Altangi's 'orientalism' is a guise for Goldsmith's 'Irishness,' for both character and author comment on [. . .] the place of the foreigner in the insular-island ethos of England."[9] Just as Goldsmith's literary landscapes are usually vehicles for sociopolitical commentary, so too is his orientalism. The story of the forlorn woman in the verse paragraph above works on several, delicately allegorical levels. It derives from contemporary garden discourse, and it draws orientalist and Irish narrative forms together to make a political point about the denudation of Goldsmith's native country.

Goldsmith's cryptic mode was well prepared by eighteenth-century critical discourse. "An allegory," wrote John Hughes in his 1715 edition of Edmund Spenser, "is a kind of Poetical Picture, or Hieroglyphick, which by its apt Resemblance conveys Instruction to the Mind by an Analogy to the Senses; and so amuses the Fancy, while it informs the Understanding."[10] The fair female, once unadorned and plain, now a garden and a grave, is the "Poetical Picture" which can be illuminated by analyzing the allegorical uses to which Goldsmith puts ostensibly Eastern narrative forms. Studied here is the manner in which the metaphor and the narrative of the *aisling*, modified according to broader contemporary intellectual exchanges between "the English tradition" and "the Chinese fashion" in landscape design, are subtly woven into the fabric of *The Deserted Village*. Chinese-ness was a vehicle for interrelated, and subversive, political and aesthetic philosophies. This chapter traces the heritage and satirical nature of Goldsmith's orientalism before demonstrating the precisely Jacobite inflections of his oriental landscapes.

East and West

Before and during the Middle Ages, China, for Europeans, was really no more than an indistinct figment of the imagination. A continent of unknown area, just beyond the eastern edge of the known world, Cathay, thus named, was ruled in the thirteenth century by Kublai Khan, the great Mongol emperor whom Marco Polo served during his Asian travels between 1275 and 1292. Polo's book *The Description of the World*, dictated in 1298 to Rusticello of Pisa, was "a combination of

CHAPTER 3

verifiable fact, random information posing as statistics, exaggeration, make-believe, gullible acceptance of unsubstantiated stories, and a certain amount of outright fabrication." Superficial, overembellished by Rusticello's writerly conceits, and ultimately combining and confusing "ignorance and precision," it would have been no different to other early accounts, but for the fact that it was the first of its kind by a westerner which claimed to be an "insider" description.

The most substantial descriptive accounts after Polo's were those of seventeenth-century Jesuit missionaries Louis Le Comte, whose *Nouveaux Memoires sur l'état de la Chine* Goldsmith consulted in the third edition (1697), and those of Jean-Baptiste Du Halde, whose *Description Geographique, historique, chronologique, politique, et physique de l'empire de la Chine* (1696) Goldsmith knew in an English translation entitled *A Description of the Empire of China*, published in two volumes by Edward Cave in 1738 and 1741. After the waning of the Catholic nations' imperial adventures, of which Polo was an emissary, Protestant powers—the Netherlands and Britain—began in the eighteenth century to seize new holds in the Far East and to explore China more fully. Of this enlightenment juncture, Jonathan Spence has theorized that, though literalness and exactitude were not strictly required, depictions of the East at least yielded more raw material for "powerful synthetic minds" to exploit for philosophical and satirical purposes.[11] China became a model for Utopian philosophes, and Goldsmith himself would become a popular and populist instrument of this example.[12]

Inspired by literary antecedents such as Montesquieu's *Lettres Persanes* (1721), Lyttelton's *Letters from a Persian in England to his friend at Ispahan* (1735) and the Marquis d'Argens' *Lettres Chinoises* (1739), and emboldened with specifically Chinese material gleaned from the writings of Le Comte and Du Halde, Goldsmith indulged the oriental vogue by writing a series of "Chinese Letters," published in the *Public Ledger, or Daily Register of Commerce and Intelligence* between January 1760 and August 1761, and collected in May 1762 as *The Citizen of the World; or Letters from a Chinese Philosopher, residing in London, to his Friends in the East*.[13] The generic predecessors which inspired—and the informative sources which nuanced—Goldsmith's Chinese letters have been well documented.[14] The literary use to which he would put those sources had clearly been in his mind for the three years before he began his Chinese letters. In an essay for *The Bee* "On the Instability of Worldly Grandeur," Goldsmith had imagined a Chinese who "once took it into his head to travel into Europe, and observe the customs of a people whom he thought not very much inferior, even to his own country men" (W1: 472). In a 1758 letter to Robert Bryanton, he wrote that, in order to display his erudition, he would "soon make our Chinese talk like an Englishman" (L: 39–40); and in the *Monthly Review* for August 1757, Goldsmith, assessing the merits of *Letters from an Armenian in Ireland, to his Friends at Trebisonde*, wrote:

> The Writer who would inform, or improve, his countrymen, under the assumed character of an Eastern Traveller, should be careful to let nothing escape him which might betray the imposture. If his aim be satirical, his remarks should be collected from the more striking follies abounding in the country he describes, and from those prevailing absurdities which commonly usurp the softer name of fashions. His accounts should be of such a nature, as we may fancy his Asiatic friend would wish to know,— such as we ourselves would expect from a Correspondent in Asia.
>
> Whether the country our Author describes was deficient in materials, and had not national follies enough for general satire, we are not to determine; but certain it is, he has by no means been cautious in his endeavours to preserve the fictitious character he has assumed. (W1: 90-1)

In these opinions, Goldsmith is echoing Voltaire's views on the pseudo-letter.[15] *The Citizen of the World* does, to the ends described above, attempt to maintain the disguise—primarily through frequent allusion to Chinese names, place-names, proverbs, maxims (Confucian and otherwise), anecdotes, festivals, manners and customs. Gradually, however, the pretence is almost entirely dropped and the letters become more determinedly satirical.[16] Though well informed compared with the speculative descriptions of the Middle Ages and Renaissance, Goldsmith's Chinese letters appear at a point when western conceptions of the orient were still hazed in a literary mystique. Edward Said has equated the "pretechnical" Orientalism of the eighteenth century with the pre-Romantic moment in Europe; this early version was a "free-floating Orient [which] would be severely curtailed with the advent of academic Orientalism."[17] Goldsmith, in his own work, acknowledged the existence of empirical lacunae with regard to the East; his impersonation of an "Oriental" uses that empirical instability, as Swift had done, to fashion geographical satire.

Hence, in the midcentury, the east afforded a screen onto which could be projected the anxieties, cultural, political, and *economic*, of the Western observer. Nigel Leask, introducing his study of the interaction of Romanticism and Orientalism, sees "the Oriental topos" in the era immediately prior to Romanticism as "the literary equivalent of an important luxury commodity," an imaginative by-product of early modern mercantilist exchanges which attended European

CHAPTER 3

maneuvers in the East Indies. Leask goes on to implicate eighteenth-century orientalism in the displacement of "the Arcadian locus amoenus of neo-classicism from a Mediterranean 'Golden-Age' to a 'contemporary' eastern site."[18] Similarly, B. Sprague Allen proposed that the catholicity that accommodated orientalism "offended the exclusive, aristocratic classicist."[19] Goldsmith was a classicist by training and inclination, and yet he was not especially exclusive or aristocratic. At times, as in his facetious review of Arthur Murphy's play *The Orphan of China* (1759), he affects a disdain for the Chinese fashion; and yet, in writing *The Citizen of the World*, he is indulging it. To critique the particularities and peculiarities of England and the English, as well as those of Europe and Europeans generally, Goldsmith uses as his ventriloquist's medium a citizen of a remote and still strange country. The satiric conflation of the remote and the domestic was a regularly activated ruse; elaborating upon the enlightenment notion that "exoticism offered home truths," G. S. Rousseau and Roy Porter have commented that Goldsmith in particular recognized the ways in which "exotic models simultaneously flattered and flayed European manners."[20] Specifically, the China produced by the European imagination could be deployed, as Ros Ballaster has remarked, "not for imperial political ends but rather for domestic narcissism or critique."[21]

In spite of a European vogue for Chinese philosophy, and the use of China as a satirical obverse, the Chinese mode of government—or as much of it was presumed to be known—was questioned by Enlightenment thinkers. Montesquieu, initially pro-China, saw its government as an aberration from his theory of the state; likewise, Jean-Jacques Rousseau thought China endemically corrupt. Despotism was seen as an emanation from the national characteristics of the Chinese, which Du Halde attempted to define in terms of their strong reverence for the family and an endemic paternalism.[22] In *The Citizen of the World*, the paternalism of the Chinese emperor is pointedly "illustrated" when members of Altangi's family are taken into custody as a result of the emperor's displeasure at his departure from China—"contrary to the rules of our government, and the immemorial custom of the empire" (W2: 38). Altangi's correspondent Fum Hoam defends the paternalism of Chinese government on the grounds of filial rectitude:

> When I compare the history of China with that of Europe, how do I exult in being a native of that kingdom which derives its original from the sun. Upon opening the Chinese history, I there behold an antient extended empire, established by laws which nature and reason seem to have dictated. The duty of children to their parents, a duty which nature implants in every breast, forms the strength of that government which has subsisted

> for time immemorial. Filial obedience is the first and greatest requisite of a state; by this we become good subjects to our emperors, capable of behaving with just subordination to our superiors, and grateful dependants on heaven; by this we become fonder of marriage, in order to be capable of exacting obedience from others in our turn: by this we become good magistrates; for early submission is the truest lesson to those who would learn to rule. By this the whole state may be said to resemble one family, of which the emperor is the protector, father, and friend. (W2: 176–7)

China thus becomes a potential allegorical example in Goldsmith's defense of monarchism. In this instance, however, Goldsmith's politics are tempered by a clear sense of the dangers which present themselves whenever the ruling figure tends arbitrarily to flex his might. Thus, when Altangi's predicament is juxtaposed with Fum Hoam's strong defense, it is evident that Goldsmith is demonstrating that he understands the arguments for and against the mode of government which he, as others, understood to be Chinese.

The cohesiveness of Chinese paternalism was linked, in the minds of some European observers, to religious and philosophical culture. In particular, Gottfried Wilhelm Liebniz, who had conducted long correspondences with Jesuits living in or returned from China, saw in Chinese beliefs the means to a social unity. In his *Novissima Sinica*, or *Latest News from China* (1699), he argued that the Chinese were more advanced than Europeans in terms of practical philosophy and applied ethics. In *The Citizen of the World*, Goldsmith reflected this view by periodically invoking maxims of Confucius which Le Comte had translated. To consolidate his critique of party and critical whimsy—the banes of *The Traveller*—Altangi reprimands the English republic of letters, where "each looks upon his fellow as a rival, not an assistant in the same pursuit," by invoking Confucianism. "Confucius observes," according to Altangi, "that it is the duty of the learned to unite society more closely, and to persuade men to become citizens of the world; but the authors I refer to, are not only for disuniting society, but kingdoms also" (W2: 85–6). And just as Confucian wisdom confounded faction, so did it mirror Christian doctrine; the precepts of the *Analects* were deemed by Jesuit observers to be close to articles of Christian faith.[23] Accordingly, Goldsmith's Altangi remarks that "the two sects of philosophers in the world that have endeavoured to inculcate that fortitude is but an imaginary virtue" are "the followers of Confucius, and those who profess the doctrines of Christ" (W2: 200–1).[24]

Philosophically, Goldsmith finds a demonstrative use for Chinese precepts; in terms of the general, undiscriminating fashion for all things Chinese, however,

[95]

CHAPTER 3

he is a little more wary. The "editor" of the Chinese letters frames the entire device in an allegory, related by way of a dream narrative, which goes toward a preliminary explanation of Goldsmith's opinion on Chinoiserie. He imagines the Thames frozen over, with the booths of a "Fashion fair" arrayed on the ice. Aware that the ice might not bear too much weight, he resolves to observe events from the shore, "having been always a little cowardly in my sleep." Finally, emboldened by the presence of so many others on the ice, the editor ventures forth:

> The furniture, frippery and fireworks of China, have long been fashionably brought up. I'll try the fair with a small cargoe of Chinese morality. If the Chinese have contributed to vitiate our taste, I'll try how far they can help to improve our understanding. But as others have driven into the market in waggons, I'll cautiously begin by venturing with a wheel-barrow. Thus resolved, I baled up my goods and fairly ventured; when, upon just entering the fair, I fancied the ice that had supported an hundred waggons before, cracked under me; and wheel-barrow and all went to the bottom. (W2: 14–5)

Goldsmith thus distinguishes between the heft of Chinese ethics and the flimsy fashions of rococo chinoiserie. The problem is that the intended audience might not appreciate "heavy" orientalism; pointedly, letter 14 describes Altangi's reception by a "lady of distinction."[25] Conveying Goldsmith's acknowledgment that Chinoiserie was a largely European invention, this letter is a cutting parody of the misguidedness of the popular Chinese taste, and the mundane racism of the orientalist dilettante. Altangi, dressed in European style, is taken for an Englishman until the lady's footman informs her that he is a Chinese guest, at which point she comes alive with exoticist curiosity:

> Bless me! can this be the gentleman that was born so far from home? What an unusual share of *somethingness* in his whole appearance. Lord how I am charmed with the outlandish cut of his face; how bewitching the exotic breadth of his forehead. I would give the world to see him in his own country dress. Pray turn about, Sir, and let me see you behind. There! there's a travelled air for you. You that attend there, bring up a plate of beef cut into small pieces; I have a violent passion to see him eat. Pray, Sir, have you got your chop-sticks about you? it will be so pretty to see the meat carried to the mouth with a jerk. Pray speak a little Chinese: I have learned some of the language myself. Lord, have you nothing pretty from China about you; something that one does not

know what to do with: I have got twenty things from China that are of no use in the world.

Altangi resists here the imputation that Chinese cultural artefacts are decorative only, and without any clear function. The lady protests that, in holding these views, Altangi may in fact be a "barbarian." She tests his "taste" by asking him about her fashionable pagods. He answers that he despises them and deflates her claims to sophistication by informing her that the Chinese temple which she has had constructed at the foot of her garden could just as easily be an Egyptian pyramid. Altangi finds it futile to contradict the lady's deluded pseudo-cosmopolitanism; and so, he is "resolved rather to act the disciple than the instructor. She took me through several rooms all furnished, as she told me, in the Chinese manner; sprawling dragons, squatting pagods, and clumsy mandarines, were stuck upon every shelf." (W2: 63–5).

The metropolitan notion of a fixed or essential cultural otherness is here parodied to the extent that any such quality is revealed ultimately to be as fungible as clothing. "Chinese-ness," at least as it is seen through European eyes, is a construction, a kitschy tissue of sartorial and decorative signifiers bereft of a definite source or application. Altangi dresses himself in the English style, and is thus seen as less authentically Chinese; equally, what is perceived to be Chinese horrifies him as a caricature of superstitions toward which the Chinese are themselves, at best, ambivalent. Hugh Honour has described decorative chinoiserie as "a European style and not, as is sometimes supposed by sinologues, an incompetent attempt to imitate the arts of China."[26] Accordingly, the description of the dubious interiors of the lady's house recalls the midcentury vogue of the *managareth*—the Chinese bedroom or dressing room—which was the indoor venue for the display of what Honour sees as a specifically English form of rococo chinoiserie.

Letter 33 exposes the bogus orientalism of the Chinese fashion still further. By this point, Altangi is exasperated by "the presumption of these islanders, when they pretend to instruct me in the ceremonies of China!" The English fail to distinguish between eastern nations; worse still, they find it difficult to credit with common sense any man "who has received his education at such a distance from London," although it is suggested to Altangi, with evident authorial irony, that he "must be some Englishman in disguise; his very visage has nothing of the true exotic barbarity." Once again, a "lady of distinction" embodies a sort of cultural myopia. She has collected all of her knowledge of the east from fictions and those oriental histories of which Altangi is disdainful. She wonders that her guest has not brought opium or a tobacco box; she gives him, in spite

CHAPTER 3

of his protestations, a cushion on the floor upon which to sit; she orders that a napkin should be put under his chin, although this is in "no way Chinese." For dinner, he is offered a choice of bear's claws or birds nests, dishes with which he is "utterly unacquainted." The company assembled for dinner is astonished that he does not eat with chop-sticks.

One gentleman guest in particular objects that Altangi does not even look like a Chinese; "in short," Altangi complains, "he almost reasoned me out of my country." Through his creation, Goldsmith delineates what he views as the more fraudulent dimensions of contemporary cultural discourse by ridiculing this English gentleman's conception of the true Chinese style in writing:

> I have written many a sheet of eastern tale myself, interrupts the author, and I defy the severest critic to say but that I have stuck close to the true manner. I have compared a lady's chin to the snow upon the mountains of Bomek; a soldier's sword, to the clouds that obscure the face of heaven. If riches are mentioned, I compare them to the flocks that graze the verdant Tefflis; if poverty, to the mists that veil the brow of mount Baku. I have used *thee* and *thou* upon all occasions, I have described falling stars, and splitting mountains, not forgetting the little Houries who make a very pretty figure in every description. But you shall hear how I generally begin. "Eben-ben-bolo, who was the son of Ban, was born on the foggy summits of Benderabassi. His beard was whiter than the feathers which veil the breast of the penguin; his eyes were like the eyes of doves, when wash'd by the dews of the morning; his hair, which hung like the willow weeping over the glassy stream, was so beautiful that it seem'd to reflect its own brightness; and his feet were as the feet of a wild deer which fleeth to the tops of the mountains." There, there, is the true eastern taste for you; every advance made towards sense, is only a deviation from sound. Eastern tales should always be sonorous, lofty, musical and unmeaning. (W2: 142–5)[27]

This passage wittily parodies the cultural presumption of the metropolitan center, anticipating latter-day critiques of Orientalist preconceptions about the literary modes and obscurantism of Asian writing, characterized, supposedly, by florid, mystic, and sometimes even mystifying simile. Against this comical ethnic calumny, Altangi issues a bemused corrective:

> I could not avoid smiling to hear a native of England attempt to instruct me in the true eastern idiom; and, after he had look'd round some time

for applause, I presumed to ask him whether he had ever travelled into the east; to which he replied in the negative: I demanded whether he understood Chinese or Arabic, to which also he answered as before. Then how, Sir, said I, can you pretend to determine upon the eastern stile, who are entirely unacquainted with the eastern writings? Take, Sir, the word of one who is *professedly* a Chinese, and who is *actually* acquainted with the Arabian writers, that what is palm'd upon you daily for an imitation of eastern writing, no way resembles their manner, either in sentiment or diction. In the east, similes are seldom used, and metaphors almost wholly unknown; but in China particularly, the very reverse of what you allude to, takes place; a cool phlegmatic method of writing prevails there. The writers of that country, ever more assiduous to instruct than to please, address rather the judgment than the fancy.

Altangi's objection to the gentleman's foolishness is augmented by his passionately made claim that the Chinese are as proficient in arts and sciences as the peoples of Europe; they should not, therefore, be accused of the same "unlettered simplicity" as their eastern neighbors. At this stage, the dinner company loses interest in its guest, and takes to whispering and yawning. Altangi leaves quickly and is not invited again, "because it was found that I aimed at appearing rather a reasonable creature, than an outlandish ideot" (W2: 145–7).

Altangi's antipathy to the useless, superficial embellishments peddled by ostensible "sinophiles" echoes Goldsmith's earlier review, published in the *Critical Review* for May 1759, of the play *The Orphan of China*, by Roscommon-born playwright Arthur Murphy. An extension of amusement into absurdity and perversion, chinoiserie is here indicted as a manifestation of luxury; relatedly, the merits of Chinese literature are downplayed in favor of classical models. Deriding Murphy's play for its lack of the Aristotelian processes, Goldsmith thought the plot lacking "a proper preparation of incident," although Murphy, to his credit, had rendered the plot more European, and hence "more perfect"—just as Voltaire had, with his 1755 version, deviated from "the calm insipidity of his Eastern original." (W1: 172, 171). Goldsmith's disdain for some aspects of Murphy's chinoiserie is, at this point, a classicist's antagonism toward the modern, exacerbated by the prologue, in which the then poet-laureate William Whitehead exclaimed: "enough of Greece and Rome. Th'exhausted store/Of either nation now can charm no more."

Murphy's work would have intrigued Goldsmith, however, because, to the politically atuned, its Chinese narrative could be read as an allegory for the plight of the exiled house of Stuart. The orphan of the play's title is the prince

CHAPTER 3

Zaphimri—clearly the Pretender—secretly raised by the mandarin Zamti in anticipation of his return and his country's deliverance. Since the royal line was broken China has been destroyed by Tartar usurpers. Preempting such an interpretation, Whitehead's prologue issues an admonition against Jacobitism. Zamti is denounced as "A patriot zealous in a monarch's cause!" Attributing the play's potential for political subversion to "China's tenets," Whitehead claims that English loyalty springs "from nobler motives." Britain, he adds, "knows no Right Divine in Kings"; loyalty to George II thus springs "from freedom's choice."[28] Though he was suspicious of the play's formal properties, Goldsmith stayed conspicuously silent on the play's monarchism in his review.

Between his review of Murphy and his own orientalist exploits, Goldsmith fell under the influence of the scholarship, though not the ideas or the politics, of Thomas Percy. Introduced to Goldsmith in February of 1759 by a colleague from the *Monthly Review*, Percy's investigations helped to broaden contemporary literary interests, to free them from the strictures of neoclassicism by translating examples of Runic, Greenlandish, Laplandish and Chinese literature.[29] The Chinese framework of *The Citizen of the World* may have been prompted by Percy's work on translating *Hau Kiou Choaan*, published in 1761.[30] In his preface to that novel was stressed the "greater regard to truth and nature" which differentiates Chinese writing from other Asiatic writing. But Percy's complements were usually backhanded; Chinese cultural artefacts, impressive in an Asian context, were paltry compared with those of the protestant west. The Jesuit accounts, as he saw it, accommodated Chinese religious culture, including Confucianism, only because of shared idolatrous tendencies; in his view, a view contrary to Goldsmith's, there was a sharp, and negative distinction to be drawn between Confucianism and Christianity. Thus, as James Watt has argued, Percy sought "to develop what he represented as a distinctively British and Protestant perspective on Chinese customs and manners," a perspective which fed into his larger antiquarian project, one which would "substantiate the distinction he drew between independence-loving Goths and benighted, superstitious—implicitly orientalized—Celts."[31] Though condescending to the "littleness and poverty of genius in almost all the works of taste of the Chinese," Percy allowed the exception of Chinese gardening, and conceded the "unity of design or fable" in Chinese art.[32] Narrative and allegorical simplicity were therefore grudgingly deemed to characterize Chinese art, but for Goldsmith such attributes, specifically as they applied in the laying out of landscape, were salutary, and he utilized them to veil a worldview quite at odds with Percy's.

Political Landscapes

Altangi claims that "the Europeans instruct by argument, and the Asiatics mostly by narration" (W2: 400). In accordance with this maxim, Goldsmith deploys the Chinese parable throughout *The Citizen of the World*; within that parabolic tradition, the instructive Chinese garden is an abiding motif. The influences of William Chambers and, in a subtler, more indirect way Edmund Burke, effect a propensity in Goldsmith to valorize the Chinese garden for its allegorical and aesthetic resonances and qualities. The influences of Chambers and Burke taper down to the metaphor of the fair female in *The Deserted Village*.

The long tradition in British garden design was one of formal, symmetrical arrangements incorporating straight lines, canals, and statuesque trees; the later eighteenth century, however, saw a shift away from formalism toward a taste for gardens which more closely imitated natural landscape.[33] William Temple's essay "Upon the Gardens of Epicurus" (1685) was among the first criticisms of that tradition. This piece was also among the first to advocate the Chinese style of *Sharawadgi*, or irregularity, which involved "contriving figures, where the beauty shall be great, and strike the eye, but without any order or disposition of parts, that shall be commonly or easily observed." The English "have hardly any notion of this sort of beauty"; the Chinese, however, have a particular word to express it, and where they find it hit their eye at first sight, they say the Sharawadgi is fine or is admirable, or any such expression of esteem."[34] Joseph Addison, in *The Spectator* for June 25, 1712, likewise criticized formal gardens and adduced the Chinese example.[35] For Addison, and for other Whig observers, naturalism best embodied the qualities of English liberty: geometrical artifice in landscape represented tyranny, either in the form of absolute monarchy, but also, as in the case of Burke later in the century, the tyranny of the mob. Burke asked whether liberty really consisted in the total destruction of monarchy: "Is every land-mark of the country to be done away in favour of a geometrical and arithmetical constitution?"[36]

There was mistaken belief abroad in the eighteenth century that naturalistic landscape gardening *per se* was of Chinese origin; in fact, naturalism existed in English gardens without necessarily including Oriental models.[37] *Sharawadgi* was a Chinese but also a partially Japanese phenomenon; much Western gardening theory, however, involved an imposition of European innovations onto Chinese ideas and vice versa.[38] The "Chinese" fashion was sometimes as much a source of amusement and decoration as an authentic artifact of cultural exchange. The decoration of gardens with fretwork, bells, dragons and serpents was a caricatured and cartoonishly superficial manifestation of the trend, and gave ammunition to the neoclassicists who bemoaned the replacement of Palladian pediments and columns with pagodas and minarets.

Goldsmith sided, personally and professionally, with those authors who proposed a wilder, less symmetrical style of landscape gardening. The personal and intellectual acquaintances involved in Goldsmith's thinking on landscape were non-English authors writing in England. William Chambers, a Swedish-born Scot, was an influence on, and a source of, Goldsmith's garden theory, specifically as it is presented in letter 31 of *The Citizen of the World* (1762). Chambers and Goldsmith would become friendly in the 1770s, and their correspondence at this time includes a telling reference to Burke. That Goldsmith and Burke were good friends is well known. They were both of Johnson's circle and were contemporaries at Trinity College, Dublin, where they were aware of each other's existence and reputation.[39] Less well known is Goldsmith's paraphrasing of a key passage—that which (in)famously describes the female form as a "deceitful maze"[40]—from Burke's *Philosophical Enquiry into the Origin of Our Ideas of the Sublime and the Beautiful* (1757) to dilate one of his oriental fables played out in landscape gardens which themselves convey, in Goldsmith's phrase, a "delicate allegory" (W2: 137), the levels of which are horticultural, ethical, political, and erotic.

William Chambers (1723–96) was the son of John Chambers, who had partnered one William Pierson in a merchant business with substantial accounts for supplying stores to the royal armies of Charles XII of Sweden, the "Jacobite hero" who plotted with the disaffected in 1716–1717.[41] Chambers was educated at the grammar school in Ripon in the North Riding of Yorkshire, and returned to England in 1755, having traveled three times to China with the Swedish East India Company between 1742 and 1749.[42] He was, for the most part, comparatively academic as a commentator and was not given to superficial exoticism.[43] He would, therefore, have earned the respect of Goldsmith, who was generally opposed to the displacement of classical formalism by shallow fashions. Not merely opposed to overwrought classical symmetry, Chambers simply opposed the too-artless naturalism of English landscape gardening, epitomized in the work of Lancelot "Capability" Brown.[44] "In England," wrote Chambers, "no appearance of art is tolerated [. . .] our gardens differ very little from common fields." Chambers objected to the "poverty of imagination in [their] contrivance"; distrusting extremes of artifice and naturalism, he advocated a via media:

> I think it is obvious that neither the artful nor the simple style of Gardening here mentioned, is right: the one being too extravagant a devia-

tion from nature; the other too scrupulous an adherence to her. One manner is absurd; the other insipid and vulgar: a judicious mixture of both would certainly be more perfect than either.

The art of the gardener is close to that of the poet, according to Chambers: both "should give a loose to their imagination, and even fly beyond the bounds of truth, wherever it is necessary to elevate, to embellish, to enliven, or to add novelty to their subject."[45] These ideas, expressed in Chambers' *Dissertation on Oriental Gardening* (1772), expand on his earlier *Designs of Chinese Buildings, Furniture, Dresses, Machines, and Utensils* (1757), where the author proclaims himself "far from desiring to be numbered among the exaggerators of Chinese excellence." He intends only to validate Chinese culture by comparing it favorably with contiguous nations in the East; he disclaims any "intention to place them in competition either with the antients, or with the moderns" of the west. He proposes that his measures and sketches might "be of use in putting a stop to the extravagances that daily appear under the name of Chinese," of which most "are mere inventions, the rest copies from the lame representations found on porcelain and paper hangings." The genuinely Chinese is at least original; and Chinese culture is qualified at least by its longevity, having "continued without change for thousands of years."[46] Thus Chambers expected that his work on China might be well received; in particular, he hoped that his chapter on "The Art of Laying out Gardens among the Chinese" might be a source of guidance for English gardeners.

This chapter, given room in the *Gentleman's Magazine* and the *Literary Magazine* in 1757, was certainly of use to Goldsmith. Letter 31 of *The Citizen of the World* makes ample use of Chamberist principles. Altangi, echoing Chambers' assertion that the Chinese model is the type at which English gardeners should have been aiming, begins his delineation of the Chinese style by pointing out an English deficiency:

> The English have not yet brought the art of gardening to the same perfection with the Chinese, but have lately begun to imitate them; nature is now followed with greater assiduity than formerly; the trees are suffered to shoot out into the utmost luxuriance; the streams no longer forced from their natives beds, are permitted to wind along the vallies; spontaneous flowers take place of the finished parterre, and the enamelled meadow of the shaven green.

The English deficiency is further evinced by its preclusion of moral, imaginative or associative allegory:

CHAPTER 3

> Yet still the English are far behind us in this charming art; their designers have not yet attained a power of uniting instruction with beauty. An European will scarcely conceive my meaning, when I say that there is scarce a garden in China which does not contain some fine moral couch'd under the general design, where one is not taught wisdom as he walks, and feels the force of some noble truth, or delicate precept resulting from the disposition of the groves, streams or grottos.

His preferences thus established, Altangi proceeds to describe his gardens at Quamsi in China. The path descending from the house is flanked by two impenetrable groves of trees and porcelain, statuary, and painting for decoration. The path leads into an open area circumscribed by a "natural" array of rocks, flowers, trees and shrubs. On either side of the lawn there are two opposing and architecturally diverse gates. At the end of the lawn is "a temple built rather with minute elegance than ostentation." The gate on the right is simple and rude, its pillars overgrown with ivy; overhung with "the baleful cyprus," it is guarded by hideous serpents and dragons, and two champions bearing clubs. The view of what lies exposed behind the gate is dark, gloomy, and foreboding.

The gate on the left is hung invitingly with wreaths of flowers and the stonework has retained its original smoothness. The vista inside seems "gay, luxuriant, and capable of affording endless pleasure." The gates offer to the visitor a moral choice: to take the gate motted "PERVIA VIRTUTI" (pervious to virtue) or that inscribed with "FACILIS DECENSUS" (the descent is easy). One must choose, in effect, between the dull and virtuous way and that of sensual, enjoyable vice. Altangi relates that, given a free choice, the visitor will choose FACILIS DECENSUS. However,

> Immediately upon entering the gate of vice, the trees and flowers were disposed in such a manner as to make the most pleasing impression; but as he walked further on he insensibly found the garden assume the air of a wilderness, the landskips began to darken, the paths grew more intricate, he appeared to go downwards, frightful rocks seemed to hang over his head, gloomy caverns, unexpected precipices, awful ruins, heaps of unburied bones, and terrifying sounds, caused by unseen waters, began to take place of what at first appeared so lovely; it was in vain to attempt returning, the labyrinth too much perplexed for any but myself to find the way back. In short, when sufficiently impressed with the horrors of what he saw, and the imprudence of his choice, I

brought him by an hidden door, a shorter way back into the area from whence at first he had strayed.

The allegory is simple enough: the visitor descends from the house into a Paradise where he can exercise free choice; he chooses easy luxury, and liberty is lost. Through recognition of his fault, he "regains" the Paradise that lies behind the gloomy gate. Goldsmith's Altangi claims: "There is no spot, tho'ever so little, which a skilful designer might not thus improve, so as to convey a delicate allegory, and impress the mind with truths the most useful and necessary" (W2: 134–7).

The allegory of the garden is not, however, "universally" moral. The topographical progress through the garden described above can be juxtaposed productively with Goldsmith's very local account, alluded to in the introduction, in which the poor patriarch of an hospitable Irish family expresses a forlorn Jacobitism. Ventriloquized in the voice of an "English Gentleman," it is an account of traveling west from Dublin through the affluent, Anglicized Pale into the Irish "interior":

> When I had got about forty miles from the capital, I found the country begin to wear a different appearance from what it before appeared to me in. The neat inclosures, the warm and well built houses, the fine cultivated grounds, were no more to be seen, the prospect now changed into, here and there, a gentleman's seat, grounds ill cultivated, though seemingly capable of cultivation, little irregular fences made of turf, and topped with brush wood, cut from some neighbouring shrub, and the peasants houses wearing all the appearance of indigence and misery. You will not be surprised, sir, as you know me, that I had curiosity enough to enter one of those mansions, which seemed by its appearance to be the habitation of despair: ordering my servant therefore to walk his horses to a neighbouring inn, I alighted and walked into the peasant's hovel. (W3: 26)

Slow gradations from cultivation to wilderness, it seems, characterize the Chinese garden and Ireland together. The progress for Goldsmith's English gentleman ends in a curiously pastoral scene, in which the peasant family is as hospitable as possible toward their visitor. Fabricant contrasted this piece's "sentimental, idealized picture that all but denies the terrible realities previously acknowledged" with Swift's harsher, anti-pastoral descriptions of the Irish midlands. She notes the "implicit criticism" in the impersonated touristic tone of this "English" gentleman's account, but claims that Goldsmith himself is relatively complicit in all of

CHAPTER 3

this.⁴⁷ The pastoralism of that scene is meant however, not to sentimentalize, but to exemplify the hospitality of the old Jacobite culture in the midlands, and to illustrate how that culture has long since been disenfranchized and improverished.

Read through a Jacobite lens, the essay's dishevelled interiors—of the country, and of the peasant family's shed—are all the more pointed and poignant. If landscapes, and the ideals which are invested in them, are bound up with notions of liberty and progress, Goldsmith's writings and correspondences on issues of garden design are all the more telling in their veiled collaborative commentary on contemporary political rhetoric. Goldsmith wrote to Chambers, in a missive discovered in 1936 by R. W. Seitz in Chambers' *Letter Books*, to thank him for supporting for Goldsmith's *She Stoops to Conquer*, which was first produced on March 15, 1773. Reciprocating Chambers' support, Goldsmith wished Chambers well with the second edition of his *Dissertation on Oriental Gardening* (1773), the first edition of which (1772) had been lampooned in "An Heroic Epistle to Sir William Chambers" (1773), a poem thought initially to have been composed by Christopher Anstey but revealed later to have been the work of William Mason. Mason derided Chambers' "plastic hand,"⁴⁸ while Walpole's introduction and notes were at once vehemently anti-Chamberist and sonorously nationalistic: "the English Taste in Gardening," he wrote, "is thus the growth of the English Constitution & must perish with it."⁴⁹ Chambers' *Dissertation* was deemed to be imaginatively extravagant and too pugnacious in its criticism of Lancelot "Capability" Brown, the chief exponent of the English style of landscape gardening. Brown had won out in the quest to design Lord Clive's villa; Chambers' invective was, therefore, seen to be petty and, worse still, unpatriotic. Mason's poem was popular, running to fourteen editions in four years. Its popularity, according to Rudolf Wittkower, accrued to its politicization of the gardening debate: "Mason, a convinced Whig, regarded Chambers, the newly appointed comptroller general, as the tool of a king who, in Mason's eyes, was a detestable Tory." Chinese gardening, then, was the aesthetic wing of "Tory tyranny."⁵⁰ His recommendation of ancient styles was deemed by Brown's supporters to be appealing to those who hankered after absolute government and outmoded, often Jacobite, notions of divine right.⁵¹

Goldsmith sought to encourage Chambers by naming Edmund Burke as an ally:

> This is the first time I had one moment to Spare to sit down and thank you for your kind Sollicitude for the fate of my play which has turned out beyond my expectation. when will your book [the second edition of the Dissertation] come out. you have read no doubt a poem with some

share of humour supposed to be written by a Mr Ansty against you. whoever the author is he is I perceive a steady Brownist. no matter, it will all in the end contribute to do you honour. most of the Companies that I now go into divide themselves into two parties the Chamberists and ye Brownists, but depend upon it you'l in the end have the Victory, because you have truth and nature on your side. Mr Burke was advising me about four days ago to draw my pen in a poem in defence of your system, and sincerely I am much warm'd in the Cause. If I write it I will print my name to it boldly. I wonder you have not excited much more envy than you do?[52]

Just as "truth and nature" were for Thomas Percy the hallmarks of Chinese art, so are these qualities attributable to the garden designs of Chambers, who replied:

> I am Glad to hear that the Virtuosi devide between Monsieur Brown and me at first the cry was all for Monsieur Brown. if they once begin to doubt there is hopes of a reformation, and if You can find leisure to draw your pen in defence of the new System there is no doubt that it will have a great effect I wish you would take Mr Burks advice, but apropos are you sure it was not a Sneer for I have always Considered Mr Burke as no favourere of my system not owing to anything he has Said, but rather to what he has not Said, pray tell me if you think he was sincere for he is a man of Judgement and his opinion counts
>
> With regard to the Poem ascribed to Ansty he is a damned Brownite to be Sure but his poem I do not admire though it has sold all the remainder of my first Edition if I took in hand to laugh at my Self I could do it much better than Mr Ansty has done.[53]

Sides, thus, were clearly taken. Goldsmith replied briefly that both Burke and Joshua Reynolds were professed supporters. Chambers' playfulness, in this letter at least, deflates criticisms of his extravagance. He himself knew that the satirical poem had publicized his work. At any rate, he was more aware of the fragility and potential transience of the Chinese fashion than Mason or Walpole would have credited; and with the classically designed gardens of Somerset House—in which Burke assisted—Chambers would eventually consolidate his reputation.[54]

Goldsmith, had, however, already celebrated in verse Chambers' work as designer and architect of the gardens at Kew, the villa of Augusta, princess dowager of Wales. Conflating classical and Chinese models, Chambers worked on the Kew project between 1757 and 1762. Following Augusta's death in 1772, Goldsmith

CHAPTER 3

was commissioned to write a poem to her memory. The second part of the poem is a pastoral overture applauding Chambers' efforts:

> Fast by that shore where Thames' translucent stream
> Reflects new glories on his breast,
> Where, splendid as the youthful poet's dream,
> He forms a scene beyond Elysium blest;
> Where sculptur'd elegance and native grace
> Unite to stamp the beauties of the place;
> While, sweetly blending, still are seen
> The wavy lawn, the sloping green;
> While novelty, with cautious cunning,
> Through every maze of fancy running,
> From China borrows aid to deck the scene. (W4: 336–7)

This passage suggests another level of allegory in Goldsmith's garden, a level at which the aesthetic supplants the didactic. The descriptive terminology, as with the word "maze," suggests contextually verifiable connections between ideas of garden aesthetics and of female beauty. In his study of allegory Angus Fletcher demonstrates that, in the eighteenth century, "the artificial landscape is treated by its theoreticians just as if it were a woman's body"; the garden may, as such, be dressed accordingly. Allegory, in Fletcher's formulation, is "a many-sided phenomenon," capable of affording "education (the didactic strain) and entertainment (the riddling or romantic strain)."[55] In order better to comprehend this proliferation of allegorical levels, it is to this second strain that attention is now given.

Letter 76 of *The Citizen of the World* consists of another allegory, related to Altangi by his son Hingpo, and conveying the latter's growing affection for Zelis, his fellow captive in Persia.[56] The subject is the preferability of grace to beauty. Hingpo's companion Zelis may lack the "regularity of feature" bestowed upon the local Circassian women; her "imperfect beauty" is, however, preferable to "finished" beauty. Unable to rationalize this preference, Hingpo resorts to an allegory which recalls the structure of the allegorical garden described above. Hingpo imagines himself placed between two landscapes: one is called the "region of beauty"; the other, "the valley of the graces." The region of beauty is "adorned with all that luxuriant nature could bestow; the fruits of various climates adorned the trees, the grove resounded with music, the gale breathed perfume, every charm that could arise from symmetry and exact distribution were here conspicuous." Predictably, the valley of the graces is, at first glance, unalluring: "the streams and the groves appeared just as they do in frequented countries; no magnificent parterres, no consort in the grove, the rivulet was edged with weed, and the rook joined its voice to that of the nightingale. All was simplicity and nature." Hingpo claims that "The most striking objects ever first allure the traveler"; he therefore enters the region of beauty. Although others have entered with the same curiosity, he sees that they leave abruptly. Hingpo stays and is eventually introduced to the goddess: "who represented beauty in person." Hingpo and several fellow-admirers quickly grow tired of the goddess" "languishing airs, soft looks and inclinations of the head." She refuses to speak and it becomes clear to those visiting the region that its goddess has no mind.

Hingpo, grown weary of hollow beauty, goes to the valley of the graces where he finds others who had, before him, tired of the mute goddess. He joins these pioneers in their search for the goddess of grace. Unable to find her too readily, the searchers wander through the valley observing the "natural," "domestic," "pleasing," "familiar and charming" minutae which decorate the garden. They are finally addressed by an unseen speaker who advises them in their quest:

> If you would find the goddess of Grace, seek her not under one form, for she assumes a thousand. Ever changing under the eye of inspection, her variety, rather than her figure, is pleasing. In contemplating her beauty, the eye glides over every perfection with giddy delight, and, capable of fixing no where, is charmed with the whole. She is now contemplation with solemn look, again compassion with humid eye; she now sparkles with joy, soon every feature speaks distress: her looks at times invite our approach, at others repress our presumption, the goddess cannot be properly be called beautiful under any one of these forms, but by combining them all, she becomes irresistibly pleasing. (W2: 314–7)

This section of the letter-allegory is as intriguing for its sources as for its substance. The first sentence is derived from Marivaux. Arthur Friedman, Goldsmith's most comprehensive editor to date, did not identify a precedent for the description of the eye gliding giddily over the female form. Goldsmith himself disingenuously flagged a Horatian precedent—"vultus nimium lubricus aspici"—which translates, approximately, as "very slippery to behold." A truer source is Burke's *Philosophical Enquiry*:

> observe that part of a beautiful woman where she is perhaps the most beautiful, about the neck and breasts; the softness; the easy and insensible swell; the variety of the surface, which is never for the smallest space

CHAPTER 3

the same; the deceitful maze, through which the unsteady eye slides giddily, without knowing where to fix or whither it is carried.[57]

For Burke, the female body is imaged as a labyrinth through which the eye of the imagination moves. Their mutual use of variations on words like "giddy" and "fix" suggests the clear influence of the chapter "On Gradual Variation" in Burke's *Enquiry* on Hingpo's allegory in *The Citizen of the World*. Goldsmith reviewed the former upon its release in the *Monthly Review* for May 1757. The substantial and discursive footnotes with which he augmented an otherwise mundane and descriptive review illustrate the extent to which he was engaged with Burke's ideas.[58]

The relationship between their aesthetics extends beyond a parallel in vocabulary, however: Goldsmith and Burke were in broad aesthetic agreement on the analogous subjects of female beauty and landscape gardening. In Goldsmith's letter, the effects of "symmetry and exact distribution" are shallow, unnatural, and short-lived. Likewise, for Burke, proportion is allied with mere convenience: it is "a creature of the understanding, rather than a primary cause acting on the senses and imagination." Proportionism is an application of art to nature; disproportionism is an application of nature to art. Writing against proponents of the former, Burke framed an allegorical reciprocation between woman and garden by extolling natural disproportion in topography as in animated nature: "our gardens, if nothing else, declare, we begin to feel that mathematical ideas are not the true measures of beauty. And surely they are full as little so in the animal as the vegetable world." Non-proportionality and imperfection (here meant as an opposite of symmetrical accomplishment) are sources of beauty, therefore; perfection and regularity are not. Indeed, to augment their attractiveness, Burke proposed that women feign imperfection: "they learn to lisp, to totter in their walk, to counterfeit weakness, and even sickness. In this they are guided by nature."[59] What is intriguing about this notion is that agency, however disingenuous, is allocated to the beautiful object. The female form, or maze, is, after all, deceitful rather than deceiving. As is Goldsmith's "fair female."

Goldsmith shared with Chambers and Burke an aesthetic interest in improving upon nature, and an organicist interest in saving nature from aesthetic excess; in this he sought, like his peers, a middle way, which Chinese gardening seemed to offer, but sometimes exceeded. With women and with gardens, nature could be dressed to a beauteous optimum. The poet William Shenstone inscribed as much on the plinth of the statue of Venus de Medici placed in the Leasowes, his famous landscape garden near Birmingham:

> Let sweet concealment's magic art
> Your mazy bounds invest;
> And while the sight unveils a part,
> Let fancy paint the rest.

Nature could, also, be dressed to an unsightly excess. Hence the insertion into the same poem of a stanza by Shenstone's friend Richard Graves which refers to the Chinese alcove erected at Stourhead by Henry Hoare:

> And far be driven the sumptuous glare
> Of gold, from British groves;
> And far the meretricious air
> Of China's vain alcoves.[60]

"Meretricious" is a key word here: the landscape "deceives" in the same way as a "harlot." The word "meretricious" itself recalls and is etymologically continuous with "an méirdreach," the generic female character in allegorical Gaelic poetry of the time.

It is appropriate to draw attention to Shenstone in relation to Goldsmith. In 1773, Goldsmith wrote an essay for *The Westminster Magazine* entitled "The History of a Poet's Garden." The garden in question was the Shenstone's Leasowes. In his essay Goldsmith charts the decline of Shenstone's garden following his death in 1763, as reported to him by "the Genius of the Place." "When the poor poet died," lamented the Genius, "his garden was obliged to be sold for the benefit of those who had contributed to its embellishment." The first owner was Mr. Truepenny, the button-maker, who valued "the more regular production of art." Hence, he clipped and cut the garden down to a tedious tidiness. The next owner in Goldsmith's chronology was a ship's captain who had a passion for building Chinese temples and summer-houses. Under his supervision the garden was changed into "a little city" (W3: 207–9) not unlike a village in the East-Indies where he made his fortune. The captain is analogous to the egotistical and ostentatious nabob-figure of *The Deserted Village*; both men have imported from their imperial adventures luxuries which have damaged the face of the landscape.

Such ostentation was, finally, the biggest potential problem with the more superficial, consumerist manifestations of the Chinese fashion. Unthinking chinoiserie was symptomatic of luxury stretched to absurdity. Nonetheless Goldsmith successfully deployed a thoughtful, more self-reflexive adaptation of—inevitably mediated—Chinese ideas and allegorical modes to think through his position as an Irish outsider in London, and to ruminate upon the fate of political traditionalism in the midst of urban modernity in the imperial metropolis.

CHAPTER 3

א

Auburn, Goldsmith's literary village, is a nostalgic, utopian depiction of a natural landscape which is home to an organic community. The poem moves knowingly from an integrated past to a ruined present in which the costly spectacle of success masks a more profound, widespread poverty. Its movement from past to present is equally a movement from England to Ireland; in this contrast, Goldsmith illustrates starkly the extent to which one nation has, through ostentation and absenteeism, undone the other. The landowner, wealthy, luxurious, and proud, has taken the wealth generated by peasant rents and labor to use for his own amusement. Part of this money he uses for landscape design in order to enhance his estates; the rest he spends on metropolitan entertainment. In sum, the wealth generated in Ireland is taken out of circulation *in* Ireland; and the country is left to wither. Yet the land, the Irish land, by luxury betrayed, attempts to dress *herself*. Ireland thus becomes a mixture of wildness and a shabby, neglected gentility. The landowner has agency, but so, in a much more limited way, does the land, figured here as a once beautiful but now neglected woman. This image is redolent of the *aisling* mode, in which Ireland is personified as a forlorn woman whose agency is limited, subject as she is to dynastic conflicts beyond her control.[61] "Like Swift," writes Murray Pittock, "Goldsmith may have had connexions with the nationalist culture which reflected itself elsewhere in the stylized protests of the *aisling*s."[62] Unlike Swift, however, Goldsmith's protest was embedded and obscured in an unlikely convergence of influences. His orientalism was an allegorical screen for his Irishness; and his version of the *aisling* was modified according to contemporary issues in gardening. Chinese gardening, if its fashion went unchecked, threatened to disrupt the preeminence of the English style; the defense of the latter was thus characterized by the chauvinist vim of such as Mason and Walpole. The English tradition they defend finds itself opposed by a coalition, in defense of the Chinese style, consisting of two Irishmen and a Scot. The political subtext of residual Jacobitism is compounded, in Goldsmith's case, by use of the *aisling* metaphor. Thus the political malaise and the ruination at the heart of *The Deserted Village* are adumbrated in the landscapes of *The Citizen of the World*. It is according to the allegorical levels delineated here, and the acquaintances that informed their mutual vocabularies, that a fair female unadorned and plain becomes a garden, and a grave.

4

GEOGRAPHIES OF RUIN: IRELAND, AMERICA, AND AUBURN'S ABSENTEES

IN HIS POSTHUMOUSLY PUBLISHED *Survey of Experimental Philosophy* (1776), Goldsmith reported that the English physicist George Cheyne "has pretended to demonstrate, that if we compare the muscular strength of two animals, that animal whose fluids circulate twice as swift, will be six times as strong."[1] For Cheyne himself, "*Health, Chearfulness* and *Activity*, (as they are bodily Affections)" require the "*easy, equable* and *regular* Performance" of the body's circulatory system.[2] Healthy circulation was strength; this truism, so perceived, had analogies beyond the medical, in political economy; thus, bodily vigor was transposed metaphorically from one realm to the other. Through the enlightenment, Roy Porter writes: "An entrenched medical materialism [. . .] pictures the pulsating body as a through-put economy; its well-tuned functioning depended upon generous input and unimpeded outflow."[3]

A bodily materialism informed equally Goldsmith's *The Deserted Village*, as acknowledged by critics then and now. John Hawkesworth's contemporary review of the poem, published in *The Gentleman's Magazine*, defended Goldsmith's economic argument by comparing a nation's wealth to "the vital fluid"; if and when the circulation of that wealth is impeded, Hawkesworth proposed, "universal corruption and ruin" follow.[4] Economic ruin was quickened wherever due attention was not paid to economic continence and self-sufficiency, to the measured sustainability of economic systems. There is, thus, a need to preserve and maintain a nation's circulatory force if its social health is to remain robust; thus, in the self-sufficient society, wealth generated by the local economy is fed back into that economy. This trope of circulation is the biological motif around which *The Deserted Village* is organized. It is evident in the frequency with which the words

CHAPTER 4

"round," "around" and "return" appear. Early in the poem, the word "round" denotes movement within a vigorously healthy pastoral scene; at the last it follows the word "ruin." For Marshall Brown, circulation "governs the lexical economy" of the poem. It becomes, in its happier, pastoral sections, "a sign of strength, with all the various circles knitting the village into a community."[5]

Ireland, however, leeched by the colonial class, by iniquities and inequities in trade, conspicuously lacked a circular flow of "generous input and unimpeded outflow"; lopsidedly, the only unimpeded outflow from Ireland was that of people and rent-incomes. The circulatory force of the Irish village economy had been undone by absenteeism—the hemorrhaging of its monetary wealth to England—and the emigration of its human wealth to America. Thus, Ireland served as a desolate example of an economy which was decidedly *not* through-put. With her wealth perverted outward, Ireland's was the epitome of an anemic body politic, her circulations depleted, her villages deserted. This is the reality in which the poem's more desolated sections deal.

The Irish origins and political geography of *The Deserted Village* will in this chapter be laid out in four parts. The first part gives a preliminary account of the problem of locating physically and specifically the poetic village of Auburn, and the ways in which this problem has, in the critical heritage, either obscured or enhanced the poem's political potential. In order to elaborate its critical possibilities, and to locate the poem more firmly in its Irish context, the rest of this chapter provides a deep chronological context for the poem, one which involves a cast of interconnected protagonists, including Burke, James Edward Oglethorpe, George Savile and the Marquess of Rockingham. The second part describes the culture of antipathy to absentee landlordism which characterized the intellectual scene of which Goldsmith was a product—that of Dublin in the 1740s. The third part deals with Irish emigration to America between the 1740s and the poem's publication in 1770, and in particular emigration to the colony of Georgia, the infernal scene which *The Deserted Village* ominously invokes. The fourth and final part details the reemergence, in the 1770s, of the debate about absenteeism, and in that context assesses and anticipates the poem's Irish resonance and afterlife.

Locating Auburn

Much scholarly effort has been spent on the correspondence of the pastoral of *The Deserted Village* to a real location, in Ireland or in England.[6] In 1786 the Irish antiquarian Joseph Cooper Walker wrote to Charles O'Conor, historian and friend to Goldsmith's uncle Thomas Contarine, requesting information for Percy's biographical endeavors: "I promised the Bishop I would beg of you to acquaint me, for his Lordship's Information, with the original & present Name of Goldsmith's immortal Auburn.—I believe it lies near Elfin."[7] Elphin, the diocesan school of which was Goldsmith's place of education for a period, was confirmed, perhaps too readily, by one Mr. Brett (probably related to John Brett, the bishop of Elphin from 1748 to 1756): "Mr. Brett informs me that the Village of Lissoy, which lies near Elfin, is the Auburn of Dr. Goldsmith. Have you ever been in that Village? And what is its present State?—Does 'Desolation sadden all its Green?'"[8]

Others went further into the poem's more immediate political context. In 1808, the miscellaneous writer Edward Mangin made an attempt at "clearing up a contested question, as to the precise scene of [Goldsmith's] 'Deserted Village.'" Mangin confessed a debt to Dr. Annesley Strean, a clergyman in the diocese of Elphin, whose letter states that the poem refers to the plight of the peasantry on the estate in that diocese of one general Robert Napper, or Napier. Having purchased extensive lands surrounding Lissoy, Napier, it is alleged, removed many local cottiers' families to make room for "the wide domain of a rich man."[9] Following Mangin, the Reverend R. H. Newell further substantiated the Napier connection in 1811, adding that all of the lands which Napier had acquired had been formerly those of the Dillon family, who "were staunch supporters and followers of the Stuart family." In 1730, Napier began to enclose his lands and to eject local respectable families, "thus at length occasioning some hundreds to emigrate to the other parts of the country, and to America."

That the poem is sourced in the plight of Jacobite families in its author's native region belies the poem's ostensibly English setting; in this discrepancy, Goldsmith, as Newell remarks, "contrived to give an English character to circumstances and objects plainly and originally Irish."[10] Equally, James Prior observes that "the flourishing state of trade, the influx of wealth and luxury, the song of the nightingale, and many other incidental details" are only true of England, while "the stream of emigration which has for a century largely and steadily flowed toward America, and much of the local scenery and objects, belong to Ireland."[11] In his account of the circumstances of the poem's creation, William Cooke recalls Goldsmith's remark two days into composition: "Some of my friends," he told Cooke, "differ with me on this plan, and think the depopulation of villages does not exist—but I am myself satisfied of the fact. I remember it in my own country, and have seen it in this."[12] These catastrophes take place in England *and* in Ireland, Goldsmith proposes—hobbling his argument with a lack of precision which critics then, as now, have fixed upon. The poem's dedication to Sir Joshua Reynolds is preoccupied with the question of veracity:

> I know you will object (and indeed several of our best and wisest friends concur in the opinion) that the depopulation it deplores is no where to be seen, and the disorders it laments are only to be found in the poet's imagination. To this I can scarce make any other answer than that I sincerely believe what I have written; that I have taken all possible pains, in my country excursions, for these four or five years past, to be certain of what I alledge, and that all my views and enquiries have led me to believe those miseries real, which I here attempt to display. (W4: 285)

Goldsmith's emphasis, throughout the dedication, is never on the real existence of the happy Auburn; it is, rather, on the phenomenon of depopulation. Many contemporary English critics, however, scoffed at the poem's more negative elements, particularly its portrayal of mass emigration. One review remarked that the poem was

> a most beautiful structure, though we think it is built upon a very sandy foundation; or rather, it is a rainbow castle in the air, raised and adorned solely by the strength of the author's imagination; for we cannot believe, that this country is depopulating, or that commerce is destructive of the real strength and greatness of a nation.[13]

Another nationalistic review seems willing to credit the poem's pastoralism, but not its politics. The reviewer doubts "whether he here shows himself as accurate a politician and philosopher, as he is a poet of a rich and elegant fancy" before claiming that "England wears now a more smiling aspect than she ever did; and few ruined villages are to be met with except on poetical ground."[14]

Thomas Babington Macaulay, similarly, sees the poem's alleged Englishness as incongruous; in adding an Irish dimension, however, he gets closer to the poem's origins:

> The village in its happy days is a true English village. The village in its decay is an Irish village. The felicity and the misery which Goldsmith has brought close together belong to two different countries, and to two different stages in the progress of society. He had assuredly never seen in his native island such a rural paradise, such a seat of plenty, content, and tranquillity, as his *Auburn*. He had assuredly never seen in England all the inhabitants of such a paradise turned out of their homes in one day

and forced to emigrate in a body to America. The hamlet he had probably seen was in Kent: the ejectment he had probably seen in Munster; but by joining the two, he has produced something which never was and never will be seen in any part of the world.[15]

Though supercilious, Macaulay is half correct. The village in decay *is* an Irish village. Goldsmith had traveled through Munster as a young man, and had seen some of the ejectments which he might add to his catalogue of abuses in the midlands. That he had tried to relate this decay to England is something which contemporary critics, and economic historians, could not credit. If the poem had described a happy, and still-happy village, English critics would have been content enough to accept the poem's verisimilitude. Auburn, the *deserted* village, however, was in Ireland. *The Deserted Village* deals with social destruction in one jurisdiction—Ireland—and the threat of self-destruction in England, but it does so through a pastoral medium which has tended to obscure both its origin and its object.

In order fully to understand why *The Deserted Village* has been so long misunderstood in England, it is worth examining an instance of its being disingenuously rewritten there. Anthony King's *The Frequented Village; A Poem Inscribed to the Late Dr Oliver Goldsmith* (1771) adapted Goldsmith's poem to its own ideological ends: "Addressed amicably to Goldsmith," writes David Fairer, "*The Frequented Village* offers a patriotic corrective to *The Deserted Village*'s pessimistic view of Britain's emigrating peasantry."[16] Like many English critics, King greatly admired Goldsmith's pastoralism; like those critics again, he wondered at the poem's negativity, and so sought to reorient its politics. "Designed originally," claims King, "as a Companion," it is in fact a travesty of the original, one which galvanizes rather than decries the concept of "Liberty":

> And thou sweet Liberty, inspire my song,
> Peculiar praises to the sound belong,
> Whose generous tongue a fettered speech disdains,
> But sweetly utters unaffected strains;
> Propitious on Britannia's sons look down,
> From whom thy genius never yet hath flown,
> Let no ideal form in freedom's guise,
> Mislead the vulgar, or deceive the wise,
> The breast with fluctating [sic] bonds enthral,
> But shine a great, a true original.[17]

CHAPTER 4

Opposing those forms of freedom born of abstract idealism, or theory, King willingly concedes that, outside of Britain, the concept had been much abused. Goldsmith's pessimistic view could not be corrected so easily, however, in the case of Ireland, where denudation and decay were demonstrably the downside of English liberty.

King was himself an Irish lawyer writing to an English audience; though even contemporary London-Irishmen commenting to compatriots at home could neglect the poem's darker side. In a letter to Richard Shackleton, Edmund Burke commended *The Deserted Village* for its "true and pretty" pastoral images (CH: 91). The pastoral images, though pretty enough, were not true of any scene. Goldsmith argues his case about trade, displacement, and dehumanization by appealing to a shared sense of a Golden Age. In the most technical sense of its being utopian, the happy pastoral scene that Goldsmith describes is *nowhere*, and of no specific time. Auburn was an imagined space, whose depiction served a particular purpose in Goldsmith's criticisms of burgeoning capitalism and its detrimental effect on the rural poor. As Rachel Crawford writes, his "utopic vision" is deployed to demonstrate "the precarious state of villagers who are dependent on the ministrations of a benevolent lord."[18] Fredric Jameson's comments on utopia as imaginary future could as easily be applied, thus, to an imaginary past, and imaginary pastoral: "imaginary or not," Jameson writes, the utopian projection "returns upon our present to play a diagnostic and a critical-substantive role."[19] Speculation regarding any other exact location is suggestive but it must be accepted that, while elements in the poem's dramatis personae, the object of its ethical-economic critique, and its topography can be linked to autobiography, *The Deserted Village* describes a happy village that is indeed ultimately utopian, and a deserted village that is depressingly real. In its happier state, thus, Auburn exists only to serve the specific purposes of a protest poem. As the thresher poet Stephen Duck showed decades before in "The Thresher's Labour" (1730), and as George Crabbe would seek to demonstrate in *The Village* (1783), literary pastoral could be guilty of an obfuscation or reification of real conditions; but pastoral could also, to adapt and apply Jameson's analysis once more, involve a "Utopian compensation for increasing dehumanisation on the level of daily life."[20] Auburn may be misremembered or misrepresented; it may in fact be nowhere. Such scenes, however, demonstrate by contrast that an accelerated and aggressive commercialism has resulted in social catastrophe.

Even the *motives* of the protest element within the poem, however, have been questioned. Raymond Williams saw *The Deserted Village* as a "self-regarding poetic exercise": a lament for the loss of the social conditions of poetry.[21] Commercial society has abstracted poetry from social relationships, and regret at the loss of rural virtues is to be understood as no more than regret for the depreciation of Goldsmith's literary vocation. This, for Williams, is a disabling point, one which demonstrates a dialectical failure on Goldsmith's part. *The Deserted Village* does end on a note of regret for the exile of poetry from commercial society; however, this sentiment is less an exercise in poetic self-regard than it is an argument against an instrumental, acquisitive logic which depreciates, not just poetry, but a more general social and cultural intelligence and sensitivity to the plight of the rural poor. The surface Englishness of the poem is reflected in Williams' criticism of it. However, as Edward Said has remarked, Williams' literary criticism was limited in its "feeling that English literature is mainly about England."[22] That Goldsmith seems to decry the effects of colonialism on the poor in England only partially obscures another geographical source for his disaffection.

In Ireland too, however, it is *still* the soft pastoralism of *The Deserted Village*, and not its political argument, which defines and delimits the poet's stance. For Seamus Deane, Goldsmith's Ireland is *not* "the Ireland of the penal Laws and of occasional famines, agrarian disturbances and judicial murders. It is an idyll, comparable to his view of Irish society of which *The Deserted Village* is the appealing remnant."[23] This reading of the poem, while understandable in the light of Yeats' later use of Goldsmith, is not fully responsive to that half of the poem which portrays a degraded contemporary reality. Yeats might have been able to adapt the poem to his imagined eighteenth-century Golden Age of Anglo-Irish benevolence; to accept that adaptation of the poem, however, is to risk repeating Yeats' aesthetic selectivity along with his willful ahistoricity. For if Goldsmith is idealizing Irish life as it actually was, the poem would surely have had a title more like Anthony King's perverse imitation.

For *The Deserted Village* is very clearly haunted by famine and landlordly oppression; and its argument must be thought of as a product of the last decades which Goldsmith spent in his native country. In the years before Goldsmith and Burke began their studies at Trinity, Ireland was, according to Philip Skelton,

> oftner visited with famine, than any other country under heaven, and every famine attended as a natural and necessary consequence, with a pestilence that sweeps away its inhabitants in prodigious numbers, who also croud out to *America*, and elsewhere, so fast, that it is in danger of being unpeopled in a little time; that as to it's wealth, it is one of the poorest countries in the world [. . .][24]

CHAPTER 4

Skelton's account is echoed in Goldsmith's reference to the "imploring famine" of 1740–1, of the "wretched matron, forced, in age, for bread, /To strip the brook with mantling cresses spread" (W4: 292).²⁵ Goldsmith's vision is of a country ruined by the waste of the peasantry's potential, the population distraught, hungry, and driven to emigration by a general neglect. This is the reality with which *The Deserted Village* grapples.

Though England is a constituency to whom Goldsmith is necessarily appealing, it is not the constituency from which his convictions emerge. The poem confuses its Irish background and its ostensible Englishness to critical effect, drawing attention to a general rupture in traditional attachments to the land. As Terry Eagleton writes, the rural poor in both countries are linked by "the same exploitative economic system."²⁶ However, Ireland's colonial predicament exacerbates that exploitation. Kevin Whelan has argued that the bucolic notion of the people's organic attachment to the land in England "had a seductive effect as a soothing sedative to excitable and deracinated radicalism," while in Ireland, "as Edmund Burke knew only too well, both intellectually and emotionally, the jagged edges of the land question chafed at the superficially smooth patina of eighteenth-century life."²⁷ In England, thus, Goldsmith's pastoralism had a nostalgic feel which appealed, but was attached to a political critique which did not. Burke understood this discrepancy; as such, his connection to Goldsmith is again crucial: their shared, and in one important instance divergent, politics help to explain the poem's contexts and motivations.

Auburn's Absentees

The most famous lines of Goldsmith's posthumously published *Retaliation* (1774) refer to Burke's narrowing his mind so that he could give up to party "what was meant for mankind" (W4: 353). Goldsmith, more than many, might have known; their acquaintance and developing friendship spanned that "narrowing." The longer context of Goldsmith's connections with Burke explains the supposedly friendly but markedly barbed swipe which implied that Burke's public spirit had been wasted on Charles Watson-Wentworth, 2nd Marquess of Rockingham.²⁸ When Burke and Goldsmith were students at Trinity College, there existed a broad patriotic culture of disgust with the absentee landlord class. While a student, Goldsmith was influenced by the political content, and in particular the anti-absentee stance, of Burke's *Reformer* (1748). Not only did Goldsmith read the *Reformer*; he may have contributed his first published poem, anonymously, to its fourth number. But the antiestablishment nature of Burke's youthful writing did not hold; and one problem with Burke's ambition and ultimate success as a politician in England, for Goldsmith, was that his stance on the absentee issue was plainly compromised by his party affiliation.

The absentee issue in Ireland had a substantial recent literary history. In 1729, the Irish Patriot Thomas Prior excoriated the wanton luxury of Irish absentee landlords, by claiming that they:

> add Insult to ill Usage; *they* reproach us with our Poverty, at the same Time, that *they* take away our Money; and can tell us, we have no Diversion or Entertainments in *Ireland* for them, when they themselves disable us from having better, by withdrawing from us.
>
> But 'tis to be hoped, that our Legislature will take Care, that these Gentlemen, who spend their Fortunes abroad, and are thereby the greatest, and almost only Cause of its Poverty and Distress, shall not be the only Persons favoured, and exempted from paying the Taxes thereof.[29]

Prior's complaint was contemporaneous with Swift's argument that absenteeism was a primary cause of Ireland's political and economic woes. As the metropolitan economy improved, prices went up. More money was spent by the Irish landowning classes in England; rack-renting and emigration ensued. "The miseries we suffer by our absentees, are of a far more extensive nature than seems to be commonly understood," concluded Swift.[30] Elsewhere, he lambasts "the Folly, the Vanity, and Ingratitude of those vast Numbers, who think themselves too good to live in the Country which gave them Birth, and still gives them Bread; and rather chuse to pass their Days, and consume their Wealth, and draw out the very Vitals of their Mother Kingdom, among those who heartily despise them."[31] In *A Modest Proposal*, famously, the argument for taxing the absentees is ironically and chillingly rejected in favor of an ostensibly more logical and efficient solution.

The culture of disdain for the absentees was broad, intense in Dublin's patriotic circles, and diffused throughout the countryside. In the contemporary poetry of Laurence Whyte, the perfidy of the absentees explains the phenomenon of emigration. Published in 1740, and again, expanded, in 1742, Whyte's *Poems on Various Subjects* was widely read in Goldsmith and Burke's Trinity milieu. In "The Parting Cup, or, The Humours of *Deoch an Doruis*," the poet remembers the culture of hospitality among the native gentry in Westmeath, one of Goldsmith's home counties, before narrating the decline of that hospitality from 1688 down to the present. The world of Whyte's poem, according to An-

CHAPTER 4

drew Carpenter, was that of "a generalized but not very aggressive Jacobitism."[32] The fourth canto of "The Parting Cup" in particular is a critique of the destruction wrought by the absentees. The narration includes a severe admonition to those landlords who spend most of their money in London, thus impoverishing the country which sustains their luxurious lifestyles. Extracting excessive rents from a tenantry toward which they demonstrate no filial affection or sense of duty, it is the landlord class which allows the dereliction of rural Ireland, thereby "Depopulating every village." The tenants are, in Whyte's description, oppressed by rents to the extent that they cannot sustain themselves in Ireland, and must therefore suffer displacement to the new world. The processes described by Whyte presage the content and language of *The Deserted Village*. For James Prior, "The Parting Cup" expresses "the common rural complaints of Ireland—the exactions of landlords, the spirit of emigration, the absenteeism of the gentry, with the neglect of their tenantry, estates, and residences." More important again for Prior is the poem's "having been supposed to impress Goldsmith's mind at an early period with strong commiseration for the state of the peasantry, and to have suggested passages in the "Deserted Village."[33]

Rather than submit to oppression and abuse at home, Whyte's villagers "trust themselves to Wind and Waves." Preferring what Goldsmith would later characterize as the hollow pomp of London and Paris masquerades, the absentees, "too well bred to live at home," are held in acidic contempt by Whyte:

> These *Absentees* we here describe,
> Are mostly of our Ir___sh Tribe,
> Who live in *Luxury* and *Pleasure*,
> And throw away their *Time* and *Treasure*,
> Cause *Poverty* and Devastation,
> And sink the *Credit* of the *Nation*,
> A *Nation* sunk for Want of *Trade*,
> A Foot-stool to her *Neighbours* made;
> And yet our *Gentry* all run wild,
> And never can be reconcil'd,
> To live at home upon their Rent,
> With any Pleasure or Content.[34]

This lines provide a plaintive echo to the patriotic satire of Swift's *Modest Proposal*; indicatively, Swift had a copy of Whyte's poems in his library when he died. It was in this Dublin and Dublin-educated world of the 1740s that Edmund Burke's views on the land, the Irish peasantry, and the landlords were most in agreement with those of Whyte, and, by extension, Goldsmith.

Out of this intellectual and literary cluster arose an important dimension of *The Deserted Village*'s deep background. On May 21, 1747, following the arrest for debt of one of their number, rioting Trinity students made their way to the Black Dog, or Newgate prison, where shots were fired by the constabulary, killing two. The college authorities publicly admonished Goldsmith for his leading part in the riot. On May 29, the students' club, of which Burke was president, affected stern disapproval of student participation in city rioting. Such disciplinary matters were not the main business of the club, however. In the evenings following their discussions of these student disturbances Burke, echoing Prior and Swift, introduced to the club a bill "to tax the absentees ten per cent of their estates," claiming such a tax to be "the only means of preserving some part of the little money in the kingdom, which, appropriated to the Dublin Society, might prove a great advantage to it."[35] This resolution was expounded in the fourth number of the *Reformer*, in which Burke argued that it was the love of the public and mankind—or "Public Spirit"—as opposed to the narrow concept of "Party," which gave rise to their enterprise. His differentiation between party and public-spiritedness provides a basis for his critique of those who, "as if conscious of the Poverty and Infamy their Behaviour raises to their Country, they fly it and bestow their Riches, where, as they are less wanted, the People are less thankful for them."[36] The problem for Burke was "luxury": a many-faceted term which, according to the context of its use could mean exploitation, insubordination, or, more instructively again, an insubordination generated by exploitation.[37]

Set against luxury was the idea of a providential social dispensation in which it was understood that different strata of society had and could hold their place, and that each stratum had its own responsibility to the society as a whole. Appearing at the end of *Reformer* no. 4 is a poem which expresses that idea. "On the Several Conditions of Life" was included by Burke for its being "moral and ingenious":

> With even hand has all disposing Fate,
> Pleasure and Pain annex'd to every State:
> Kings who Dominion with their Maker share,
> Tho' free to govern, live the Slaves of Fear;
> While Peasants whom no regal Cares invade
> Find their Contempt with Safety well repaid;
> Content when lodg'd within the poor man's Breast,
> Equals his worst of Fortunes with the best;

CHAPTER 4

> While the rich Wretch whose Wishes nought confines
> In Midst of Plenty as in Want repines.
> To heal his Wounds the Soldier gets a Name,
> And dies in battle but to live in Fame;
> The Hopes of Heaven cheers the suff'ring Saint,
> While keen Remorse the Sinner's Pleasures taint;
> The Bard whose Labours are with Genius crown'd,
> Oft sees his Worth in Seas of Envy drown'd,
> Saint-like he voluntary Want must chuse,
> Nor reap, till dead, the Profits of his Muse.[38]

The monarch, like the peasant, has his cares; the latter enjoys, at least, a philosophical equanimity which offsets the lowliness of his social status. Equally, the prospect of posthumous fame might compensate the injured soldier, and the poet plagued by a factional culture of criticism. The rich and luxurious are, in spite of the appearance of wealth, singled out as more profoundly miserable because their acquisitiveness is never done.

The broader sentiments of this piece echo Alexander Pope's *Essay on Man* (1734–5). Pope's "cosmic Toryism," his providential sense of order was, like his characteristic deployment of the heroic couplet, an abiding influence on Goldsmith's poetry.[39] "On the Several Conditions of Life" is very probably the first manifestation of this influence; accordingly, A. P. I. Samuels first raised the possibility that Goldsmith may have furnished the piece to *The Reformer*.[40] If it is by Goldsmith, and it is highly likely (Burke's opposition to Goldsmith's riotous behaviour notwithstanding), this piece would be his earliest published work. Objections have been lodged to that attribution, however. In his present-centered critique of "retrospective localism" in Irish studies of Goldsmith, W.J. McCormack, writing against what he perceives to be a form of "neo-romanticism," questions both the Irish contextualization of *The Deserted Village* and the specific attribution of "On the Several Conditions of Life" to Goldsmith. In so doing, McCormack draws due attention to an alliterative bum note in the phrase "rich wretch."[41] Though jarring, that infelicity is not enough to disqualify the piece as a possible early indication of Goldsmith's poetic style, or indeed his ethical scheme. With that scar of youthful overwrite acknowledged and admitted, the rest of the poem is smoothly and evenly composed. Quite apart from the promising stylistic similarities to both of his major poems, the philosophy of the poem adumbrates *The Traveller*, in which the once merely acquisitive section of society has become society's greatest threat. "On the Several Conditions of Life" deals in what would become Goldsmith's perennials: contentment, responsibility, and such entities' inevitable contrast with a socially abject wealth. Also, *The Deserted Village* develops one image in particular, in which the surviving soldier weeps "o'er his wounds and tales of sorrow" in a scene of bucolic generosity and limited local fame. The image of the reward as "crowning" is also one which figures in idealized scenes of calm retirement in the later poem.

The implication of all three poems is that the form of government best suited to oversee social equanimity depends upon a protective kingly prerogative. Goldsmith paints a pastoral order wherein everyone has their load to bear; wherein, more importantly, everyone knows which load is *theirs*. For every benefit of power, there is responsibility. For every simple pleasure of rustic working life, there is limitation. The duty and obligation of the powerful to the poor is essential, though in Ireland normative rather than actual. *The Traveller* internationalizes the thesis of "On the Several Conditions of Life" to demonstrate that what holds within countries also holds comparatively. The appearance of "On the Several Conditions of Life" in an especially sharp number of the *Reformer*, wherein the absentees are vilified, gives the poem a political charge which, intrinsically, it lacks—just as the idyllic scenes of *The Deserted Village* develop a critical edge when described alongside the social disasters which the poem more pointedly narrates.

This pervasive notion of "content"—or contentment—is a motif which runs throughout the oeuvre, and is linked, in antagonism, to the hollow and showy allure of economic luxury.[42] In the *Reformer*, Burke's idea of real national wealth is precisely Goldsmith's; Goldsmith's, at this point, precisely Burke's: "The Riches of a Nation are not to be estimated by the splendid Appearance or luxurious Lives of its Gentry; it is the uniform Plenty diffused through a People, of which the meanest as well as the greatest partake, that makes them happy, and the Nation powerful."[43] In *Reformer* No. 7, published on March 10, 1748, poverty and destitution are again linked to the luxury of the absentees. Their ostentation gives the country only an appearance of wealth. Echoing Swift's *Short View of the State of Ireland* (1727), Burke observes that wealth is not diffused as it should be through the population, and claims that few countries in Europe can equal Ireland for the poverty of its peasantry, all the more scandalous when thrown into sharp relief by the excesses of the rich. Irresponsibly accrued wealth, as Goldsmith would put it, is "but a name/That leaves our useful products still the same" (W4: 297). For Burke and Goldsmith, as for Swift, it is the rich man who displaces the rural poor with his expansive landscape garden who stands accused; but such villainy is general—inspired equally by the absentee who, in luxurious oblivion, drives his tenants to emigration. The absentees lack any sense of responsibility to the future of the localities they own and control; as such, the antagonism of Burke's *Reformer* resonates even through his *Reflections on the Revolution in France*:

> But one of the first and most leading principles on which the commonwealth and the laws are consecrated, is lest the temporary possessors and life-renters in it, unmindful of what they have received from their ancestors, or of what is due to their posterity, should act as if they were the entire masters; that they should not think it amongst their rights to cut off the entail, or commit waste on the inheritance, by destroying at their pleasure the whole original fabric of their society; hazarding to leave to those who come after them, a ruin instead of an habitation—and teaching these successors as little to respect their contrivances, as they had themselves respected the institutions of their forefathers.

In the *Reflections*, there is admiration for true nobility, for those who behave demonstrably in accordance with "the customs of mankind, taught by their nature; that is, with modest splendour, with unassuming state, with mild majesty and sober pomp." This moderate responsibility is contrasted—and here the *Reflections* are explicitly inspired by *The Deserted Village*—with the luxury of the egomaniacal individual: "the wealth and pride of individuals at every moment makes the man of humble rank and fortune sensible of his inferiority, and degrades and vilifies his condition."[44] In Goldsmith, this is the "unwieldy wealth and cumbrous pomp" (W4: 290) which oppresses the contiguous rural poor:

> The man of wealth and pride
> Takes up a space that many poor supplied;
> Space for his lake, his park's extended bounds,
> Space for his horses, equipage and hounds;
> The robe that wraps his limbs in silken sloth
> Has robbed the neighbouring field of half their growth;
> His seat, where solitary sports are seen,
> Indignant spurns the cottage from the green;
> Around the world each needful product flies,
> For all the luxuries the world supplies:
> While thus the land, adorned for pleasure all,
> In barren splendour feebly waits the fall. (W4: 298)

The peasant's cottage is spurned from the green by the creation of the private pleasure garden; this is an economic modernity which has come to threaten the notion of there being such a thing as communally or collectively inherited space.

In his *Estimate of the Manners and Principles of the Times* (1757), John Brown anticipated Goldsmith's poem when he diagnosed a false liberty which gave rise to individual ambition and the decline of public spirit. All that remains, according to Brown, is "the Pride of *Equipage*, the Pride of *Title*, the Pride of *Fortune*, or the Pride of *Dress*, that have assumed the Empire over our Souls, and Levelled *Ambition* with the *Dirt*."[45] In his later *Thoughts on Civil Liberty* (1765), Brown distinguished further between real and false liberty, linking the former to an extension of the "social Passions of Individuals [. . .] to include the Welfare of the *whole* Community, as their *chief* and *primary* Object. This Affection is distinguished by the name of *public Spirit*, or the *Love* of our *Country*; the highest passion that can sway the human heart, considered as a permanent Foundation of true Liberty."[46] Goldsmith's poetry echoes Brown's disdain for party, corruption and luxury. This is precisely the type of view which Burke later proclaimed to be old-fashioned—symptomatic, in his *Thoughts on the Present Discontents* (1770), of an outmoded Toryism. Goldsmith knew by this point that Burke had given up on certain aspects of his own earlier outlook for the exigencies of party politics. In 1773, as I will narrate and analyze later in this chapter, Goldsmith had quietly engaged himself on a renewed campaign in favor of a tax on the Irish absentees, while Burke, reversing his earlier position, had sided, on this topic at least, with the parasitic, colonial stratum to which was attributed the general malaise of poverty, depopulation and American emigration.

To Distant Climes

In 1769, the year before the publication of *The Deserted Village*, a group of emigrants arrived at Savannah, Georgia. Their petition to the provincial council read

> that they were chiefly farmers; that being of late years greatly oppressed by rents in Ireland, so that the most exerted industry scarcely afforded a comfortable subsistence to their families, they determined to seek relief by moving to the American colonies. That being informed by sundry letters from their friends, who came to settle in this province from Ireland last year in the ship Prince George, that a certain portion of land was laid out and appropriated for the purpose of settling a township in this Province, the consideration of the great privileges and advantages

CHAPTER 4

afforded them by the Governor and General Assembly were powerful inducements to their immediately resolving to leave their native country.⁴⁷

The township in question was the Queensborough township, now Louisville in Jefferson County, near the Ogeechee River, settled initially by the Irish slave trader John Rea. Between 1760 and 1769, the decade which provides the immediate context for the poem, twenty-three vessels sailed from the north of Ireland to South Carolina and Georgia, with immigrants attracted to those parts by the South Carolina Bounty of the 1730s. By 1790, the colony had "the highest proportion of inhabitants of Irish birth or ancestry in the 13 states, with estimates ranging above 26 percent."⁴⁸ Most Irish settled near Savannah; and many others spread out along the banks of the Savannah and Altamaha Rivers and their tributaries. This migration was important for Goldsmith, whose specific invocation of Georgia—*The Deserted Village* refers to "wild Altama"—as a destination for villagers is salient for two reasons: it was the destination of a great many Irish émigrés through the middle of the eighteenth century; and its founder was James Edward Oglethorpe, a crypto-Jacobite, and later a friend of Goldsmith, who supported the political argument of *The Deserted Village* in the face of English scepticism.⁴⁹

Oglethorpe has been celebrated by biographers as an "imperial idealist." Familially and, to some, *actually* a Jacobite, he was one of England's first determined prison reformers: a point of sympathetic agreement with Goldsmith—*The Vicar of Wakefield* is, in several sequences, concerned with issues of dehumanizing incarceration.⁵⁰ Oglethorpe's appeal for prisoners' rights was, in his own mind, congruent with his broader imperial mission. He obtained the royal charter for Georgia in 1732 with the intention of creating there a state where the destitute at home, including imprisoned debtors' and persecuted Protestants on the continent, could have a second chance abroad. The mission, in theory, was threefold. According to the philanthropic motive, poor English people and persecuted Protestants were to be persuaded to take the refuge and opportunity which Georgia afforded. The second motive was mercantile: Georgia could provide raw materials as well as a market for finished goods. Finally, Georgia was militarily important. Hence, a body of Jacobite Highlanders from Inverness traveled to and settled at Darien (defiantly named after William Paterson's failed Scottish investment scheme at the Isthmus of Darien of 1698) twelve miles along the Altamaha.⁵¹ The law of the new colony limited the extent of agrarian landholdings, a legal stipulation intended to make Georgia a haven from the culture of enclosure which had ruined the rural underclass at home. Both rum and slavery were also banned, but this was an aspect of Oglethorpe's idealism which irked other mercantile interests in the colonies.

Georgia appears in *The Deserted Village* as the obverse of happy pastoral; it is an exaggeratedly infernal scene, in which climate and all of animated nature seem to threaten:

> Ah, no. To distant climes, a dreary scene,
> Where half the convex world intrudes between,
> Through torrid tracts with fainting steps they go,
> Where wild Altama murmurs to their woe.
> Far different there from all that charm'd before,
> The various terrors of that horrid shore.
> Those blazing suns that dart a downward ray,
> And fiercely shed intolerable day;
> Those matted woods where birds forget to sing,
> But silent bats in drowsy clusters cling,
> Those poisonous fields with rank luxuriance crowned
> Where the dark scorpion gathers death around;
> Where at each step the stranger fears to wake
> The rattling terrors of the vengeful snake;
> Where crouching tigers wait their hapless prey,
> And savage men more murderous still than they;
> While oft in whirls the mad tornado flies,
> Mingling the ravaged landscape with the skies. (W4: 300–1)

These striking images do not derive from the reports of emigrants but from Goldsmith's hurried readings in contemporary geographies. A selection of creatures, including the misnamed or mislocated tiger—there were none in Georgia—are compiled in an emblematic natural history to instil a naïve terror in the reader. Buffon had claimed that all creatures had degenerated in the new world climate; and this applied to people as much as to parrots.[52] Accordingly, extremes of cold and moisture had rendered the American Indians unloving, cruel, surly, and, as a further consequence, incapable of emotions conducive to song. Their gruff speech, according to Buffon, set a bad example for the birds—thus, there arose in the eighteenth century an ornithological fallacy, reproduced in the poem, that American species produced no birdsong.[53] In *The Deserted Village*, the natives are "savage men more murderous still" (W4: 301) than the animals with which they share a country where, as *The Traveller* had earlier phrased it, "beasts with man divided empire claim" (W4: 268). As Laura Brown has argued of the eighteenth century, "new paradigms in biology, zoology, and natural history raised controversial questions

CHAPTER 4

about the nature of the physiological and developmental links among animals, or between animals and men."[54] Goldsmith, having plagiarized his way through an essay on "The Effects which Climates have upon Men, and Other Animals" in 1760, had at least a passable understanding of these paradigms. The climate produced a vicious threat from animals and men alike, and it was understood that the Irish would act as a buffer between the English and the dangers hidden in the wilderness.[55] The poem's conflation of crouching tigers, hidden Indians, angry snakes and cataclysmic tornadoes is adapted from Buffon's natural history and embellished with additional terrors to fashion a colonial sublime, wherein pity for the displaced villagers is intermingled with terror at what they face. The depiction is bound up in politics rather than in any desire for verisimilitude. Goldsmith's "unkind portrait of America in the poem," writes Laurence Goldstein, "is not meant to be realistic any more than the America of Blake's prophecies."[56]

In his two-volume *Account of the European Settlements in America* (1757), William Burke, substantially assisted by his kinsman Edmund, stated that the American colonies were, at that time, "only known to the rest of the world for about two centuries'; as such, the topic did "not naturally afford matter for many volumes." They warned the reader to be wary of contemporary accounts: "some are loaded with a lumber of matter that can interest very few," while others "obscure the truth in many particulars, to gratify the low prejudice of parties, and I may say of nations." Even accounts by the English must be read "with great caution; because very few of them write without a bias to the interest of the particular province to which they belong, or perhaps to a particular faction in that province."[57] The work was topical given the outbreak of war over the colonies in 1756, and was hurriedly published by the Dodsleys for that reason. A compendium of contemporary and near-contemporary information regarding the Americas, the *Account* is, in some respects, hackwork. The compiled materials are, however, commented upon in an engaged manner; such analysis is very probably Edmund Burke's work. Though never fully accepted as part of his oeuvre, the *Account* adumbrates some thoughts on America which would appear in Burke's later speeches.

The Burkes' preface confessed its deepest debt to John Campbell's *Concise History of the Spanish America* (1741), and his *Complete Collection of Voyages and Travels* (1744–49). F. P. Lock suggests that these and other sources, such as Amédée-Francois Frézier's *Voyage to the South-Sea* (1717), Charles-Marie de la Condamine's *Succinct Abridgement of a Voyage Made within the Inland Parts of South America* (1747), and George Anson's *A Voyage Round the World* (1740–44), were editorialized upon by Edmund in a more philosophical manner than William could have managed. On this point, Lock cites Burke's treatment of the establishment of Georgia as an "analysis in the manner of Montesquieu."[58] When he assembled his compilation on *The Present State of the British Empire in Europe, America, Africa and Asia* (1768), Goldsmith directly transplanted large tracts of the Burkes' book.[59] Expediency did not demand that he examined their work for the prejudices of which they warned. Though not terribly well informed in any solidly empirical way of American reality himself, Goldsmith would have had a vague and impressionistic sense of the threats faced by emigrants to the new world. His views on the state of society in the old world, however, led him to dramatize American terrors to create an almost gothic effect.

Demonstrating the Burkes' thesis on the politicized nature of representations of America, Goldsmith's depiction of Georgia contrasts starkly with that of the Whig poet James Thomson, whom Goldsmith considered to be, "in general, a verbose and affected poet" (W5: 325), an opinion borne out by "The Prospect," the fifth part of *Liberty* (1736):

> 'Lo! Swarming southward on rejoicing Suns,
> 'Gay COLONIES extend; the calm Retreat
> 'Of undeserv'd Distress, the better Home
> 'Of Those whom *Bigots* chase from foreign Lands.
> 'Not built on *Rapine*, *Servitude* and *Woe*,
> 'And, in their turn, some petty Tyrant's Prey;
> 'But, bound by Social Freedom, firm they rise;
> 'Such as, of late, an Oglethorpe has form'd,
> 'And, crouding round, the charm'd *Savannah* sees.[60]

Georgia, thus, was a poetically contested *topos*. The differences between Goldsmith and Thomson's versions of Georgia are political as well as poetical: one disdains empire, the other celebrates it. For Thomson, in his famous song concluding *Alfred: A Masque* (1740), Britons would rule the waves and never be slaves; for Goldsmith, Britain was making slaves of its own citizens and of others: "The wealth of climes, where savage nations roam," he writes in *The Traveller*, had been "Pillag'd from slaves, to purchase slaves at home" (W4: 266). This sentiment is tellingly repeated in his *History of England*, with reference to Clive's victories in India, where the English have been "gratified in their avarice [. . . and] that wealth which they had plundered from slaves in India, they were resolved to employ in making slaves at home" (HE4: 382). The repeated phrasing captures the connectedness and cohesiveness of Goldsmith's anti-imperial thesis, and the reference to Lord Clive slyly alludes to the fact that his

CHAPTER 4

victories won him extensive tracts of land in the counties of Clare and Limerick, where he would himself become a profligate absentee landlord.[61]

Temperamentally averse to Thomson's Whiggish version of the Georgia experiment, Goldsmith also wrote against contemporary romanticizations of native American society and Oglethorpe's dealings with it. Indians were romanticized by the man himself and by commentators since; writing in 1899, Austin Dobson gushed that "Oglethorpe's management of the Indians deserves the highest praise, and he speedily inspired them with a confidence which they never lost."[62] Oglethorpe's benign relationship with the Yamacraw Tomochichi, his closest personal point of contact with the native Americans, was quickly idealized and became a staple of Georgian folklore, influencing the Romantic and revolutionary poetry of Philip Freneau. Alongside "The Dying Indian. Tomo-Chequi" and "The Indian Burial Ground," Freneau also penned "The American Village" (1772), an homage to Goldsmith, which saw the latter's deserted Auburn rise again as a pastoral scene in the American wilderness. The wilderness in Freneau's poem is foreboding to the European, but it is one in which a fierce American population—native *and* new—is superior to the dangers in the landscape:

> What tho' thy woods, America, contain
> The howling forest, and the tiger's den,
> The dang'rous serpent, and the beast of prey,
> Men are more fierce, more terrible than they.[63]

For Oglethorpe and Freneau, the Indians embodied the frugal, hardy virtues of the Roman Republic. Rather than a negative term, "Terrible" here implies the sort of physical strength and resilience required to survive in a wild land. Goldsmith's descriptions of the Indians are less complementary, and have more in common with the Burkes, who, drawing on Joseph-Francois Lafitau's *Moeurs des Sauvages Americains* (1724), painted a terrifying picture of cannibalizing native-American savagery. That the Indians are "savage" is for Goldsmith indicative, not of their nobility, but of their murderousness. Violent in their own defense, they are not to be admired or patronized by the European; they are to be feared. Effectively, Goldsmith is arguing that the climate of empire is withering and dangerous for those who should *not* inhabit it. As was the case with the Burkes' analysis of Georgia, Goldsmith was influenced by Montesquieu's views on the suitability of peoples and laws for climates, and vice versa.

The Burkes' *Account* was written to appeal to partisan sentiments produced by the Seven Years' War. For Burke the unsuitability of the European for the

Georgian climate is a problem that can be remedied by refined regulations. For Goldsmith, their unsuitability is more seriously and immediately threatening than that; and the environmental dangers which they face demonstrate all the more lucidly the tragedy of their displacement. Goldsmith, unlike Oglethorpe, and in this instance unlike the Burkes also, is writing from an explicitly anti-imperial stance. In this regard, he has more in common with Diderot and Raynal's *Histoire Des Deux Indes* than with the *Account*. That said, Raynal adapted the Burkes' analysis of Georgia's failures in his own history of the British in America; he also subtly implied that the benevolent idealism of Oglethorpe's Georgia venture was partially an egotistical matter of "maintaining the reputation" which the general had acquired in parliament "by his taste for great designs, by his zeal for his country, and his passion for glory."[64]

Burke admired Oglethorpe's commitment to the Georgian project but was troubled by its utopian component. The ban on slavery he interpreted as having an ulterior and misguided motive of keeping the numbers of potentially rebellious Africans in check. The idealistic standard of frugality was intended to counter luxury and to make the colony militarily stronger; and the ban on rum, while intended to avoid the disorders of other colonies, was made "without sufficiently consulting the nature of the country, or the disposition of the people which they regarded." The work of building the colony was deemed too strenuous for the whites alone, while the leveling frugality supposed to characterize the venture discouraged people "of substance" from settling there. The ban on rum caused widespread illness, as the unwholesome waters "wanted the corrective of a little spirit, as the settlers themselves wanted something to support their strength in the extraordinary and unusual heat of the climate, and the dampness of it in several places disposing them to agues and fevers." These grievances had the effect of denuding Georgia as settlers made for other colonies. Eventually, the trustees did away with the original regulations and Georgia partook of the same legal culture as the Carolinas. Such changes saved the colony. The Burkes criticized the regulations as first laid out; though commendable in principle, they were misguided because of the "fault of mankind in general," but also because of the particular conditions which prevailed in Georgia: "We want political regulations, and a steady plan in government, to remedy the defects that must be in all things, which depend merely on the character and disposition of the people."[65]

For Burke, Georgia was a problematic destination for emigrés for practical reasons of sustainability. Goldsmith's poetic portrait is more dramatically damning; however, his description of the colony is actually less a critique of Georgia,

CHAPTER 4

its climate or natives, than it is a critique, for the readers at home, of commercial oligarchy and colonialism. Oglethorpe understood the first critique, which is why he defended a poem which otherwise denigrated the scene of his imperial efforts. Oglethorpe led imperialism, hence Thomson's poetic approval; Goldsmith decried it. Oglethorpe was paternalistic to the "noble savages" from whom his colonialism subtly stole; Goldsmith's poem promoted fear of the "murderous savages" lurking in an environment for which Europeans had no native aptitude. Oglethorpe's was a primitivism which might seek to cosset the natives from the march of ostensible progress. Goldsmith resisted that primitivism, painting instead a scene of colonial violence, not to denigrate the Indians, but figuratively to warn against the dangers of neglect closer to home. His oppositions of Auburn and America, nostalgia and terror, utopia and dystopia, of rustic folk and murderous savages entangle the various strands, political and generic, historical and natural-historical, of his reading and output. On the surface, *The Deserted Village* idealizes pastoral husbandry and frugality; but a celebration of these qualities alone would make for an unnecessary poem. Ruin and emigration to America serve to activate the poem's nostalgia, but it is a deliberately fake nostalgia for an unreal society, made radical by its applicability to the contemporary political situation. Only the destructive processes are real; ruination is rendered all the more clearly when contrasted with a happier scene such as Auburn. This dialectic propels the poem, geographically and politically.

And Home Again

Thomson's *Liberty* pays Georgia's founder an extravagant compliment on his colonial endeavor. Goldsmith seems at first glance to be disparaging by association the man who would encourage innocent old-world villagers to travel to such a terrible destination. It is all the more intriguing, then, that Oglethorpe should have championed Goldsmith. Their differences on the issue of imperialism aside, it makes perfect sense that Oglethorpe was the only high-profile Englishman to defend Goldsmith's *Deserted Village* when it was published. In the *Adams Letters* published in the *Morning Chronicle*, of 1773 and 1774, Oglethorpe expatiated upon one of his favorite topics: the relationship of luxury, via land enclosure, to migration:

> Your Majesty, as a man of letters, has no doubt read Dr. Goldsmith's amiable poem of the "Deserted Village." On the cause of that desertion I mean to address you. I mean to endeavour, to shew that the basis of that

poem is *truth*, and to point out the particular means which have been the cause of that general emigration from the country, and the cause of the capital being filled with objects of distress and nuisance [. . .] The rage of inclosing, too much encouraged, is the foundation of these evils.[66]

Oglethorpe's lifelong Jacobite politics are primarily evident in his concern about enclosures and depopulation. He decided on principle against walling in his own estate in Haslemere in Surrey because he felt that such enclosures resulted in the expulsion of the rural peasantry to the cities. In 1732, "John Cowper, farmer" dedicated to Oglethorpe his *Essay, Proving, that Inclosing Commons, and Commonfield-Lands, is Contrary to the Interest of the Nation*. Arguing against the view that enclosure led to efficiency and economic growth, Cowper bemoaned the departure of the rural laborers from their habitations, and their necessary wanderings to other localities where enclosures had not yet taken hold. But if enclosure was to become general policy, argued Cowper, the prospects for the laborer would be dismal: "They must become Vagabonds, be driven from one Country to another; be reduced to Beggary or Starving; or be forced to leave their Native Land, in Hopes of meeting with better Treatment in a strange Country," all this to humor "the Pride and Luxury of a few, whose Fortunes are already too large for their Souls." Cowper concluded with a dire warning: enclosure would result in the destruction of the Kingdom, and he foresaw "what a miserable condition we must be in, when all our inland Towns and Villages are deserted."[67]

This was equally the argument of the preface, almost certainly written by Goldsmith, to John Newbery's famous children's tale *The History of Little Goody Two-Shoes* (1765):

> This is not the book, Sir, mentioned in the title, but the Introduction to that book; and it is intended, Sir, not for those sort of Children, but for children of six feet high, of which, as my friend has justly observed, there are many millions in this kingdom; and these reflections, Sir, have been rendered necessary by the unaccountable and diabolical scheme which many gentlemen now give in to, of laying a number of farms into one, and very often of a whole parish into one farm; which in the end must reduce the common people to a state of vassalage worse than that under the barons of old, or of the clans in Scotland; and will in time depopulate the kingdom.[68]

Goldsmith is proposing here that, however oppressive in their own way, the hierarchical ways of old—the Scottish clan system is explicitly included—were

CHAPTER 4

superior to what had been taking hold gradually since the Glorious Revolution: the acceleration of enclosure—and, in Scotland following the Jacobite rebellions, the Highland clearances. For Oglethorpe and for Goldsmith, the luxury of the few had been legitimated by 1688. As late as 1783, Oglethorpe would express to Samuel Johnson his opinion that parliament had "usurped" the nation's money to tyrannical ends: "Government is now carried on by corrupt influence, instead of the inherent right of the King." Johnson, ever susceptible to the emotional pull of Jacobitism, agreed that the lack of inherent right in the King was a source of social disorder, but speculated that, even though it broke the constitution, the Glorious Revolution was necessary. Oglethorpe's response was terse: "My father did not think it was necessary."[69] It was clear to Johnson, and others, that Oglethorpe's Jacobite family background had always infused his traditionalist politics. On that basis, Oglethorpe argued for an alternative form of progress which would encourage cultural sensitivity on the part of landowners and facilitate the well-being of the peasantry in Ireland. These measures might in turn ameliorate the tendency to agrarian violence:

> [. . .] nay surely the example of that worthy man, Sir George Savile, in Ireland, would be a sufficient lesson, his tenants there are numerous and well supplied with all the necessaries of life; they have not joined the rioters, but are happy and contented; can this arise from any other than a conviction that his method is right? His farms are small, the culture of the country is considered, and plenty and peace are the consequence.[70]

Oglethorpe's invoking of the politician and landowner George Savile (1726–84) is telling. Savile held land in the Ulster counties of Fermanagh and Tyrone; thus it would have been unlikely that his tenants would have joined in the land agitations of the 1760s and 1770s—the riots to which Oglethorpe refers—which took place primarily in Munster. These were the Whiteboy disturbances whose immediate cause was enclosure, the denial in Ireland of the "bare-worn common" (W4: 299) to which Goldsmith's poem alludes. But even though Oglethorpe is inexact in his Irish political geography, his reference to Savile's management as an alternative to culturally insensitive modes of modernization was in keeping with the latter's generally applauded ethical rectitude on Irish issues. Savile would come to advocate the restoration of Catholic freedoms in Ireland, a stance which earned him the respect of Burke, with whom he collaborated on Catholic relief legislation. A figure of generally acknowledged eccentricity and benevolence, Savile's growing reputation in the midcentury may have prompted the naming of the benevolent

Sir William Thornhill in *The Vicar of Wakefield* (Savile's ancestor was Sir William of Thornhill, near Wakefield, in Yorkshire).[71] Savile's sense of responsibility in Irish matters figured again in the 1770s, when the issue of a tax on Irish absentee resurfaced. He supported in principle the tax on absenteeism in Ireland, which provided an occasion for disagreement with Burke, who had sided decisively with his employer, the second Marquess of Rockingham (1730–82).

In 1773, the Irish House of Commons, following on a proposal from the patriot Colonel John Blaquiere (1732–1812), proposed, as Burke had done decades before, a tax of two shillings on every pound of net rents earned by Irish estates owned by landlords who did not reside in Ireland for six months of every year. It was quietly agreed at a poorly attended cabinet meeting that, should the Irish send over such a proposal, the North Ministry would urge the king to authorize it. The prominent landholders to be damaged by such a tax would include Rockingham, whose town house in Grosvenor Square would become the center of opposition to the tax. Rockingham, Horace Walpole recorded, was one of those chiefs of the English Opposition, who "forgetting their patriotism in both countries, grew very clamorous against the project."[72] Since 1765, Burke had been Rockingham's private secretary. Thus, in the opposition to the absentee tax, Burke was the primary agitator, accumulating petitions and assisting in the drafting of letters representative of the absentees' interests.

There are two interpretations of Burke's mature opposition to the absentee tax: one places his opposition in the context of party affiliation and ambitious self-interest; the other in the context of his adhesion to a general imperial principle. Burke was himself an absentee at this stage, though on a very small scale. He inherited his brother Garrett's estate in Clogher, in Cork, in 1765, the same year as he allied with the Rockingham Whigs. By the time of the 1773 proposal, Rockingham's estates in Ireland yielded 14000 pounds a year; Burke's, the considerably smaller sum of 500. "It may therefore seem plausible," writes Conor Cruise O'Brien, always alert to Namierite insinuation, "that the opposition to the Bill [. . .] was dictated by their material interests, in particular, Rockingham's."[73] For O'Brien's Burke, however, it was the principle of the thing, a principle of stability through union; looking ahead, O'Brien sees Wolfe Tone operating on opposing, separatist, principles. In this view, Burke's aim, with Ireland and America, was to minimize exploitation and oppression in the context of the imperial connection, not to break the connection itself.

For Burke, unease in the American colonies loomed large, and it was crucial that the center held. "The position which he took on this Irish business," writes

CHAPTER 4

Thomas Mahoney, "was in perfect consonance with that which he had been holding in reference to America."[74] Only England could exercise power in ways which would keep the empire unified. If any other parliament took it upon itself to authorize and collect taxes for its own administration, the empire as a whole would gradually fracture, with Ireland setting a legislative precedent. Such imperatives were deemed by Burke properly to reside in England itself; anything else would result in a dilution of the imperial system. The tax would also discourage intra-imperial mobility. Citizens of the empire should be able to reside wherever they wished, according to Burke, in any of His Majesty's dominions. He wrote to Rockingham on September 29, 1773, that he thought the proposed tax preposterous. It would prevent absentees from residing in England, close to the imperial center. His opponents, he anticipated, would be duped by its "superficial appearance of Equity," thereby failing adequately to assess its real dangers. The proposal, Burke argued, was symptomatic of "a mere visionary Theory."

A tax on absenteeism, in Burke's view, acknowledged that Ireland and England were separate political and administrative entities. Absentee landlords would be driven back to Ireland and would therefore not be in a position to represent the interests of Ireland to parliament in England. The broader cultural effect would be the loss of bonds of affection and inheritance: those factors which for Burke were the essence of international relations. His arguments are by turn alarmist and affective, as in his letter of October 30, 1773, to Charles Bingham in Dublin:

> We shall be barbarized on both sides of the water if we do not see one another now and then. *We* shall sink into surly, brutish Johns, and *you* will degenerate into wild Irish. It is impossible that we should be wiser, or the more agreeable; certainly we shall not love one another the better for this forced separation, which our ministers, who have already done so much for the dissolution of every other sort of good connexion, are now meditating for the further improvement of this too well-united empire. Their next step will be to encourage all the colonies, about thirty separate governments, to keep their people from all intercourse with each other and with the mother country. A gentleman of New York, or Barbadoes, will be as much gazed at as a strange animal from Nova Zembla or Otaheite; and those rogues the travellers will tell us what stories they please about poor old Ireland.

A tax as proposed is "a virtual declaration that England is a foreign country." "Is there a shadow of reason," he asked Bingham, "that because a Lord Rockingham, a Duke of Devonshire, a Sir George Saville [sic], possess property in Ireland, which has descended to them without any act of theirs, they should abandon their duty in parliament, and spend their winters in Dublin?"[75] The question was more rhetorical than it should have been. Absentees would not necessarily have to return to Dublin; they would just have to pay tax on their lands' earnings in Ireland for Irish supply.

Savile himself acknowledged as much. And though invoked by Burke in his letter to Bingham, Savile agreed with neither Burke nor Rockingham on the issue. Though a Whig himself, Savile had refused an invitation to take part in the Rockingham administration; less interested in party affiliation, he preferred to remain an independent member of Parliament. His record on colonial matters was consistent. Vocally opposed to imperial exploitation, he declined a role on the select committee on East Indian affairs, proclaiming himself to be opposed to the whole system of abuse in India. He was generally against territorial acquisitions, which he considered to be a form of public theft. With Burke he moved to introduce a bill for the relief of Roman Catholics in 1778, with the result that his house was burned and looted during the Gordon riots two years later. Unlike Burke, however, he did not oppose the Irish absentee tax. Though he owned property in Fermanagh and Tyrone, Savile refused to sign up with the tax's opponents because he doubted that the measure was a bad one for Ireland, though it certainly was for England and for the absentees. On November 5, 1773, he explained himself to Rockingham:

> We are two nations, not one. In money matters absolutely, in some matters hostile, for we have a separate purse. If *you* was to be taxed in Northamptonshire for not living there, it would be absurd; but if Northamptonshire had a separate purse, and all her landlords went and enriched neighbour counties, I don't know exactly how far I should think I might go if I were a Northamptonshire man.

Savile was similarly unconvinced by what he saw as Burke's shrill, convoluted and sophistical objection that the measure would prevent Irish landowners from traveling to England to represent themselves at the metropolitan center: "I am a prisoner, it is true, if I am forbid by the state to use my right of travelling about, but a tax upon wheels is not an infringement upon liberty." With marked prescience, and a sensitivity to the Atlantic situation which would have interested Burke, Savile envisioned a situation in which "England might double tax all persons who, having English estates, live in Ireland. When America begins to entice our rich, as it does now our people, we shall have this last proposition more fairly before us."[76] It was Burke's stance, in Savile's eyes, which was theoretical: the equality of all citizens of the empire was a fine idea, but for however long it was the *British* empire, the colonies would always be at the mercy of the imperial center when it came to matters of taxation and supply. Wealth generated in Ireland and America would always tend to benefit that center; the ultimate incommensurability of equality and empire meant that the situation would never work the other way around.

Savile was, according to "Marius," a correspondent in the *Public Advertiser*, a man of "strict Principles," whose honesty in this matter was to be compared positively with the private and party interest of Rockingham, and, by implication, Burke. Rockingham had, for Marius, a cheek "to interest the Public in his Private Affairs."[77] "Philo-Marius" augmented this argument two days later:

> We know, Sir, that Ireland has been principally ruined by the Management of the Retainers of the English Proprietors of vast Tracts of Land in that Country. The unfortunate People, by having the whole Fruits of their Industry carried out of the Country by the avaritious Exactions of men, who farm whole Estates from such as the Marquis, are first reduced to Beggary and Distress, and then are obliged to trust themselves to the Ocean to seek in a foreign Country that Relief which their own had denied. Hence proceed those emigrations that have deprived Ireland of a third Part of her Inhabitants; and hence those extensive Deserts which cover the best Parts of that unfortunate Kingdom.
>
> When the Proprietor resides upon his Estates he barters back his rents for the Industry of his Tenants; but when the whole is carried to another Country, the Heart for want of the Return of the Blood, loses its Pulse, and the Body Politic languishes, and at last expires.[78]

Philo-Marius here gives in prose the thesis of *The Deserted Village*, recapitulating most plainly and effectively the poem's argument about the dereliction of the body politic, the desertion of villages and the depletion of the nation's energy.

Savile was not alone in being an Irish landowner unopposed to the tax. William Petty, the second Earl of Shelburne, also abstained from joining the Rockingham campaign, though his stance was, to many observers, less principled. Indeed, Shelburne's duplicity in the absentees affair was documented with a jaundiced eye by Horace Walpole. In reality opposed to the tax, like Rockingham, for reasons of personal finance, he claimed to have been convinced of its merits by William Pitt, the First Earl of Chatham (1708–1778), who argued that the Irish parliament had not exceeded its remit, and that the solicited interference of the British parliament would be unjust, unconstitutional, and injurious to Anglo-Irish relations. Thus, Shelburne played the role of double agent. Even though he publicly acceded to Chatham's "old-fashioned" Whig philosophy, he encouraged Burke to write against the tax to save the absentees, including himself, money.[79] He was, in short, remarkably two-faced on the issue.

Shelburne and Savile, then, both absentees, stood aloof from the Rockingham campaign against the tax—Savile for reasons of thought-out principle; Shelburne, for opportunist and ethically elastic reasons: to hedge his bets and not to oppose the Court interests with which he sought political favor. Rockingham had called to Shelburne, and Shelburne to Rockingham twice to discuss the issue, but Shelburne stuck to his abstention: to Chatham he declared his principle that he did "not conceive that Ireland or America can ever gain by the interposition of parliament" in Westminster: "The Ministers, I understand, are come round to join with the most violent in condemning the policy, and I suppose will not be less ready to join them in upholding Poyning's [sic] Act, and all the old doctrine of the dependence of Ireland upon England, in all cases whatsoever."[80] Though he understood the larger and longer resonances of the issue in Anglo-Irish politics—as evidenced by his reference to Sir Edward Poynings' law of 1494, which subordinated the Irish parliament to English prerogative—Shelburne's views of the tax were conflicted: his personal finances jostled grubbily with his political ambition. Against Rockingham, however, he enlisted the services of Goldsmith, who, perhaps naïve about Shelburne's intentions, was more determinedly in favor of the proposition. The evidence for Goldsmith's active support for the tax is contained in a letter from Joseph Hickey to Rockingham on November 7:

> Your Lordship will pardon my mentioning what I have very strong reason to believe, tho' no certain Authority, That Lord Shelburne has employed Dr. Goldsmith to write in favor of it. The Dr is become a great advocate for it & has even condescended to consult *me*, as to my thoughts.[81]

One of Burke's closest associates at Grosvenor Square, Hickey was active in circulating lists of absentees in opposition to the tax, and of those who might politically be influenced by them. His was the ear closest to the proverbial ground on the issue. Whether and where Goldsmith did actually write in favor of the tax would be difficult to ascertain; more important, and verified by Hickey, is the fact that he strongly supported its imposition. Naïve in his support for Shelburne, and just as naïve in asking Hickey for his thoughts, Goldsmith's enthusiasm for the tax would

CHAPTER 4

have irked Burke, as much as Burke's opposition would have dismayed Goldsmith. That Burke had changed his mind is the subject of nationalist critique, according to which his stance merely exemplified his commitment to empire: "In playing the part he did in this instance," writes Mahoney, "Burke was clearly placing himself in opposition to the sentiment prevalent among the majority of his former countrymen."[82] Equally, Seamus Deane acknowledges that Burke's later position was "heretical" from a nationalist or republican standpoint.[83]

A tax which should have been generally popular, however, ultimately disappeared without any great noise. The proposal was defeated, after a muddled debate, in the Committee of Ways and Means of the Irish House of Commons on November 25, 1773. It transpired that many Irish tenants were subject to clauses which made them liable for all new taxes. The burden of the absentee tax would, in effect, be passed on to the tenant. Thomas Campbell later wrote that the 1773 proposal was

> defeated by the cabals of faction. A land tax, if it were raised as a substitute for others, which oppress the poor, would be a desirable thing in this country, as it would oblige the absentee to pay something. If on the other hand it should fall on the tenant, it would serve only to fill up the measure of oppression.[84]

That the tax could potentially be visited upon the most vulnerable merely accentuated the injustices which inhered in the culture of absenteeism. It was thus doomed by the iniquitous legal and political situation into which it would have been produced. "Laws grind the poor, and rich men rule the law" (W4: 266), as Goldsmith wrote in *The Traveller*, rephrasing Altangi's earlier criticisms of penal laws, which "grind every rank of people, and chiefly those least able to resist oppression" (W2: 327).

On the absentee issue much had changed for Burke and Goldsmith in the period between 1748 and 1773. Burke's disdain for the absentees had been superceded by the necessities of working for them. Goldsmith, meanwhile, would support the tax on anti-imperial and generally anti-oligarchical principles. As he saw it, the landowning class had neglected its duties, leaving the land to ruin, causing famine and the peasantry's emigration to an inhospitable colonial America. Discourses surrounding absenteeism, emigration, and the responsibility of landowners provide the long context for *The Deserted Village*. Points of political agreement and disagreement about land, land ownership, emigration and the relationship of Ireland to England explain, even more than any speculation about the location of Auburn, the poem's origins and argument. *The Deserted Village* travels from the imaginary utopia of Auburn to a hellish and equally imaginary America to make this simple, oppositional point about the obligations of the rich to the rest. Goldsmith is closer to the Burke of the *Reformer*, closer also to Savile and the crypto-Jacobite Oglethorpe, than to Burke the Rockingham Whig. If Burke, as Luke Gibbons has argued, was "a man deeply divided against himself," then the absentee issue is clearly one episode in a conflict between his later party prerogatives and his earlier convictions.[85] The last decade which Burke and Goldsmith spent in Ireland provides the most clarifying backdrop, not just to *The Deserted Village*, but to that long process whereby Burke had given up to the Rockingham Whigs some of what, in Goldsmith's phrase, was meant for mankind.

Auburn's afterlife

On May 5, 1792, a correspondent styling himself "Gulielmus Valsas" wrote to the editor of the *Northern Star*, the paper of the founding members of the Society of United Irishmen, recalling precisely the sentiments expressed by "Philo-Marius" in the *Public Advertiser* almost twenty years before:

> I have been led to the following reflections, by observing the embarcation of a considerable number of passengers on board a lighter going down to the Ship Wilmington, bound for America. The quay was covered with their baggage, and the number of passengers was very considerable, but of this the public need not be informed. These, said I, are going to America; and indeed I cannot blame them; but I lament the loss that my native country hereby suffers. This loss is much greater than is generally imagined; it is the loss of very considerable property, but this bears no proportion to the loss of inhabitants; they are the bones, nerves, and sinews of a country, and Ireland, not yet half peopled, is deprived of its vital strength.

Claiming to have personally witnessed this dreary scene, Valsas numbers the causes of emigration. They have not much changed since the first half of the century. "There must," he claims, "be many things wrong and oppressive" in Ireland for its people to leave the country to which they have "a natural predilection." Ireland has been misrepresented as being in "a very flourishing and prosperous condition; but as there is a diversity of opinion on this subject, as well as a diversity of condition in the inhabitants." The prosperity consists only in "a numerous and luxurious aristocracy," which is to say that it does not exist in any real sense. The argument of

CHAPTER 4

Bernard Mandeville's *Fable of the Bees* (1714)—that private vices engender public benefits—is disproved for Valsas by the colonial case of Ireland:

> most of our great men who receive our rents, have chosen another stage to act their Tragedies and their Comedies; and England if it is injured by their vices, if they have any, is benefited by their cash—we are injured by their non-residence, whether they act their parts well or ill, the rents of their estates are spent abroad, chiefly in England, after they have rode post through the principal Towns of the Continent, which expeditious travelling is commonly called making the Tour of Europe.

The loss of Ireland's strength to America is explained for Valsas, not just by absenteeism in particular, but more generally by the English connection: "it is from English influence and ascendancy; it is from protestant ascendancy that protestants are flying." Emigration is to be prevented "by kindness, by good leases, by encouragement, but above all, by *General Liberty.*" General Liberty here consists, not in the liberty of the few to advance their wealth at the expense of others, but in a relationship of trade among independent equals: "Let no British minister and his Irish junto, dare to say, you have a right to trade, we confess, but you shall not do it, because forsooth it would hurt a monopolising English Company; let, I say, Ireland be free, and there will no emigration of any consequence."[86]

Laments in prose for the loss of population were obviously Goldsmithian. But these resonances were even more plainly identifiable in the patriotic poetry of the 1790s. "Irish Absentees, &c." was addressed from Trinity College, and published in 1793 in *Anthologia Hibernica*:

> One serious ill, indeed, arrests my view,
> Would it were lighter, would it were less true!
> The richest nobles of Ierne's isle
> Leave those domains where health and beauty smile,
> Where a 'bold peasantry' might sing their praise
> And wish them peace, and health, and length of days,
> Where every prospect that enchants the sight,
> Each heart-felt pleasure, and each true delight,
> Might crown their wishes, where the splendid board,
> And all that grandeur, all that wealth afford
> Attend their call—yet these and more they slight
> For noon-day beds, and revelry at night—
> They slight them, and at fashion's dire command

> Squander their riches in a foreign land.
> Shame! when the storm-toss'd Swiss, and Highland boor,
> Adore their countries, tho' despised, tho' poor,
> Love their low huts—and their native soil
> The spot where heaven's most cheering blessings smile.

With its invocation of the rude patriotism of the Swiss peasant, positioned opposite the fickle absentee, the poem marries elements of *The Traveller*'s geography with the critical pastoral of *The Deserted Village*:

> Alas! review the Irish peasant's cot,
> Want is his portion, misery his lot—
> Nor these the worst, for whilst his thoughtless lord
> Tastes all the pleasures foreign courts afford,
> A rack-rent minion stints his stripe of ground,
> And all the honours of a gaol confound!—
> So when the shepherd leaves the fleecy care
> To strive with tempests and inclement air,
> The storm descends, the timorous victims fly,
> The wolf appears—they bleat their last—and die.[87]

Goldsmith's men of wealth and pride are conjured again, as they were in the poetry of his precursor Laurence Whyte, as rack-renting absentee landlords. More vividly pastoral in its use of shepherding images, the 1790s poem reproduces the desertion of Auburn in the image of the deserted flock, left to the elements and to the wolf. Such poems renew the critical potential of *The Deserted Village*, and serve to readdress the actuality of the original poem's complaint in a more explicitly Irish context toward the end of the century. Though Goldsmith's English audience could not have known it, the background of want and misery, added to the abiding threat of famines vividly remembered from the midcentury, made his poem, however peaceful-seeming to Yeats two centuries later, a ready influence for the United Irishmen.

In the decades following Goldsmith's poem, then, a renewed critique of the role of the absentees fed into the disaffection of patriots and the growing ranks of reform-minded, but also revolutionary, observers. The United Irishmen sought to stem the hemorrhaging of revenue and population which had depleted the nation, and to break the connection which had so ravaged the Irish body politic. Apparently conservative, superficially English, the themes and motifs of Goldsmith's poems were taken up and modified in the peculiarly Irish confluence of a waning Jacobitism and the rising republicanism of the 1790s and beyond.

ILL FARES THE LAND: CONCLUSION

THE LATE POLITICAL PHILOSOPHER and historian Tony Judt took for the title of his last work a couplet in *The Deserted Village*: "Ill fares the land, to hastening ills a prey/Where wealth accumulates, and men decay." The lines express more pointedly than any others Goldsmith's abiding social concerns, his pushing back against ideologies of liberty and the shallower appearances of improvement. Judt's book is an impassioned plea to understand the mistakes of liberalism in the wake of the 2008 crash and the subsequent financial crisis. It was written as a cycle of thirty years rotated to a miserable low, a cycle during which, in his analysis, no one seemed to know what anything was worth, and where questions of fairness, justice, and morality were subservient to questions of efficiency and profit. Chiming with the sentiments of the poem from which he takes his title, and its author's jaundiced view of the rhetoric of liberty, Judt argues that liberalism is "like a well-designed outer coat, it conceals more than it displays." To liberalism, and its cheerleading cohort sheltering under "the Washington consensus," is opposed social democracy: "the possibility and virtue of collective action for the collective good." The Washington consensus "was everywhere greeted by ideological cheerleaders: from the profiteers of the 'Irish miracle' (the property-bubble boom of the "Celtic Tiger") to the doctrinaire ultra-capitalists of former communist Europe." In Ireland, as wealth accumulated, something was definitely decaying: "Of Ireland there is little to say. The so-called economic miracle of the "plucky little Celtic tiger" consisted of an unregulated, low-tax regime which predictably attracted inward investment and hot money." Social democrats of today, argues Judt, are "like the eighteenth-century critics of 'commercial society,'" in that they too "were offended at the consequences of unregulated competition. They were seeking not so much a radical future as a return to the values of a better way of life."

As well as providing a titular and thematic contour for Judt's work, Goldsmith's poem has inspired comment on the recent economic collapse in Ireland specifically. Writing in the *Irish Times* in March of 2011, one commentator, following Judt's lead, argued that Goldsmith's lines "summarize the sad story of Ireland over the past decade" in which a general oligarchical recklessness laid the nation low, and in which only one section of the population managed to produce spectacular wealth while the rest partook of an illusory fiction of the freedom to borrow. We have learned "to our great cost," this observer continued, "the idea that Ireland had become one of the wealthiest countries in the world was an illusion, a house of cards."[1] The demonstrations of wealth were everywhere, but serve now only as a reminder of other lines from *The Deserted Village*:

> Ye friends to truth, ye statesmen who survey
> The rich man's joy's increase, the poor's decay,
> 'Tis yours to judge, how wide the limits stand
> Between a splendid and an happy land. (4: 297)

The current crisis, for Judt and for others, forces a rethink of how economic "liberty," however it is defined or designed, can sit alongside the notion of social sustainability. This was the central question which exercised Goldsmith throughout his career, and especially in his two major poems. For Goldsmith, the nation effectively *was* its peasantry. If the neglect and recklessness of a rack-renting and ostentatious landowning class forced that peasantry abroad, the country would be left immeasurably and indefinitely weakened. Freedom might mean greater wealth in the short term for those "Who call it freedom, when themselves are free" (4: 265); in the longer view, however, and for most, that freedom was and is, to quote Samuel Johnson, "little more than the choice of working or starving."[2]

Goldsmith, like Johnson, understood the difference between the rhetoric and the reality of freedom. Goldsmith's social criticisms, however, did not entail a fatalistic adherence to thorough or unmovable hierarchy. To return to this book's point of departure, for instance: it is not known whether Goldsmith and Tom Paine did meet, or whether they did enjoy that bottle of wine in 1772. At one gathering of Johnson's literary club in late April 1773, however, Goldsmith, sounding Painite, proposed to talk of equality. Burke joked: "Here's our monarchy man growing Republican," in response to which Goldsmith explained: "I'm for monarchy to keep us equal."[3] In their shared egalitarianism, Paine and Goldsmith may have found some common ground; and though Paine may have baulked at Goldsmith's monarchism, the latter's politics are, from an Irish perspective, more coherent than Paine would have appreciated, or than Burke jokingly implied. Three years later, in *Common Sense*, Paine, sounding uncannily Goldsmithian, admitted that absolute monarchy had one positive point:

> Absolute governments (tho' the disgrace of human nature) have this advantage with them, that they are simple; if the people suffer, they know the head from which their suffering springs, know likewise the remedy, and are not bewildered by a variety of causes and cures. But the constitution of England is so exceedingly complex, that the nation may suffer for years together without being able to discover in which part the fault lies, some will say in one and some in another, and every political physician will advise a different medicine.[4]

If Paine's condemnatory aside were subtracted from this paragraph, it could have read as a critique of the legacy of 1688, of a piece with Goldsmith's Jacobite aversion to the new oligarchy. In such a context, Jacobitism itself had a radical edge. In England and Europe, Jacobitism and monarchism were counterrevolutionary; but in Ireland, as Conor Cruise O'Brien has argued, "the Jacobite aspiration is objectively revolutionary, since it is an expression of the will of a conquered people to shake off its servitude."[5] Equally, Goldsmith's hope that monarchy would keep the people equal was as much a statement on the relationship between Ireland and England as it was a curious form of proto-socialism. Issues of divine or inherited right were largely irrelevant to his paternalistic belief that monarchy was the single institution which could preside over a more profound equality. But he also understood that the negligent monarchies threatened their own implosion; if the French "have but three weak Monarchs more successively on the Throne," he wrote three decades before the French Revolution, "the mask will be laid aside and the country will certainly once more be free" (W2: 235). But *that* freedom, like the freedoms generated in 1688, would have been, to someone of Goldsmith's traditionalist temperament, rhetorical only. The Glorious Revolution caused inequality within and between Ireland and Britain because it subordinated monarchy to the prerogatives of a faction for whom advantage in trade and politics was more important than good governance. Since 1688, Goldsmith observed, power was diffused and its abuses harder to locate and counter. Britain had as a result become a commercial, imperialist state; this was his abiding complaint. Thus, Burke's insinuation was literally true: Goldsmith's politics bridged monarchism and republicanism. What was deemed tyranny for others was really the potential for strong, centralized and answerable rule. What was deemed "liberty" was for Goldsmith synonymous with trade's empire, and constituted the ideological justification for the neglect of the laborer, urban and rural. In those years when Paine's influence was at its most pronounced in Ireland, the tones of Goldsmith's poems echoed most forcibly.

Goldsmith's major works partake of English traditions, to be sure; stylistically and thematically, his writing is involved with, but crucially and intriguingly devolved from, English norms. His career testifies to the troubled historical intermingling of a nascent scientific and political modernity and an anxious cultural and political intelligence. As natural historian, as "philosophic vagabond," and as oriental philosopher in London, Goldsmith mixed his genres, his geographies and, with that, inevitably, his political registers. In his writings, enlightenment discourses jostled, in a complex dialectic, with his Jacobitism. Locating Goldsmith is thus no straightforward task; his surveys of peoples were half immersed in the Anglocentrisms and Eurocentrisms which prevailed in the enlightenment information and publishing revolutions; and yet he balanced against those narcissisms a considered appreciation of cultural difference. In his human geography, Goldsmith reproduced classical and neoclassical errors and prejudices while simultaneously and often in a contradictory manner expounding a pluralism at odds with his pseudo-scientific facetiousness. Likewise, his manipulation of the generic prospect poem in *The Traveller* significantly defied convention with its critique of national self-congratulation. His Chinese letters deployed *and* satirized oriental allegory to subversive ends, while *The Deserted Village*, his most enduring literary achievement, subordinated elegiac pastoral to a very current political complaint regarding the condition of the peasantry.

The duality and exchange between convention and intervention in Goldsmith's oeuvre is inevitably that of an author whose political convictions were involved in a fraught and ongoing trade-off with the generic and professional contours within which he worked. The diversity of tones and approaches through Goldsmith's literary and scientific output, therefore, must be placed in material, intellectual, and historical context so that the substance and the unavoidable contradictions of his oeuvre might be understood. His career is resistant to the liberal conception of the artist as an autonomous individual with a single, or singular, identity; so too are his politics difficult to comprehend to an equally liberal interpretation more inclined to think of Jacobitism (or monarchism) and egalitarianism as mutually exclusive. His poetic appeal on behalf of the integrity of the people's attachment to their native space, their organic and affective sense of community, would be reexpressed and varied upon in Ireland throughout nineteenth- and twentieth-century arguments and agitations for land rights and self-determination. As John Montague once dryly remarked, *The Deserted Village* is a poem "much loved and quoted in Ireland, even by Ministers of Agriculture."[6] Its appeal to the ministerial stratum in the new Free State would probably have intrigued Yeats; and Éamon DeValera's idyllic vision of a rural, self-sufficient republic, as eloquently expressed in his 1943 St Patrick's Day speech as it has been disdained since for fey, patriarchal rusticity, owes much to Auburn.[7] Goldsmith's emphasis on self-sufficiency and economic integrity had its limitations, but it also had its own Janus-like prescience, just as the fraught politics of his output, taken as a whole, resonate with Ireland's anxious, perennial negotiations between ideals of tradition and community and an ever more precarious economic modernity.

NOTES

Introduction

1. Quoted in Thomas Percy, *Life of Oliver Goldsmith*, ed. Richard L. Harp (1801; Salzburg: Institüt f[ü]r Englische Sprache und Literatur, 1976), 96–8; see also John Keane, *Tom Paine: A Political Life* (New York: Grove, 1995), 74–5. Keane takes the communication as the beginning of a firm friendship between the two men, though for this there is no evidence. See also Chester Chapin, "Oliver Goldsmith and Thomas Paine," *American Notes and Queries* 11 (1998), 22–3.

2. Patrick Gordon, *Geography Anatomized: Or, A Compleat Geographical Grammar* (London: Printed for Robert Morden and Thomas Cockerill, 1693), preface.

3. David N. Livingstone and Charles J. Withers, "Introduction: On Geography and Enlightenment," in *Geography and Enlightenment*, ed. Livingstone and Withers (Chicago: University of Chicago Press, 1999), 3.

4. See Miles Ogborn and Charles W. J. Withers, "Introduction," in *Georgian Geographies: Essays on Space, Place and Landscape in the Eighteenth* Century, ed. Ogborn and Withers (Manchester: Manchester University Press, 2004), 1–23. For a review of scholarly work on geography in the eighteenth century, see Withers and Robert J. Mayhew, "Geography: Space, Place and Intellectual History in the Eighteenth Century," *Journal for Eighteenth-Century Studies* 34 (2011), 445–452.

5. Edward Heawood, *A History of Geographical Discovery in the Seventeenth and Eighteenth Centuries* (Cambridge: Cambridge University Press, 1912), 13.

6. Colin Smethurst, "Introduction," in *Romantic Geographies: Proceedings of the Glasgow Conference, September 1994*, ed. Smethurst (Glasgow: University of Glasgow Publications, 1996), viii.

7. Samuel Johnson, *A Dictionary of the English Language* (1755; London: Times Books, 1979). Johnson's definition is taken from and ascribed to Isaac Watts, *Logick: Or, The Right Use of Reason in the Enquiry after Truth* (London: Printed for John Clark and Richard Hett, Emanuel Matthews, and Richard Ford, 1725), 98. For a more specific, educational treatise in the geographical field by that author, see Watts, *The Knowledge of the Heavens and the Earth Made Easy: Or, The First Principles of Astronomy and Geography* (London: Printed for J. Clark and R. Hett; E. Matthews, and R. Ford, 1716).

8. Arthur Friedman repeatedly footnotes as a geographical reference *A Complete System of Geography*, 2 vols. (London: Printed for William Innys, Richard Ware, Aaron Ward, J. and P. Knapton, John Clarke, T. Longman and T. Shewell, Thomas Osborne, Henry Whitridge, Richard Hett, Charles

NOTES

Hitch, Stephen Austen, Edmund Comyns, Andrew Millar, James Hodges, Charles Corbett, and Jo. and Ja. Rivington, 1747), compiled from Herman Moll's *Complete Geographer* and containing maps by Emanuel Bowen. There is no evidence that Goldsmith used this compendium as a source, though it has in common with Goldsmith's *Survey of Experimental Philosophy* general chapters on the shape of the earth, on the magnet (or loadstone), on springs, fountains, and rivers, on the sea and tides, on the air and its properties, on rainbows, and on winds.

9. Christopher Fox, "How to Prepare a Noble Savage: The Spectacle of Human Science," in *Inventing Human Science: Eighteenth-Century Domains*, ed. Fox, Roy Porter, and Robert Wokler (Berkeley: University of California Press, 1995), 3.

10. See Derek Gregory, *Geographical Imaginations* (Oxford: Blackwell, 1994), 15–6. Gregory is influenced by Foucault's account of the concept of natural history. See Michel Foucault, *The Order of Things: An Archaeology of the Human Sciences*, no tr. given (London: Tavistock, 1970), 132; idem, "Questions on Geography," in *Power/Knowledge: Selected Interviews and Other Writings, 1972–77*, ed. Colin Gordon, trans. Colin Gordon et al. (Brighton: Harvester Press, 1980), 63–77. For a general survey of the relationship between geography and imperialism, although in the nineteenth century, see Felix Driver, "Geography's Empire: Histories of Geographical Knowledge," *Environment and Planning D: Society and Space* 10 (1992), 23–40; see also Chris Philo, "Foucault's Geography," *Environment and Planning D: Society and Space* 10 (1992), 137–61.

11. Edward Said, *Orientalism* (Harmondsworth: Penguin, 1978).

12. On the orientalism controversy, see Aijaz Ahmad, *In Theory: Classes, Nations, Literatures* (New York: Verso, 1992); and *Orientalism and the Postcolonial Predicament*, ed. Carol A. Breckenridge and Peter van der Veer (Philadelphia: University of Pennsylvania Press, 1993). The best compendium to elucidate the debates regarding colonial discourse theory and historical specificities is *Orientalism: A Reader*, ed. A. L. MacFie (Edinburgh: Edinburgh University Press, 2000).

13. In a section entitled "The Foucault connection: methodological criticisms," Bill Ashcroft and Pal Ahluwalia address the critique of Said's use of Foucaultian discourse theory. See *Edward Said: The Paradox of Identity* (New York: Routledge, 1999), 76–82. See also Edward Said, "Afterword to the 1995 Printing," *Orientalism: Western Conceptions of the Orient* (London: Penguin, 1995), 329–54.

14. Joseph Lennon, *Irish Orientalism: A Literary and Intellectual History* (Syracuse: Syracuse University Press, 2004), xxvi.

15. Max Horkheimer and Thoedor W. Adorno, *Dialectic of Enlightenment: Philosophical Fragments*, ed. Gunzelin Schmid Noerr, trans. Edmund Jephcott (Stanford: Stanford University Press, 2002), xvi.

16. Roy Porter, *Enlightenment: Britain and the Creation of the Modern World* (London: Penguin, 2000), xxi.

17. Sankar Muthu, *Enlightenment against Empire* (Princeton: Princeton University Press, 2003), 1–4.

18. Montesquieu, *Persian Letters*, trans. C. J. Betts (1721; London: Penguin, 1993).

19. Raynal, *A Philosophical and Political History of the Settlements and Trade of the Europeans in the East and West Indies*, trans. J. Justamond, 5 vols. (London: Printed for T. Cadell, 1776), 1: 483–84.

20. On Burke's conception of "geographical morality," and his "peculiar universalism," see Jennifer Pitts, *A Turn to Empire: The Rise of Imperial Liberalism in Britain and France* (Princeton: Princeton University Press, 2005), 59–100.

21. Lynn Festa and Dan Carey, "Introduction—Some Answers to the Question: What Is Postcolonial Enlightenment?" in *The Postcolonial Enlightenment: Eighteenth-Century Colonialism and Postcolonial Theory*, ed. Carey and Festa (Oxford: Oxford University Press, 2009), 7.
22. Clement Hawes, *The British Eighteenth Century and Global Critique* (Houndmills: Palgrave Macmillan, 2005), xiii, 168, 168, 170.
23. James Watt, "Goldsmith's Cosmopolitanism," *Eighteenth-Century Life* 30 (2005), 71.
24. See John McVeagh, "Goldsmith and Nationality," in *All Before Them: English Literature and the Wider World, Volume 1: 1660–1780*, ed. McVeagh (London: Ashfield, 1990), 217–31.
25. R. W. Seitz, "The Irish Background of Goldsmith's Social and Political Thought," *Publications of the Modern Language Association* 62 (1937), 411.
26. Dustin Griffin, *Patriotism and Poetry in Eighteenth-Century Britain* (Cambridge: Cambridge University Press, 2002), 206.
27. Rachel Crawford, *Poetry, Enclosure, and the Vernacular Landscape, 1700–1830* (Cambridge: Cambridge University Press, 2001), 3.
28. James Chandler, "A Discipline in Shifting Perspective: Why We Need Irish Studies," *Field Day Review* 2 (2006), 27, 26, 31. See also Claire Connolly's expansion on Chandler's themes: Connolly, "Ugly Criticism: Union and Division in Irish Literature," *Field Day Review* 4 (2008), 115–131.
29. See Carole Fabricant, *Swift's Landscape* (Notre Dame: University of Notre Dame Press, 1982); Luke Gibbons, *Edmund Burke and Ireland: Aesthetic, Politics, and the Colonial Sublime* (Cambridge: Cambridge University Press, 2003); Seamus Deane, *Strange Country: Modernity and Nationhood in Irish Writing since 1790* (Oxford: Oxford University Press, 1997), 1–48; and Deane, *Foreign Affections: Essays on Edmund Burke* (Cork: Cork University Press, 2005).
30. W. B. Yeats, "The Seven Sages," *The Poems*, ed. Daniel Albright (London: Everyman, 1990), 291–2.
31. Ricardo Quintana, "*The Vicar of Wakefield*: The Problem of Critical Approach," *Modern Philology* 71 (1973), 60.
32. Quintana, *Oliver Goldsmith: A Georgian Study* (New York: Macmillan, 1967), 136. J. A. Downie writes: "Goldsmith is essentially a satirist. That is his "genius." But it is not satire in the manner of Swift who, as he put it himself, wrote in a 'hum'rous biting Way.'" Downie, "Goldsmith, Swift and Augustan Satirical Verse," in *The Art of Oliver Goldsmith*, ed. Andrew Swarbrick (London: Vision, 1984), 134.
33. Seamus Deane, "Oliver Goldsmith: Miscellaneous Writings 1759-74," in *The Field Day Anthology of Irish Writing*, ed. Seamus Deane, 3 vols. (Derry: Field Day, 1991), 1: 659–60.
34. Barrell, *The Dark Side of the Landscape: The Rural Poor in English Painting 1730–1840* (Cambridge: Cambridge University Press, 1980), 78. Luke Gibbons adapts Barrell's concept of critical pastoral in *The Deserted Village*—"a form of radical nostalgia"—to John Ford's *The Quiet Man*. Gibbons, *Ireland into Film: The Quiet Man* (Cork: Cork University Press, 2002), 13.
35. Fabricant, *Swift's Landscape*, 19.
36. In his recent essay, Nigel Wood admits of Goldsmith's Irishness, but comes to noncommittal, and deliberately non-identitarian, conclusions: "Goldsmith's Irishness," writes Wood," is rarely an overt

ingredient in his imaginative work; it is, however, implicit in many of the analyses of displacement that assail his protagonists." Wood, "Goldsmith's English Malady," *Studies in the Literary Imagination* 44 (2011), 67.

37. John Lucas, *England and Englishness: Ideas of Nationhood in English Poetry, 1688–1900* (London: Hogarth Press, 1990), 5.

38. Seamus Deane, *Foreign Affections*, 24.

39. See Ian Higgins, *Swift's Politics: A Study in Disaffection* (Cambridge: Cambridge University Press, 1994), which goes against the view of J. A. Downie, *Jonathan Swift: Political Writer* (London: Routledge, 1984).

40. Johnson was, according to Linda Colley, "a Tory who sometimes leaned towards emotional Jacobitism." Colley, *Britons: Forging the Nation, 1707–1837* (New Haven: Yale University Press, 1992), 76. Murray G. H. Pittock has argued: "It appears more likely [. . .] that Johnson was a man of Jacobite ideals who distrusted their reality." Pittock, *Poetry and Jacobite Politics in Eighteenth-Century Britain and Ireland* (Cambridge: Cambridge University Press, 1994), 132. While acknowledging the force of some of Johnson's intermittent anti-Hanoverian sentiment, Nicholas Hudson has also questioned the substance of any Jacobite inclination on Johnson's part. See Hudson, *Samuel Johnson and the Making of Modern England* (Cambridge: Cambridge University Press, 2003), 79–85. The term "emotional Jacobitism" was coined by Douglas Brooks-Davies: *Pope's Dunciad and the Queen of Night: A Study in Emotional Jacobitism* (Manchester: Manchester University Press, 1985). Brooks-Davies has been contradicted in his view of Pope as Jacobite by J. A. Downie, "1688: Pope and the Rhetoric of Jacobitism," in *Pope: New Contexts*, ed. David Fairer (New York: Harvester Wheatsheaf, 1990), 9–24.

41. Patrick Murray, "The Riddle of Goldsmith's Ancestry," *Studies* 63 (1974), 186.

42. John O'Donovan's *Letters Containing Information Relative to the Antiquities of the County of Roscommon. Collected During the Progress of the Ordnance Survey of 1837*, are cited in Murray, 186, 189n. "Sliocht Mhagarlaidhe an tSean Bhráthar" translates roughly as "the progeny of the testicles of the old brother."

43. Seamus Fenton, *It All Happened: Reminiscences* (Dublin: M.H. Gill, 1949), 129.

44. Louis Cullen, "Catholics under the Penal Laws," *Eighteenth-Century Ireland: Iris an dá Chultúr* 1 (1986), 28.

45. W. J. McCormack, "Goldsmith, Biography and the Phenomenology of Anglo–Irish Literature," in *The Art of Oliver Goldsmith*, ed. Swarbrick, 183.

46. Thomas Babington Macaulay, "Life of Goldsmith" (1856), in Walter Scott, Thomas Babington Macaulay, and William Makepeace Thackeray, *Essays on Goldsmith*, ed. G. E. Hadow and C. B. Wheeler (Oxford: The Clarendon Press, 1918), 20–1.

47. Fenton, *It all Happened: Reminiscences*, 130–1.

48. James Boswell, *Life of Johnson*, ed. G. B. Hill and L. F. Powell, 6 vols. (1791; Oxford: The Clarendon Press, 1934), 2: 224, 238, 238.

49. "A Protestant Jacobite interest [. . .] survived in Dublin among some rurally based Protestant clergy." Eamonn O'Ciardha, *Ireland and the Jacobite Cause, 1685–1766: A Fatal Attachment* (Dublin: Four Courts, 2004), 377.

50. "Memoirs of the Life and Writings of the late Ch Oconor of Belanagare Esqr. M.R.I.A., to which is prefixed a short Historical Account of the Family of O'Conor From the Invasion of Henry 2. Compiled Principally from Notes and Extracts taken by Himself From Ancient Writers on Irish History And other Sources hitherto unexplored or not generally known," included in the Gilbert Collection MS 203, Dublin City Library, Pearse St, 163–4. Contarine was "the strongest, best, and most enduring influence exercised on Goldsmith in his early days." Michael F. Cox, "The Country and Kindred of Oliver Goldsmith," *Journal of the National Literary Society* 1 (1901–1903), 81–111.

51. David Dickson, "Jacobitism in Eighteenth-Century Ireland: A Munster Perspective," *Éire–Ireland*, 39 (2004), 69, 70.

52. Cited in Romney Sedgwick, *The History of Parliament: The House of Commons 1715–1754*, 2 vols. (New York: Oxford University Press, 1970), 1: 69.

53. Graham Gargett, "Plagiarism, Translation and the Problem of Identity: Oliver Goldsmith and Voltaire," *Eighteenth-Century Ireland: Iris an dá Chultúr* 16 (2001), 95.

54. Boswell, *Life of Johnson*, 3:253.

55. Thomas Percy, *Life of Oliver Goldsmith*, ed. Richard L. Harp (Salzburg: Institüt f[ü]r Englische Sprache und Literatur, 1976), 79.

56. See Claire Harman, "Partiality and Prejudice: The young Jane Austen's 'Hatred of all those people whose parties or principles do not suit with mine,'" *Times Literary Supplement*, no. 5470 (February 1, 2008), 14–15.

57. Robert Bataille, *The Writing Life of Hugh Kelly: Politics, Journalism, and Theater in Late-Eighteenth-Century London* (Carbondale: Southern Illinois University Press, 2000), 19.

58. Roger Lonsdale, "A Garden and a Grave: The Poetry of Oliver Goldsmith," in *The Author in His Work: Essays in a Problem in Criticism*, ed. Louis L. Martz and Aubrey Williams (New Haven: Yale University Press, 1978), 9.

59. See Peter Dixon, *Oliver Goldsmith Revisited* (Boston: Twayne, 1991); Richard C. Taylor, *Goldsmith as Journalist* (London: Associated University Presses, 1993).

Chapter 1. The Cultural Climate: Natural Histories of National Character

1. This essay first appeared in the *Royal Magazine* between June and September of 1760. R. S. Crane attributes it to Goldsmith because many phrases echo or presage phrases in the acknowledged writings. The attribution seems all but certain. For bibliographical details, as well as for notes on similarities with Buffon and on thematic repetition within the Goldsmith corpus, see in Goldsmith, *New Essays* (Chicago: University of Chicago Press, 1927), 12–55n.

2. Laurence Goldstein, *Ruins and Empire: The Evolution of a Theme in Augustan and Romantic Literature* (Pittsburgh: University of Pennsylvania Press, 1977), 100.

3. Wolfgang Zach, "Oliver Goldsmith on Ireland and the Irish: Personal Views, Shifting Attitudes, Literary Stereotypes," *Studies in Anglo-Irish Literature*, ed. Heinz Kosok (Bonn: Bouvier Verlag, 1982), 28, 32.

NOTES

4. On the history of this concept in the enlightenment, see Paul B. Wood, "The Science of Man," *Cultures of Natural History*, ed. Nicholas Jardine, J. A. Secord, and Emma Spary (Cambridge: Cambridge University Press, 1996), 197–210.

5. R. S. Crane argues that another piece which also features the phrase "citizen of the world," entitled "Reflections on National Prejudices," published in the *British Magazine* for August 1760, was Goldsmith's work and a development of the theme which he outlines in his "Comparative View." Arthur Friedman disagrees with the ascription. While Friedman may be correct in claiming that there is "no evidence of Goldsmith's hand"—the essay has been ascribed elsewhere to Tobias Smollett—the argument is notably Goldsmithian and is worthy, at least, of consideration. See "Reflections on National Prejudices. In Response to a Chauvinist Englishman looking for Verification," *The British Magazine, or Monthly Repository for Gentlemen and Ladies* 1 (1760), 460–62; see Arthur Friedman, "Essays from the *British Magazine* (1760), Introduction" (W3: 87–90); and for Crane's attribution, see Goldsmith, *New Essays*, 17n.

6. David Bell, *The Cult of the Nation in France: Inventing Nationalism, 1680–1800* (Cambridge: Harvard University Press, 2001), 143–4.

7. Hippocrates, "Airs, Waters, Places," *Writings*, ed. G. E. R. Lloyd, trans. J. Chadwick et al. (Harmondsworth: Penguin, 1983), 159–60. For a survey of connections between race, climate and biology, see George W. Stocking, "Bones, Bodies, Behaviour," in *Bones, Bodies, Behaviour: Essays on Biological Anthropology*, ed. George W. Stocking (Madison: University of Wisconsin Press, 1988), 3–15. For an historical treatment of "ethnoclimatology" (the relationship between climate and human anatomy) and "anthropometric cartography" (mapping of variations in human physiognomy) see Livingstone, "The Moral Discourse of Climate: Historical Considerations on Race, Place and Virtue," *Journal of Historical Geography* 17 (1991), 413–34.

8. In a chapter on "Of the Most Obvious Effects of Air Upon the Human Body," Goldsmith wrote: "the air produces several effects upon the body in proportion as it is charged with vapours and exhalations. This was well known to Hippocrates, and several succeeding physicians have given us histories of those disorders which are produced by the badness of air." *A Survey of Experimental Philosophy, Considered in Its Present State of Improvement*, 2 vols (London: Printed for T. Carnan and F. Newbery jun., 1776), 2: 20. Hippocrates' racial typology did not move past the Scythians and the Egyptians; it was not until Pliny took account of "monstrous races"—the African Androgini, the Libyan Blemmyae, the Indian Sciopods and Cynocephali—that the issue became one of categorizing the "human" and the "non–human." These typologies, and the categorical schemes that inspired them, are pervasive in eighteenth-century ideas of nature and culture. See the second volume of Pliny (the Elder), *Natural History*, ed. E. H. Warmington, trans. H. Rackham, 10 vols (Cambridge: Harvard University Press, 1969). For a useful catalogue of these Plinian races, see John Block Friedman, *The Monstrous Races in Medieval Art and Thought* (Cambridge: Harvard University Press, 1981), 5–25. Clarence J. Glacken, in his extensive study, bridges the classical and the neo-lassical in human geography; in so doing, he teases out a multitude of intellectual traditions, connections, and debts. See Glacken, *Traces on the Rhodian Shore: Nature and Culture in Western Thought from Ancient Times to the End of the Eighteenth Century* (Berkeley: University of California Press, 1967).

9. William Temple, "An Essay upon the Ancient and Modern Learning" (1690), *Essays On Ancient and Modern Learning and On Poetry*, ed. J. E. Spingarn (Oxford: The Clarendon Press, 1909), 15.

10. Temple, "Of Poetry" (1690), *Essays on Ancient and Modern Learning and On Poetry*, 74.

11. William Congreve, "Concerning Humour in Comedy" (1695), *Critical Essays of the Seventeenth Century*, ed. J. E. Spingarn, 3 vols. (Bloomington: Indiana University Press, 1957), 3: 252.

12. George Farquhar, "A Discourse upon Comedy in Reference to the English Stage" (1702), *The Complete Works*, ed. Charles Stonehill, 2 vols. (Bloomsbury: Nonesuch, 1930), 2: 337.

13. See Jonathan Swift, *The Intelligencer* No. 3 [probably May 25, 1728], *The Intelligencer*, ed. James Woolley (Oxford: The Clarendon Press, 1992), 61–2.

14. Denis Hay cites enduring Hippocratic ideas about European and non–European peoples in his historical treatment of an emerging "idea of Europe." He refers to "the completely developed 'Europeanism' of Montesquieu, for whom, in brief, Europe represented progress, Asia stagnation." *Europe: The Emergence of an Idea* (New York: Harper and Row, 1966), 3, 122.

15. David Hume, "Of the Rise and Progress of the Arts and Sciences" (1742), *Essays Moral, Political and Literary* (Oxford: Oxford University Press, 1963), 121.

16. Hume, "Of National Characters" (1748), *Essays Moral, Political and Literary*, 206, 209, 218, 220. In 1775 Lord Kames wielded a similar argument; see Henry Home, Lord Kames, *Sketches of the History of Man in Four Volumes* (Dublin: Printed for James Williams, 1775). For a critical variation on Kames's approach, see Samuel Stanhope Smith, *An Essay on the Causes of the Variety of Complexion and Figure in the Human Species. To which are added, Strictures on Lord Kaim's Discourse, on the Original Diversity of Mankind* (London: Printed for John Stockdale, 1789).

17. Charles de Secondat, Baron de Montesquieu, *The Spirit of Laws*, 2 vols. (1748; tr. London: Printed for J. Nourse, and P. Vaillant, 1750), 1: 317.

18. This essay first appeared in the *British Magazine* in May of 1760. It was ascribed to Goldsmith by R. S. Crane on the basis that Goldsmith was, at that time, a regular contributor to the *British Magazine*. Also, there was the perennial influence of Buffon. Crane describes this piece's many thematic similarities to Goldsmith's introductions to Richard Brookes' *New and Accurate System of Natural History* (1763) and his own *Animated Nature*. See Crane's notes in Goldsmith, *New Essays*, 5–11n. The attribution of the essay to Goldsmith is not absolutely certain, and has been the subject of stylometric investigation since. See David Mannion and Peter Dixon, "Authorship Attribution: The Case of Oliver Goldsmith," *The Statistician* 46 (1997), 1–18; and "Goldsmith and the *British Magazine*," *Literary and Linguistic Computing* 13 (1998), 37–49.

19. See François–Ignace Espiard de la Borde, *The Spirit of Nations. Translated from the French*, no trans. given (London: Printed for Lockyer Davis and R. Baldwin, 1753), 21–23. Goldsmith was not the only person to plagiarize de la Borde. In 1769 the novelist Jean-Louis Castilhon republished the work, with a more republican inflection, under his own name and with a new title: *Considerations sur les causes physiques et morales*.

20. Bell, *The Cult of the Nation in France*, 10.

21. Espiard de la Borde, *The Spirit of Nations*, iii–vii.

22. "The Effects which Climates Have Upon Men, and Other Animals," (W3: 112–13). Buffon made the same observation: "Mais lorsque le froid devient extrême, il produit quelques effets semblables à ceux de la chaleur excessive." Georges-Louis LeClerc, Comte de Buffon, *Histoire Naturelle*, 15 toms (Paris, 1749), 3: 527.

NOTES

23. Raynal, *A Philosophical and Political History of the Settlements and Trade of the Europeans in the East and West Indies*, 1: 246.

24. These three last examples, along with the Italian example quoted above, are plagiarized from de la Borde. For a full account of these borrowings, see Michael Griffin, "Oliver Goldsmith and François–Ignace Espiard de la Borde: An Instance of Plagiarism," *The Review of English Studies* 50 (1999), 59–63.

25. Montesquieu, *Persian Letters*, 216.

26. Ralph M. Wardle, *Oliver Goldsmith* (Lawrence: University of Kansas Press, 1957), 283.

27. Goldsmith thanked Nourse in February 1774 for *over*payment. See *CL*, 136–37. On the contents and circumstances of the publication, see James Hall Pitman, *Goldsmith's Animated Nature: A Study of Goldsmith* (1924; Hamden: Archon, 1972), 7–17. See also John Forster, *The Life and Times of Oliver Goldsmith*, 2 vols. (London: Chapman and Hall, 1871), 2: 413–4.

28. Quoted in James Boswell, *Life of Johnson*, 2: 237, 3: 84n; 2: 232–233.

29. Goldsmith would have been familiar with the following: John Ray, *Synopsis Methodica Animalioum Quadrupdum et Serpentini Generis* (1693); *Synopsis Methodica Avium & Piscium* (1713); Iacobi Theodori Klein, *Quadrupedum Dispositio Brevisque Historia Naturalis* (1751); Mathurin Jacques Brisson, *Ornithologia* (1760). Linnaeus, *Systema Naturæ in quo Naturæ Regna Tria, Secundum Classes, Ordines, Genera, Species, Systematice Proponuntur* (1740); *Amoenitates Academicae* (1749). An English physico–theologist and natural historian, Ray in particular was a central source in R. Brookes' *New and Accurate System of Natural History* (London: Printed for J. Newbery, 1763), which Goldsmith reviewed and for which he was contracted to write prefaces. In one review he accuses Klein and Linnaeus, though not Ray, of dullness: "It is true, that Linnaeus, Klein, and others, have classed natural objects with much greater assiduity and minuteness; but those systematic divisions, which were originally introduced with the science, to assist the learner's memory, serve at present, by their number, to create embarasment [sic], and repress his curiosity" (W1: 138).

30. Goldsmith to John Bindley, July 1766, cited in Katharine C. Balderston, "New Goldsmith Letters," *The Yale University Library Gazette* 39 (1964), 71–2. For a detailed account of Linnaeus' reception in Britain in the mid-to-late eighteenth century, see Frans A. Stafleu, *Linnaeus and the Linnaeans: The Spreading of Their Ideas in Systematic Botany, 1735–1789* (Utrecht: Oesthoek, 1971); and John Gascoigne, *Joseph Banks and the English Enlightenment: Useful Knowledge and Polite Culture* (Cambridge: Cambridge University Press, 1994), 98–107.

31. See Buffon, "Variétés dans l'espèce humaine," *Histoire Naturelle*, 3: 371–530. See also Phillip R. Sloan, "The Idea of Racial Degeneracy in Buffon's *Histoire Naturelle*," in *Racism in the Eighteenth Century*, ed. Harold E. Pagliaro (Cleveland: Case Western Reserve University Press, 1973), 293–321; and Sloan, "The Gaze of Natural History," in *Inventing Human Science*, ed. Christopher Fox, Roy Porter, and Robert Wokler, 112–151. Goldsmith's comparative treatments of the faculties of seeing, hearing, smelling, feeling, and tasting, consist of a good deal of direct (and acknowledged) translation of corresponding sections in Buffon. Wherever Goldsmith intervenes with his own observations or his own additions to Buffon's descriptions, he identifies himself by placing his ideas within inverted commas.

32. Nicholas Hudson, "From 'Nation' to 'Race': The Origin of Racial Classification in Eighteenth-Century Thought," *Eighteenth-Century Studies* 29 (1996), 248.

33. Felicity A. Nussbaum, *Torrid Zones: Maternity, Sexuality, and Empire in Eighteenth-Century English Narratives* (Baltimore: The Johns Hopkins University Press, 1995), 8.

34. Goldsmith makes another point on the relativity of beauty in his introduction to *The Bee*: "A traveller, in his way to Italy, found himself in a country where the inhabitants had each a large excrescence depending from the chin; a deformity which, as it was endemic, and the people little used to strangers, it had been the custom, time immemorial, to look upon as the greatest beauty. Ladies grew toasts from the size of their chins, and no men were beaux whose faces were not broadest at the bottom" (W1: 357).

35. The famous anthropologist (and phrenologist) Johann Friedrich Blumenbach, while emphasizing the tendency to arbitrariness in any such system, was to remark on the credibility of Goldsmith's conflation of the two authors' schema. "On the Natural Variety of Mankind" (1776), *The Anthopological Treatises*, trans. and ed. Thomas Bendyshe (London: Longman, 1865), 99.

36. Daniel Beeckman, *A Voyage to and from the Island of Borneo in the East–Indies* (London: Printed for T. Warner and J. Batley, 1718), 185. On the subject of such motifs and of "grotesquerie" in colonial literature (and on Jonathan Swift's parodies thereof), see R. W. Frantz, "Swift's Yahoos and the Voyagers," *Modern Philology* 29 (1931), 54–5. See also Clement Hawes, "Three Times around the Globe: Gulliver and Colonial Discourse," *Cultural Critique*, no. 18 (Spring 1991), 193–94. See also Claude Rawson's chapter, "The Savage with Hanging Breasts: Gulliver, Female Yahoos, and 'Racism,'" in *God, Gulliver, and Genocide: Barbarism and the European Imagination, 1492–1945* (Oxford: Oxford University Press, 2001), 92–182.

37. William Lithgow, *The Totall Discourse, of the Rare Adventures, and Painful Peregrinations of Long Nineteene Yeares Travailes from Scotland, to the most Famous Kingdomes in Europe, Asia, and Africa* (London: I. Okes, 1640), 436.

38. Epitomized in Francois–Xavier's *Histoire du Paraguay*, which Goldsmith reviewed in 1757: "The author further informs us, that they are almost all naturally stupid, savage, perfidious, voracious, and addicted to drunkenness, without precaution or forecast, even with respect to the necessaries of life; that they are lazy, and indolent, to the last degree, except in some places; that pillage, and revenge, often render them furious, without making them brave; that they are generally cowards; and that even such of them as have preserved their liberty, owe it solely to those inaccessible parts of the country which they inhabit" (W1: 52).

39. Benjamin Bissell, *The American Indian in English Literature of the Eighteenth Century* (New Haven: Yale University Press, 1925), 214.

Chapter 2. The Lie of the Land: Liberty and Travel

1. Montesquieu, *Persian Letters*, 90.

2. Katherine C. Balderston, *The History and Sources of Percy's Memoir of Goldsmith* (Cambridge: Cambridge University Press, 1926), 15.

3. Katherine Turner, *British Travel Writers in Europe 1750–1800: Authorship, Gender and National Identity* (Aldershot: Ahsgate, 2001), 14–5.

NOTES

4. John G. Hayman, "Notions of National Characters in the Eighteenth Century," *Huntington Library Quarterly* 35 (1971), 14.

5. See Pat Rogers, "The Dialectic of *The Traveller*," *The Art of Oliver Goldsmith*, ed. Andrew Swarbrick (London: Vision, 1984), 107–25.

6. Walpole, "To WEST, Sunday 2 October 1740," *Correspondence with Thomas Gray, Richard West and Thomas Ashton*, ed. W. S. Lewis, George L. Lam and Charles H. Bennett (New Haven: Yale University Press, 1948), 231. "Before Goldsmith," writes Katherine Turner, "the primary poetic models for European travel had been Addison's *A Letter from Italy* (1703) and Lord Lyttelton's Addisonian verse epistles from abroad." *British Travel Writers in Europe 1750–1800*, 13.

7. John G. Hayman, "Notions of National Characters in the Eighteenth Century," 5.

8. See Heinz–Joachim Müllenbrock, "The Political Implications of the Grand Tour: Aspects of a Specifically English Contribution to the European Travel Literature of the Age of Enlightenment," *Trema*, no. 9 (1984), 7–21.

9. Ciaran Murray, *Sharawadgi: The Romantic Return to Nature* (San Francisco: Rowman & Littlefield, 1999), 53.

10. Joseph Baretti, *An Account of the Manners and Customs of Italy; with Observations on the Mistakes of Some Travellers, with Regard to that Country*, 2 vols. (London: Printed for T. Davies, L. David, and C. Rymers, 1768), 2: 317, 1: 42.

11. Joseph Addison, *A Letter from Italy, to the Right Honourable Charles Lord Halifax in the Year MDCCI* (1701), *The Miscellaneous Works*, ed. A. C. Guthkelch, 2 vols. (London: G. Bell, 1914), 1: 51, 55, 57. See also *Remarks on Several Parts of Italy*, *The Miscellaneous Works*, 2: 13–235.

12. Richard Blackmore, *The Nature of Man. A Poem. In Three Books* (London: Printed for Sam. Buckley, 1711), ii–iii.

13. Leo F. Storm, "Conventional Ethics in Goldsmith's *The Traveller*," *Studies in English Literature, 1500–1900* 17 (1977), 466, 474–5.

14. Edgecombe, "Regionalisms Ancient and Modern," *Classical and Modern Literature: A Quarterly* 14 (1993), 44–5.

15. For an informative, general study of these dynamics in literature of the Grand Tour, see Jeremy Black, *The British Abroad: The Grand Tour in the Eighteenth Century* (New York: St. Martin's Press, 1992).

16. See William Cooke, "Table Talk; or, Characters, Anecdotes, etc. of Illustrious British Characters, during the last Fifty Years: Dr. Goldsmith," *European Magazine* 24 (1793), 93.

17. See Roger Lonsdale's headnote to *The Traveller* in Thomas Gray, William Collins, and Oliver Goldsmith, *The Poems*, ed. Lonsdale (London: Longman, 1969), 622.

18. For Goldsmith's general views on criticism, see "The Futility of Criticism" (1760), W3: 51–3; elsewhere, in *An Enquiry into the Present State of Polite Learning in Europe*, Goldsmith proposes "the rescuing of genius from the shackles of pedantry and criticism" (W1: 258).

19. There is a correlation between this passage and three others in the oeuvre: see *The Bee* (W1: 370); *The Citizen of the World* (W2: 303); and *The Vicar of Wakefield* (W4: 163). These lines also

echo Matthew Prior: "My destin'd Miles I shall have gone,/ By THAMES or MAESE, by PO or RHONE,/ And found no Foot of Earth my own." Prior, "Written at Paris, 1700. In the beginning of Robe's Geography," *Literary Works*, ed. H. Bunker Wright and Monroe K. Spears, 2 vols. (Oxford: The Clarendon Press, 1959), 1: 189.

20. "Let observation with extensive view,/ Survey mankind, from China to Peru;/ Remark each anxious toil, each eager strife,/ And watch the busy scenes of crowded life." Samuel Johnson, *The Vanity of Human Wishes* (1748), *Poems*, ed. E. L. Mc Adam with George Milne (New Haven: Yale University Press, 1964), 91–2.

21. Ingrid Horrocks suggestively proposes that Goldsmith's particular use of vantage points allows for, and provides, "a more egalitarian 'prospect of society.'" Horrocks, "'Circling Eye and Houseless Stranger'": The New Eighteenth-Century Wanderer (Thomson to Goldsmith)," *English Literary History* 77 (2010), 666–667.

22. This is Pat Rogers' term. Rogers, "The Dialectic of *The Traveller* ," 107–25.

23. Wilson's *Pastoral Scene in the Campagna* is reproduced as an appendix in Luke Herrmann, *British Landscape Painting of the Eighteenth Century* (London: Faber, 1973). See page 54 for Herrmann's commentary.

24. Cited in William L. Pressly, "On Classic Ground: James Barry's 'Memorials' of the Italian Landscape," *Record of the Art Museum, Princeton University* 54 (1995), 14, 17. See also Jane Munro, "Italian Landscape Drawings by James Barry," *Master Drawings* 29 (1991), 307–310.

25. James Thomson, "Liberty" (1735), *Liberty, The Castle of Indolence, and Other Poems*, ed. James Sambrook (Oxford: The Clarendon Press, 1986), 97; and John Dyer, *The Ruins of Rome. A Poem* (London: Printed for Lawton Gulliver, 1740), 1.

26. George, Lord Lyttelton condensed this wisdom in one of his epistles: "Unhappy Italy! whose alter'd state/ Has felt the worst severity of Fate." Lyttlelton, "To Mr Pope" (1930), *The Poetical Works* (London: Cadell and Davies, 1807), 83.

27. Paul Langford, *Englishness Identified: Manners and Character 1650–1850* (Oxford: Oxford University Press, 2000), 275.

28. See Arnd Bohm, "From Politics to Aesthetics: Goldsmith's "'The Traveller" and Goethe's "Der Wandrer',," *The Germanic Review* 57 (1982), 138–42. On Goldsmith's aesthetic appreciation, and political depreciation, of the Italian picturesque, see Elizabeth Wheeler Manwaring, *Italian Landscape in England: A Study Chiefly of the Influence of Claude Lorrain and Salvator Rosa on English Taste, 1700–1800* (New York: Oxford University Press, 1925), 118.

29. "In my Journal the place and moment of conception are recorded; the fifteenth of October 1754, in the close of evening, as I sat musing in the Church of the Zoccolati or Franciscan fryars, while they were singing Vespers in the Temple of Jupiter on the ruins of the Capitol." Edward Gibbon, *Memoirs of My Life*, ed. Georges A. Bonnard (1796; London: Nelson, 1966), 136.

30. Steven Turner, "Enlightenment Topographies: Scotland, Switzerland, the South Seas," *The Eighteenth Century* 38 (1997), 231–46.

31. See James Prior, *Life of Oliver Goldsmith, M. B.*, 2 vols. (London: John Murray, 1837), 1: 185.

NOTES

32. Voltaire himself resided in Ferney, a few miles outside of Geneva, when he was no longer allowed to live in France (even though Ferney was technically on French soil). His Ferney residence was a port of call for many English intellectuals. See Mavis Coulson, *Southwards to Geneva: 200 Years of English Travellers* (Gloucester: A. Sutton, 1988), 29–49.

33. Cited in A. D. McKillop's brief but useful account of the Swiss dimension within the primitivist aesthetic. See McKillop, *The Background of Thomson's Seasons* (Hamden: Archon, 1961), 122–24. See also George B. Parks, "The Turn to the Romantic in the Travel Literature of the Eighteenth Century," *Modern Language Quarterly* 25 (1964), 22–33.

34. James Thomson, *Liberty*, 100n.

35. Prior, *Life*, 1: 179.

36. A. Lytton Sells, *Oliver Goldsmith: His Life and Works* (London: Barnes and Noble, 1974), 56.

37. See Constantia Maxwell, *The English Traveller in France, 1698–1815* (London: Routledge, 1932), 41.

38. See Goldsmith, *An Enquiry into the Present State of Polite Learning in Europe*, W1: 291.

39. Quite unlike the close observations of cultural detail contained in the poet's 1754 letter from Leyden to Thomas Contarine. See *Letters*, 19–25. Those observations might themselves have been mediated, as has been noted above, by the example of Thomas Nugent, *The Grand Tour, or, A Journey through the Netherlands, Germany, Italy, and France*, 3rd ed, 4 vols. (1749; London: Printed for J. Rivington and Sons, B. Law, T. Caslon, G. Robinson, T. Cadell, W. Goldsmith, J. Bew, S. Hayes, W. Fox, and T. Evans , 1778), 1: 40–8.

40. In "The Revolution in Low Life," Venice, Genoa, and Holland "are little better at present than retreats for tyrants and prisons for slaves" (W3: 197). In letter 35 of *The Citizen of the World*, modern Persia is also described in these terms. The phrase may have originated, as Friedman notes, in the *Literary Magazine* in 1756, where Jamaica is characterized as "a den of tyrants, and a dungeon of slaves" (W2: 152n).

41. A. J. Barnouw, "Goldsmith's Indebtedness to Justus Van Effen," *Modern Language Review* 8 (1913), 318. The third paragraph of Goldsmith's "Letter from a Traveller" in *The Bee* (1759) is substantially translated from the sixth letter of Van Effen's *Relation d'un Voyage de Holland en Suède*, printed first in 1729 in *Le Misanthrope*, a collection of essays in imitation of the *Tatler* or *Spectator*. See Barnouw, 314–23.

42. Thomson, "Liberty, a Poem. V. The Prospect," 130.

43. On this point, see John Lucas, *England and Englishness*, 55–70.

44. In 1902, Bertram Dobell discovered a draft, thus titled and 310 lines long, which contained, albeit with verses in an erroneously shuffled order, most of what would become *The Traveller*. See Oliver Goldsmith, *A Prospect of Society*, ed. Bertram Dobell (London: by the editor, 1902).

45. John Ginger, *The Notable Man: The Life and Times of Oliver Goldsmith*, (London: Hamilton, 1977), 86–90.

46. Prior, *Life*, 1: 172.

47. Holberg, *A Journey to the World Under-Ground. By Nicholas Klimius* (London: Printed for T. Astley and B. Collins, 1742), 74, 257.

48. James Joyce, *Letters, Volume II*, ed. Richard Ellman (London: Viking Press, 1966), 99. Joyce was evidently a keen reader of Goldsmith. He wrote to the American artist Theodore Spicer-Simon on June 8, 1910, to congratulate him on an evening in honor of Laurence Sterne. He added: "I would like to have been present and I hope your club may play a like honour to some other fellow-countrymen of mine who stand higher than L.S., for example, Jonathan Swift (who could preside over a very fantastic night) or Oliver Goldsmith" (285).

49. After its initial appearance in 1766, two further Dublin editions were published in 1767; a fourth edition appeared in December 1769 (dated 1770), and a fifth in 1773, with several pirated editions published in the intervening years. In the final quarter of the eighteenth century there were at least 23 more London editions and 21 editions in English published elsewhere. It was translated into French and German the year after its initial publication, and into Dutch in 1768.

50. "Embellishments of English books have usually been characterised by those powers of art which appeal more particularly to the eye. The object aimed at in this in this attempt to illustrate the most popular of GOLDSMITH'S Works is, that character and composition may, with the aid of drawing, appeal directly to the understanding." *The Vicar of Wakefield*, with thirty–two illustrations, by William Mulready, R. A. (London: John Van Voorst, 1843), no page number. For a comprehensive survey of illustrations of scenes from Goldsmith's works, particularly *The Vicar of Wakefield* and *The Deserted Village*, see Richard D. Altick, *Paintings from Books: Art and Literature in Britain, 1760–1900* (Columbus: Ohio State University Press, 1985), 405–410.

51. See *Once Upon a Time: The Fairy Tale World of Arthur Rackham*, ed. Margery Darrell (New York: Heinemann, 1972); and Derek Hudson, *Arthur Rackham, His Life and Work* (New York: Charles Scribner, 1974).

52. Samuel Curwen reflects the satirical understanding of *The Vicar* when, on May 30, 1777, he writes of his visit to Wakefield in Yorkshire: "It has a very large Episcopal church, with a remarkably lofty tower and spire. The principle character in the Novel called The Vicar of Wakefield was taken from the late vicar of this church, named Johnson, whose peculiarly odd and singular humour has exposed his memory to the ridicule of that satire." Curwen, *Journal and Letters, from 1775–1784* (New York: C.S. Francis and Co., 1842), 131. Curwen's information on the source of the Vicar is too literal; his description of the book reflects its satirical reception in some quarters in the decades following its publication.

53. On the production of the book, see Boswell, *Life of Johnson*, 1: 415–16. See also Friedman's notes, which address the question of the book's completion, or lack thereof, between its sale and publication (W4: 4–9).

54. Richard Helgerson, "The Two Worlds of Oliver Goldsmith," *Studies in English Literature, 1500–1900* 13 (1973), 517.

55. Samuel Woods, "*The Vicar of Wakefield* and Recent Goldsmith Scholarship," *Eighteenth-Century Studies* 9 (1976), 437.

56. Chapter 19, for James Carson, "is central rather than incidental to *The Vicar of Wakefield* [. . .] Primrose there enunciates what are fundamentally Goldsmith's own political views." Carson, "'The Little Republic' of the Family: Goldsmith's Politics of Nostalgia," *Eighteenth-Century Fiction* 16 (2004), 175. Carson sees mixed in Goldsmith's monarchism an element of classical

republicanism; both strands of Goldsmith's political thought are for Carson opposed to modern republicanism emphases on "liberty."

57. This interpretation runs counter to the argument of Robert Welch, who reads Goldsmith's novel, bizarrely, as a Williamite allegory, seemingly on the basis that Thornhill's first name is William. See Welch, "The Strange Enigma of Oliver Goldsmith," in *The Sieges of Derry*, ed. William Kelly (Dublin: Four Courts Press, 2001), 81.

Chapter 3. Delicate Allegories: Ireland and the East

1. On this theme, see Laura Brown, *Ends of Empire: Women and Ideology in Early Eighteenth-Century English Literature* (Ithaca: Cornell University Press, 1993).

2. Jonathan Swift, "A Proposal for the Universal Use of *Irish* Manufacture, &c." (1720), *Swift's Irish Pamphlets: An Introductory Selection*, ed. Joseph McMinn (Savage, MD: Barnes and Noble Books, 1991), 50.

3. Robert Graves, "Lecture II: The Age of Obsequiousness," *The Crowning Privilege: Collected Essays on Poetry* (1955; New York: Books for Libraries Press, 1970), 50.

4. Translated as "The Vision": "Then answered the lady Aoibhill, of aspect bright,/ they had cause to light three candles above the harbours:/ in the name of the faithful king who is soon to come/ to rule and defend the triple realm for ever." *An Duanaire—An Irish Anthology 1600–1900: Poems of the Dispossessed*, ed. Seán Ó Túama, trans. Thomas Kinsella (Philadelphia: University of Pennsylvania Press, 1981), 155. See also John Montague, "The Sentimental Prophecy: A Study of *The Deserted Village*," in *The Art of Oliver Goldsmith*, ed. Andrew Swarbrick, 91.

5. Joseph McMinn, "Literature and Religion in Eighteenth-Century Ireland: A Critical Survey," in *Irish Writers and Religion*, ed. Robert Welch (Gerrards Cross: Smythe, 1992), 25–6.

6. Scholars such as Laura L. Howes, Anne Heskell, and Cristina Malcolmson have studied the extent to which the enclosure of gardens is, in Geoffrey Chaucer and Andrew Marvell, analogous to marriage. Apropos of Chaucer, Laura L. Howes wrote: "Walled gardens and parks enclose and contain several women in the Tales, and come to represent in context the conventional roles that prescribe the activities of medieval women, particularly as wives or as prospective wives." Howes, *Chaucer's Gardens and the Language of Convention* (Gainesville: University of Florida Press, 1997), 83. See also Ann Heskell, "Chaucerian Women, Ideal Gardens, and the Wild Woods," in *A Wyf Ther was: Essays in Honour of Paule Mertens–Fonck*, ed. Juliette Dor (Liège: Liège Language and Literature, 1992), 193–8; and Cristina Malcolmson, "The Garden Enclosed/The Woman Enclosed: Marvell and the Cavalier Poets," in *Enclosure Acts: Sexuality, Property, and Culture in Early Modern England*, ed. Richard Burt and John Michael Archer (Ithaca: Cornell University Press, 1994), 251–69.

7. See James G. Turner, "The Sexual Politics of Landscape: Images of Venus in Eighteenth-Century English Poetry and Landscape Gardening," *Studies in Eighteenth-Century Culture* 11 (1982), 343–66; and Carole Fabricant, "Binding and Dressing Nature's Loose Tresses: The Ideology of Augustan Landscape Design," *Studies in Eighteenth-Century Culture* 8 (1979), 109–35.

8. Tao Zhijian, "Citizen of Whose World? Goldsmith's Orientalism," *Comparative Literature Studies* 33 (1996), 29.

9. Christopher Brooks, "Goldsmith's Citizen of the World: Knowledge and the Imposture of "Orientalism'," *Texas Studies in Language and Literature* 35 (1993), 134. To Brooks' suggestion could be added Ralph Wardle's further qualification that, in 1760, "an Irishman's reaction to English life would have interested no one, while it was fashionable to regard the Chinese as paragons of wisdom." *Oliver Goldsmith* (Lawrence: University of Kansas Press, 1957), 111. For a more recent treatment of the issue of persona in *The Citizen of the World*, one which focuses not on nationality so much as the failure of Goldsmith the professional author to morally instruct his audience, see Megan Kitching, "The Solitary Animal: Professional Authorship and Persona in Goldsmith's *The Citizen of the World*," *Eighteenth-Century Fiction* 25 (2012), 175–198.

10. John Hughes, "An Essay on Allegorical Poetry. With Remarks on the Writings of Mr. Edmund Spenser," in Edmund Spenser, *The Works*, 6 vols. (London: Printed for Jacob Tonson, 1715), 1: xxviii–xxix.

11. Jonathan Spence, *The Chan's Great Continent: China in Western Minds* (London: Penguin, 1999), 1, 12, xiii.

12. Goldsmith "served as a conduit for British readers to receive ideas from the French *Philosophes*, the older generation of deists like Montesquieu and Voltaire, but even more extensively from the younger generations of atheists, especially D'Argens, although most of these works were also quickly translated into English so that the general ideas of the Philosophes were directly available to the eighteenth-century British reader." Samuel H. Woods Jr, "Images of the Orient: Goldsmith and the Philosophes," *Studies in Eighteenth-Century Culture* 15 (1986), 257.

13. Martha Pike Conant, in her valuable work, demonstrates that Goldsmith borrowed "certain names and incidents" from Lyttelton. See Conant, *The Oriental Tale in England in the Eighteenth Century* (New York: Columbia University Press, 1908), 185. Other predecessors, influences and sources—such as Horace Walpole's *Letter from Xo-Ho, a Chinese Philosopher at London, to his friend Lien Chi, at Peking* (1757), from which Goldsmith took the name of his Chinese correspondent—are traced and catalogued in Hamilton Jewett Smith, *Oliver Goldsmith's The Citizen of the World: A Study* (New Haven: Yale University Press, 1926). Smith lists the sources—supposed and proven—of *The Citizen of the World* in two sections: "Works in which a foreigner is pictured satirizing the country he visits in a series of letters made public in alleged translation from the original tongue," 39–85; and "Works not on the plan of *The Citizen of the World*, which were used by Goldsmith for concrete material," 85–114. On the subject of Goldsmith's direct translation of sentences, paragraphs and letters from D'Argens' *Lettres Chinoises*, see Smith and R. S. Crane, "A French Influence on Goldsmith's *Citizen of the World*," *Modern Philology* 19 (1921–22), 83–92. This information is included, wherever applicable, in Friedman's notes. Philip Harth has shown that Goldsmith used the 1755 edition of the *Lettres Chinoises*; see Harth, "Goldsmith and the Marquis d'Argens," *Notes and Queries* 198 (1953), 529–30. Friedman himself collates Goldsmith's use of this source using the 1751 edition. See also David Wei-Yang Dai, "A Comparative Study of D'Argens *Lettres Chinoises* and Goldsmith's *Citizen of the World*," *Tamkang Review* 10 (1979), 183–97.

14. On Goldsmith's use of these two sources, see H. J. Smith, *Oliver Goldsmith's The Citizen of the World*, 85–95; and A. L. Sells, *Les Sources Francaises de Goldsmith* (Paris, 1924), 98–100.

NOTES

15. Elsewhere, Goldsmith quotes Voltaire's remark on Montesquieu's *Persian Letters*: "The satire which in the mouth of an Asiatic is poignant, would lose all its force when coming from a European." "To the Authors of the *Monthly Review*" (W1: 104). Likewise, in his essay "On the Contradictions of the World," in *The Bee*, Goldsmith utilizes a translation of Voltaire's views on pseudo-letters to the same effect (see W1: 467–70). Interestingly, and influentially as far as Goldsmith's orientalism is concerned, Voltaire's *Essai sur les moeurs et l'esprit des nations*, or *History of the Manners and Spirit of Nations* (1756), began with a treatment of China, a novel point of departure for a work whose explicit aim was to report on the genius of nations with which Europe had traded.

16. *The Citizen of the World* has been described as belonging to a tradition of "geographical satires." Thomas M. Curley, *Samuel Johnson and the Age of Travel* (Athens: University of Georgia Press, 1976), 51.

17. Said, *Orientalism*, 118–9.

18. Nigel Leask, *British Romantic Writers and the East: Anxieties of Empire* (Cambridge: Cambridge University Press, 1992), 19–20.

19. B. Sprague Allen, *Tides in English Taste (1619–1800): A Background for the Study of Literature*, 2 vols. (Cambridge: Harvard University Press, 1937), 2: 40.

20. G. S. Rousseau and Roy Porter, "Introduction," in *Exoticism in the Enlightenment*, ed. Rousseau and Porter (Manchester: Manchester University Press, 1990), 11.

21. Ros Ballaster, *Fabulous Orients: Fictions of the East in England 1662–1785* (Oxford: Oxford University Press, 2005), 253.

22. For a brisk summary of the Chinese national character which emphasizes these familial virtues, see Du Halde, *A Description of the Empire of China and Chinese Tartary* [no trans. gvn: Samuel Johnson?], 2 vols. (London: Printed by T. Gardner, 1738, 1741), 1: 281. A contemporary response to Du Halde's relatively happy depictions of China and the Chinese was staunch in its British nationalism: "I see now no cause to esteem the *Chinese* Government [. . .] It is *Britain* only, I except no other Country on earth, that is happy by Constitution." [Anonymous], *An Irregular Dissertation, Occasioned by the Reading of Father du Halde's Description of China* (London: Printed for J. Roberts, 1740), 108.

23. On the broad issue of Jesuit interpretations of Chinese culture, particularly in this eighteenth-century context, where "the Jesuit was the voice of the East to the West and also the interpreter of the Occident to the Orient," see Arnold H. Rowbotham, *Missionary and Mandarin: The Jesuits at the Court of China* (Berkeley: University of California Press, 1942), vii.

24. In spite of Altangi's opinions, his creator was not acquainted firsthand with Confucius' *Analects*. His knowledge of Confucianism was absorbed through cultural osmosis and via Du Halde and Le Comte. Friedman suggests that Goldsmith's equation of Confucianism and Christianity was an English commonplace of the period; see W2: 200n. Also, W. W. Appleton suggests that the character of Confucius embodied, for the English, "an amalgam of the qualities of the good men of the eighteenth century: the detachment and wit of the Spectator, the personal devoutness and purity of William Law, the human compassion and understanding of Parson Adams." Appleton, *A Cycle of Cathay: The Chinese Vogue in England during the Seventeenth and Eighteenth Centuries* (New York: Columbia University Press, 1951), 124.

25. Martha Pike Conant has pointed to a parallel between this framing device and that of the sixty-eighth of Lyttelton's *Letters from a Persian in England to His Friend at Ispahan*. See Conant, *The Oriental Tale in England in the Eighteenth Century*, 183–5.

26. Hugh Honour, *Chinoiserie: The Vision of Cathay* (London: John Murray, 1961), 1. For a catalogue of Chinoiserie textiles, painted wallpapers, ceramics, furniture and *objets d'art*, see Madeleine Jarry, *Chinoiserie: Chinese Influence on European Decorative Art, 17th and 18th Centuries* (New York: Vendome Press, 1981).

27. These points are derived from Voltaire, whom Goldsmith translated: "False taste is very different from false wit, as the latter always proceeds from affectation, from an effort to go wrong; on the contrary, the other is an habit of going wrong without design, and following, as if by instinct, some bad, though established model. The incoherent exuberance of an oriental imagination is a false taste, and an improper example to imitate: however, they more frequently transgress in this respect, rather from a poverty than a copiousness of real genius. Falling stars, splitting mountains, rivers flowing to their sources, the sun and moon dissolving, false and unnatural comparisons, and nature everywhere exaggerated, form the character of these writers; and this arises from their never, in these countries, being permitted to speak in public. True eloquence has never been cultivated there, and it is much easier to write in a turgid strain, than with ease and delicate simplicity." "On Wit. From Voltaire" (W1: 410–1).

28. William Whitehead, "Prologue," in Arthur Murphy, *The Orphan of China, a Tragedy* (London: Printed for P. Vaillant, 1759), no page nos.

29. Thomas Percy's sources were, among others, a four-volume English translation of Du Halde's *Description de la Chine* entitled *The General History of China* (1736), by Richard Brookes, and the second, two-volume translation—*A Description of the Empire of China and Chinese-Tartary* (1738, 1741), on which Johnson worked. The latter is the edition that Percy used most copiously: "Du Halde's work on China and its translations were often quoted without acknowledgement [. . .] Goldsmith was one of the many who plagiarized. Percy was more scrupulous." T. C. Fan, "Percy and Du Halde," *Review of English Studies* 21 (1945), 328. However, Percy, rather disingenuously, did not always give credit to previous English translations, credit that, on the evidence of Fan's article, is clearly due. "The Little Orphan of the House of Chao," in *Miscellaneous Pieces Relating to the Chinese*, was, claimed Percy, a new translation into English of Du Halde, truer to the linguistic peculiarities of the Chinese original. Fan argues that Percy's translation follows the English translation already in existence, although occasional references to the French version can be found. Percy did not, any more than his contemporaries, have any serious knowledge of the "Chinese original."

30. Although: "at any rate Goldsmith soon outgrew it." Alda Milner Barry, "A Note on the Early Literary Relations of Oliver Goldsmith and Thomas Percy," *The Review of English Studies* 2 (1926), 60.

31. James Watt, "Thomas Percy, China, and the Gothic," *The Eighteenth Century: Theory and Interpretation* 48 (2007), 99, 103.

32. Thomas Percy, "Preface," *Hau Kiou Choaan or the Pleasing History. A Translation from the Chinese Language. To which are added, I. The Argument or Story of a Chinese Play, II: A Collection of Chinese Proverbs, and III. Fragments of Chinese Poetry*, 4 vols. (London: Printed for R. And J. Dodsley, 1761), 1: xiv, xii, xiv.

33. For a narration of this transition, and a discussion of its literary impact, see David C. Streatfield and Alistair Duckworth, *Landscape in the Gardens and the Literature of Eighteenth-Century England* (Los Angeles: William Andrews Clark Memorial Library, 1981).

34. William Temple, "Upon the Gardens of Epicurus; or of Gardening in the Year 1685," *Upon the Gardens of Epicurus, with other XVIIth Century Garden Essays*, int. Albert Forbes Sieveking (London: Chatto and Windus, 1908), 54.

35. Addison's garden pieces have been collected together in *The Genius of the Place: The English Landscape Garden 1620–1820* ed. John Dixon Hunt and Peter Willis (Cambridge: MIT Press, 1988), 139–47.

36. Edmund Burke, *Reflections on the Revolution in France, and on the Proceedings in Certain Societies in London Relative to that Event*, ed. Conor Cruise O'Brien, 1790 (Harmondsworth: Penguin, 1969), 144; see also Ciaran Murray, *Sharawadgi*, 252.

37. As Thomas Gray acknowledged: "that the Chinese have this beautiful Art in high perfection, seems very probable from the Jesuit's Letters [. . .] but it is very certain, we copied nothing from them, nor had anything but nature for our model. It is not forty years, since the Art was born among us; and it is sure, that there was nothing in Europe like it, & as sure, we then had no information on this head from China at all." "Gray to How: Cambridge; Sept. 10. 1763," *The Correspondence*, ed. Paget Toynbee and Leonard Whibley, 3 vols. (1935; Oxford: The Clarendon Press, 1971), 2: 814.

38. Temple may have misunderstood the exact meaning of the term. Suggesting a Japanese origin for the idea, Takua Shimada argues that Sharawadgi has less to do with asymmetry as such, and more to do with simple naturalism. See Shimada, "Is *Sharawadgi* Derived from the Japanese Word *Sorowaji*," *The Review of English Studies* 48 (1997), 350–52; see also Y. Z. Chang, "'A Note on Sharawadgi," *Modern Language Notes* 45 (1930), 221–224.

39. See Donald Cross Bryant, *Edmund Burke and His Literary Friends* (St Louis: Washington University Studies, New Series – Language and Literature, no. 9, 1939), 83–98. It was probably Burke who recollected Goldsmith's having been "distinguished at college." Goldsmith similarly "recollected more of that friend's early years, as he grew a greater man." *Life of Johnson*, 3: 168.

40. Edmund Burke, *A Philosophical Inquiry into the Origin of Our Ideas of the Sublime and the Beautiful*, in Burke, *The Writings and Speeches: Volume 1: The Early Writings*, ed. T. O. McLoughlin and James T. Boulton (Oxford: The Clarendon Press, 1997), 275.

41. In his *History of England*, Goldsmith writes that Charles XII "maintained a close correspondence with the disaffected subjects of Great Britain; and a scheme was formed for the landing a considerable body of Swedish forces, with the king at their head, in some part of the island, where it was expected they would be joined by all the malcontents in the kingdom" (4: 231). Ian Higgins writes that support for Charles XII of Sweden was sometimes construed as covert anti–Hanoverianism. See Higgins, *Swift's Politics*, 79.

42. Chambers wrote in 1774 about the "lovely bowers of innocence and ease, seats of my Youth, where every sport could please," before going on to confess that "Rippon has now no charms for me, those I once knew and loved, are dead or dispersed, and the town is a melancholy desert, where I know not a soul but my physical cousin, and two old women, famous for telling long stories." Influenced by Goldsmith's death that year, these reminiscences are mediated by, and adapted from,

The Deserted Village. Cited in John Harris, *Sir William Chambers: Knight of the Polar Star* (London: A. Zwemmer, 1970), 4.

43. See R. C. Bald, "Sir William Chambers and the Chinese Garden," *Journal of the History of Ideas* 11 (1950), 287–320.

44. "Capability" Brown was so called because he was known to refer to the "capability" of an uncultivated field. On Brown's life and work, see Dorothy Stroud, *Capability Brown* (1950; London: Faber and Faber, 1965); see also Roger Turner, *Capability Brown and the Eighteenth-Century English Landscape* (Chichester: Phillimore, 1999).

45. William Chambers, *A Dissertation on Oriental Gardening* (London: Printed for W. Griffin, T. Davies, J. Dodsley; Wilson and Nicoll; J. Walter, and P. Elmsley, 1772), v, vii, 19.

46. William Chambers, *Design of Chinese Buildings, Furniture, Dresses, Machines, and Utensils* (London: [s.n.], 1757), preface. Arthur O. Lovejoy writes: "Originality, in short, was sought after by Chinese artists. But originality, except in the expression of the same standardized idea, was inconsistent with neo-classical aesthetic theory; and it was scarcely less inconsistent with the ideal of imitating 'natural' effects." Lovejoy, "The Chinese Origin of a Romanticism," in *Essays in the History of Ideas* (Baltimore: The Johns Hopkins University Press, 1948), 129. Lovejoy's essay is often cited for its convincing attribution of nascent Romanticism to the ascendancy of Chinese gardening in Europe.

47. Fabricant, *Swift's Landscape*, 88–9.

48. William Mason, "An Heroic Epistle to Sir William Chambers, knight, &c." (1773), *Satirical Poems*, ed. Horace Walpole (Oxford: The Clarendon Press, 1926), 52. Mason was, in "An Heroic Postscript to the Public, Occasioned by their favourable Reception of a Late Heroic Epistle to Sir William Chambers, Knt., &c." (1774), more conciliatory, admitting that Chambers, in spite of his treasonable Chinese gardening, "is, and means to be his country's friend." Mason, *Satirical Poems*, 78.

49. Horace Walpole, "Notes to the Author's Preface" [To Mason, "An Heroic Epistle"], *Satirical Poems*, 45. For a background to Walpole's depreciation of the Chinese vogue, see Isabel Wakelin Chase, *Horace Walpole: Gardenist* (Princeton: Princeton University Press, 1943), 187–202.

50. Rudolf Wittkower, "English Neo-Palladianism, The Landscape Garden, China, and the Enlightenment, *L'Arte* 2 (1969), 32. See also Judith Colton, "Merlin's Cave and Queen Caroline: Garden Art as Political Propaganda," *Eighteenth-Century Studies* 10 (1976), 1–20; and Richard Drayton, *Nature's Government: Science, Imperial Britain, and the "Improvement" of the World* (New Haven: Yale University Press, 2000), 37–49.

51. See Jane Brown, *The Omnipotent Magician: Lancelot "Capability" Brown, 1716–1783* (London: Chatto and Windus, 2011), 244–6.

52. Quoted in R. W. Seitz, "Goldsmith to Sir William Chambers" (1773), *Times Literary Supplement* no. 1808 (September 1936), 772.

53. Quoted in R. W. Seitz, "Goldsmith to Sir William Chambers," 772.

54. Though the nature of the assistance is vague: "many thanks for your kind assistance in the business of Somerset House, 'tis a child of your own, and 'tis but right you should see it fledged before you leave it." William Chambers to Edmund Burke, May 5, 1782. Rockingham MS Bk 2/543, 1/802.

NOTES

55. Angus Fletcher, *Allegory: The Theory of a Symbolic Mode* (Ithaca: Cornell University Press, 1964), 260, 23.

56. The structure and content of the letter was, as Friedman, following A. Lytton Sells, pointed out, derived from the second paper in Marivaux's *Cabinet du philosophe*. See W2: 314–18n.

57. Burke, *A Philosophical Enquiry*, 274–5.

58. Goldsmith's review concludes that Burke's *Enquiry* is "branched out more extensively on the subject than any modern work of this kind, within our recollection" (W1: 35).

59. Burke, *A Philosophical Enquiry*, 270.

60. William Shenstone, [Inscription] "XVI. On a Statue of Venus de Medicis," *The Poetical Works* (Edinburgh: James Nichol, 1854), 282. On Shenstone, see also James G. Turner, "The Sexual Politics of Landscape: Images of Venus in Eighteenth-Century English Poetry and Landscape Gardening," 343–66. See also Carole Fabricant, "Binding and Dressing Nature's Loose Tresses: The Ideology of Augustan Landscape Design," 109–35. Fabricant cites Alexander Pope's epistle to Burlington as an example of this trope: "But treat the Goddess like a modest fair,/ Nor over dress, nor leave her wholly bare;/ Let not each beauty ev'ry where be spy'd,/ Where half the skill is decently to hide." Pope, "Epistle IV: To Richard Boyle, Earl of Burlington" (1731), *Epistles to Several Persons (Moral Essays)*, ed. F. W. Bateson (New Haven: Yale University Press, 1951), 142.

61. The role of female figure in the eighteenth-century *aisling* was more passive than before: "She must await the moment of liberation, allowing her body to become a site of contest between true and false lords, but taking no positive action herself." Declan Kiberd, *Irish Classics* (London: Granta, 2000), 184. Kiberd is in this instance writing on Brian Merriman's *Cúirt an Mheán Oíche (The Midnight Court)*, a ribald antidote to the pieties of the mainstream eighteenth-century *aisling*.

62. Pittock, *Poetry and Jacobite Politics in Eighteenth-Century Britain and Ireland* (Cambridge: Cambridge University Press, 1994), 200.

Chapter 4. Geographies of Ruin: Ireland, America and Auburn's Absentees

1. Goldsmith, *A Survey of Experimental Philosophy, Considered in Its Present State of Improvement*, 1: 246–47.

2. George Cheyne, *The Natural Method of Cureing the Diseases of the Body, and the Disorders of Mind Depending on the Body* (London: Printed for G. Strahan, John and Paul Knapton, 1742), 58.

3. Roy Porter, *Flesh in the Age of Reason* (London: Penguin, 2004), 235–36.

4. *The Gentleman's Magazine* 11 (1770), 272. Hawkesworth probably wrote the review of the poem for *The Monthly Review* also.

5. Marshall Brown, *Preromanticism* (Stanford: Stanford University Press, 1991), 128.

6. Instances of attempts to locate Auburn in England include that of Mavis Batey, who argues that Auburn is Nuneham Courtenay in Oxfordshire. In 1760 and 1761, Lord Harcourt cleared that village to build his pleasure-grounds. Harcourt had inherited lands and a fortune from Lord Chancellor Harcourt, his grandfather; he had added to this with returns on his own investment in the

East India Company. Batey, "Oliver Goldsmith: An Indictment of Landscape Gardening," in *Furor Hortensis: Essays on the History of the Landscape Garden in Memory of H.F. Clark*, ed. Peter Willis (Edinburgh: Elysium Press, 1974), 57–71. In her biography of Lancelot "Capability" Brown, who designed Harcourt's pleasure garden, Jane Brown suggests that the displacement at Nuneham Courtenay merely prompted Goldsmith's thoughts on Irish villages which had been "plantationed." See Brown, *The Omnipotent Magician*, 312. Other attempts include K. J. Fielding's proposition, which follows a local tradition in the pages of the Norfolk and Norwich Archaeological Society journal in 1877, that Goldsmith was referring to Houghton Hall, the Norfolk palace of Robert Walpole, who is said to have encouraged trade at the expense of agriculture. Fielding himself also suggests, however, that *The Deserted Village* comes too late for it to refer to Walpole. See Fielding, "*The Deserted Village* and Sir Robert Walpole," *English* 12 (1959), 130–2. Edmund Durrant suggested that Auburn might be Springfield, Essex, where, it is alleged, Goldsmith actually composed the poem. See Durrant, "The Deserted Village," *Notes and Queries,* 5th ser., 11 (1878), 88. Another less creditable attempt to find Auburn is George Winchcombe's equation of the poetic village with Aldbourne and nearby Draycot Foliot in Wiltshire, an equation based on the wrongful attribution to Goldsmith of an essay entitled "A Geographical Description of Wiltshire," published in the *Universal Magazine* in 1762. See *Oliver Goldsmith and the Moonrakers* (London: Thab, 1972), 28–32.

7. Joseph Cooper Walker to Charles O'Conor, >July 8, 1786, Huntington Library, Stowe MS 1366.
8. Joseph Cooper Walker to Charles O'Conor, >Nov, 1787, Huntington Library, Stowe MS 1379.
9. Edward Mangin, *An Essay on Light Reading, as it may be Supposed to Influence Moral Conduct and Literary Taste* (London: Printed for James Carpenter, 1808), 140–41.
10. R. H. Newell, "Remarks, Attempting to Ascertain, Chiefly from Local Observation, the Actual Scene of The Deserted Village," in Oliver Goldsmith, *The Poetical Works* (London: Printed for Suttaby, Evance and Company, 1811), 72, 66.
11. Prior, *Life*, 2: 261.
12. William Cooke, "Table Talk": 171–2.
13. Anonymous review of "*The Deserted Village. A Poem. By Dr*. Oliver Goldsmith," *The Town and Country Magazine; or, Universal Repository of Knowledge, Instruction, and Entertainment*, 2 (1770), 168.
14. Anonymous review of "*The Deserted Village. A Poem. By Dr*. Oliver Goldsmith," *The Critical Review*, 29 (1770), 436–42.
15. Thomas Babington Macaulay, "Life of Goldsmith," in Walter Scott, Thomas Babington Macaulay, and William Makepeace Thackeray, *Essays on Goldsmith*, 30.
16. David Fairer, *English Poetry of the Eighteenth Century 1700–1789* (London: Longman, 2003), 200. On the reception of Goldsmith's poem in English and American contexts more generally, see Alfred Lutz, "The Politics of Reception: The Case of Goldsmith's 'The Deserted Village,'" *Studies in Philology* 95 (1998), 174–96. Lutz gives an insightful and comprehensive survey of critical and poetic responses to the poem, positive and negative, which either amplified, or failed to recognize—as did George Crabbe's famous anti-pastoral *The Village* (1783)—the political charge of Goldsmith's original.

NOTES

17. Anthony King, *The Frequented Village. A Poem, By a Gentleman of the Middle Temple* (London: Printed for J. Godwin, 1771), 26. King was himself a liberal Irish lawyer, intermittently resident in London in the late 1760s and early 1770s. Thirteen years later the poem was revised for a Dublin readership as *The Frequented Village; A Poem, Inscribed to the Late Dr Oliver Goldsmith. A New Edition, Improved with Additions* (Dublin: Reprinted by R. Marchbank, 1784).

18. Crawford, *Poetry, Enclosure, and the Vernacular Landscape, 1700–1830*, 43.

19. Fredric Jameson, "The Politics of Utopia," *New Left Review* 25 (2004), 38.

20. Jameson, *The Political Unconscious: Narrative as a Socially Symbolic Act* (London: Routledge, 1981), 27.

21. Raymond Williams, "Nature's Threads," *Eighteenth-Century Studies* 2 (1968), 53.

22. Said, *Culture and Imperialism* (London: Chatto and Windus, 1993), 14.

23. Deane, "Oliver Goldsmith: Miscellaneous Writings 1759-74," *The Field Day Anthology of Irish Writing*, 1: 660.

24. Philip Skelton, *The Necessity of Tillage and Granaries. In a Letter to a Member of Parliament Living in the County of ____* (Dublin: [s.n.], 1741), 59.

25. Evidence of recourse "to collecting the classic foods of famine," which David Dickson lists as "docks, cresses, nettles, seaweed, and the blood drawn from live cattle." "The Other Great Irish Famine," *The Great Irish Famine*, ed. Cathal Póirtéir (Cork: Mercier Press, 1995), 54–5. See also idem, *Arctic Ireland: The Extraordinary Story of the Great Frost and Forgotten Famine of 1740–41* (Belfast: White Row Press, 1997); and Michael Drake, "The Irish Demographic Crisis of 1740–41," in *Historical Studies VI*, ed. T. W. Moody (London: Routledge & Kegan Paul, 1968), 101–24.

26. Terry Eagleton, *Crazy John and the Bishop, and Other Essays on Irish Culture* (Cork: Cork University Press, 1998), 115.

27. Kevin Whelan, *The Tree of Liberty: Radicalism, Catholicism and the Construction of Irish Identity 1760–1830* (Cork: Cork University Press, 1996), 4.

28. The immediate occasion is well known: unfinished by the time of Goldsmith's death on April 4, 1774, *Retaliation* was begun in January of that year, instigated by epigrammatic sparring with the actor David Garrick at St James' Coffee House. See Roger Lonsdale's headnote, *The Poems*, 741–745n. See also Richard J. Dircks, "The Genesis and Date of Goldsmith's *Retaliation*," *Modern Philology* 75 (1977), 48–53.

29. Thomas Prior, *A List of the Absentees of Ireland, and the Yearly Value of Their Estates and Incomes Spent Abroad. With Observations on the Present Trade and Condition of That Kingdom*, 2nd edn (Dublin: Printed for R. Gunne, 1729), 33. The List is "one of the most important pamphlets of the period. To write and publish it was a courageous step, for it pilloried his own class and many of his intimate friends." Desmond Clarke, *Thomas Prior, 1681–1751: Founder of the Royal Dublin Society* (Dublin: R.D.S., 1951), 16.

30. Swift, "Maxims Controlled in Ireland: The Truth of Some Maxims in State and Government, examined with reference to Ireland" (1762), *Swift's Irish Pamphlets: An Introductory Selection*, 136–8.

31. Swift, "Sermon: Causes of the Wretched Condition of Ireland," *Swift's Irish Pamphlets*, 154.

NOTES

32. Andrew Carpenter, "Introduction," in *Verse in English in Eighteenth-Century Ireland*, ed. Andrew Carpenter (Cork: Cork University Press, 1998), 25.

33. James Prior, *Life of Goldsmith*, 1: 40.

34. Laurence Whyte, "The Parting Cup, or, The Humours of *Deoch an Doruis*, alias *Theodorus*, alias Doctor *Dorus*, an old *Irish* Gentleman famous (about 30 Years ago) for his great Hospitality, but more particularly in *Christmas* Time," *Poems on Various Subjects* (Dublin: Printed for L. Dowling, T. Brown, and Ed. Hamillton, Mr. J. Hoey and Oli. Nelson, G. Falkiner; and by the author, 1740), 92, 97–9.

35. Declan Budd and Ross Hinds, *The Hist and Edmund Burke's Club: An Anthology of the College Historical Society, the Student Debating Society of Trinity College Dublin, from Its Origins in Edmund Burke's Club 1747–1997* (Dublin: Lilliput Press, 1997), 165.

36. Edmund Burke, *The Reformer* [No. 4], *The Writings and Speeches, Volume 1: The Early Writings*, 84.

37. For an influential and scholarly account of these precedents, see John Sekora, *Luxury: The Concept in Western Thought, Eden to Smollett* (Baltimore: The Johns Hopkins University Press, 1977), pp. 23–62. The second half of Sekora's study deals with Tobias Smollett's critique of luxury. However, the broader eighteenth-century debate on luxury is excellently documented: see 63–131.

38. *The Reformer* [No. 4], 87.

39. On the concept of "Cosmic Toryism," see Basil Willey, *The Eighteenth-Century Background: Studies on the Idea of Nature in the Thought of the Period* (Harmondsworth: Penguin, 1940), 47–59.

40. "Can it be by Goldsmith? When in Trinity he made a little money by occasionally resorting to ballad writing, and found a market for his productions. He may have responded to the invitation of the *Reformer*. There seems to be notes in the poem which are heard in the *Traveller* and *Deserted Village*, and the dedication of the *Traveller* to his brother Henry shows that 'the several conditions of life' were with him a considered theme." Arthur P. I. Samuels, *The Early Life, Correspondence and Writings of the Rt. Hon. Edmund Burke* LL.D. (Cambridge: Cambridge University Press, 1923), 170.

41. McCormack testily attributes this "neo-romanticism" of Irish readings of Goldsmith to "outriders of Field Day" such as Luke Gibbons. McCormack, "Oliver Goldsmith's *Deserted Village* (1770) and Retrospective Localism," in *Longford: History and Society. Interdisciplinary Essays on the History of an Irish County*, ed. Martin Morris and Fergus O'Ferrall (Dublin: Geography Publications, 2010), 270. For McCormack's critique of my work on Goldsmith, see 276–7.

42. The trope of the peasants' "content" also has its own tradition in Westmeath: in Laurence Whyte's poem, the absentees refuse to live at home "with any pleasure or content"; similarly, Samuel Whyte's later "Impromptu, written on the back of a trencher in the cottage at the crooked Wood, County Westmeath, August, 1773" celebrates content over luxury: "Let wealth regale itself on costly plate,/ cares will intrude and happiness prevent;/ but peasants, who off humble trenchers eat,/ with rosy health enjoy supreme content." In *A Georgian Celebration; Irish Poets of the Eighteenth Century*, ed. Patrick Fagan (Dublin: Branar, 1989), 145.

43. *The Reformer* [No. 7], 96.

44. Burke, *Reflections*, 192, 197.

45. Brown, *An Estimate of the Manners and Principles of the Times*, 2nd edn (London: Printed for L. Davis, and C. Reymers, 1757), 58–9.

46. John Brown, *Thoughts on Civil Liberty, on Licentiousness and Faction* (Dublin: Printed for A. Leathley, J. Exshaw, W. Watson, and S. Watson, 1765), 24.

47. Quoted in Michael J. O'Brien, *A Hidden Phase of American History: Ireland's Part in America's Struggle for Liberty* (New York: Dodd, Mead & Company, 1919), 366–7.

48. Kerby A. Miller, Arnold Schrier, Bruce D. Boling, David N. Doyle, *Irish Immigrants in the Land of Canaan: Letters and Memoirs from Colonial and Revolutionary America, 1675–1815* (Oxford: Oxford University Press, 2003), 85–6.

49. James Edward Oglethorpe (1696–1785) was a friend to Goldsmith between 1770 and the author's death. He offered him the use of his estate at Cranham Hall as a refuge in which to complete his natural history. Commended by Alexander Pope for his "strong benevolence of soul," Oglethorpe was the son of Sir Theophilus Oglethorpe and Eleanor Wall, described variously by Oglethorpe's foremost biographer as "a famous Irish beauty," and a "winsome Irish colleen," and by her friend, the rather less nebulous Jonathan Swift, as "so cunning a devil." Amos Aschbach Ettinger, *Oglethorpe: A Brief Biography* (Macon, Georgia, 1984); *James Edward Oglethorpe: Imperial Idealist* ([n. pl.]: Archon Books, 1968), 17; Jonathan Swift, *Journal to Stella*, ed. Harold Williams, 2 vols. (Oxford: The Clarendon Press, 1948), 437. A staunchly Royalist Tipperary woman, Eleanor (nee Wall) had been laundress to Charles II; her family had lost its estate after the revolution. A confidante of James II, Eleanor Wall's support for the House of Stuart would be constant right up to her death in 1732. Eleanor placed her son James Edward under the pronounced Jacobite influence of Bishop Thomas Turner at Corpus Christi College, Oxford. See also Eveline Cruickshanks, *The Oglethorpes: a Jacobite Family 1689–1760* (London: Royal Stuart Society, 1995).

50. See Alex Pitofsky, "The Warden's Court Martial: James Oglethorpe and the Politics of Eighteenth-Century Prison Reform," *Eighteenth-Century Life* 24 (2000), 88–102.

51. This scheme fell foul of English commercial opposition, exacerbating Scottish suspicions of the Williamite dispensation. See *An Enquiry into the Causes of the Miscarriage of the Scots Colony at Darien* (Glasgow: [s.n.], 1700), variously attributed to James Hodges, Walter Harris, Archibald Foyer, or George Ridpath: "if the ill usage that we meet with from the Court of *England* should force us again into a *French* or other Alliance, the World cannot blame us; since the Laws of nature and Nations are for us [. . .] If the State of Affairs in *Ireland* be consider'd, it will appear to be such, as may make it dangerous to suffer the *Scots* to be oppress'd and provok'd in this manner. It is well enough known that the People of Ireland are not very well pleas'd with their treatment by some in *England*," 45, 46. Eamonn O'Ciardha attributes the pamphlet to Andrew Bell. Its publication by Patrick Campbell in the north of Ireland O'Ciardha adduces as evidence that "The popular press occasionally catered for [an active Irish] Protestant Jacobite group." *Ireland and the Jacobite Cause*, 164.

52. "Buffon stressed the differences between quadrupeds in the Americas and in the Old World and concluded that like physical conditions had not produced or favoured like forms everywhere; he suggested that external circumstances had caused the differences in the species that lived in them." James Larson, "Not without a Plan: Geography and Natural History in the Late Eighteenth Century," *Journal of the History of Biology* 19 (1986), 451.

53. See John Robert Moore, "Goldsmith's Degenerate Song-Birds: An Eighteenth-Century Fallacy in Ornithology," *Isis: An International Review Devoted to the History of Science and Civilization* 34 (1943), 324–27.

54. Laura Brown, *Fables of Modernity: Literature and Culture in the English Eighteenth Century* (Ithaca: Cornell University Press, 2001), 224.

55. The Irish were, according to *The Intelligencer*, No. 19, "as a Screen between his Majesty's English Subjects and the Savage Indians." Cited in Claude Rawson, *God, Gulliver and Genocide: Barbarism and the European Imagination 1492–1945* (Oxford: Oxford University Press, 2001), 81.

56. Laurence Goldstein, *Ruins and Empire*, 104.

57. [William and Edmund Burke], *An Account of the European Settlements in America*, 2 vols. (London: Printed for R. and J. Dodsley, 1757), 1: preface.

58. F. P. Lock, *Edmund Burke, Volume 1, 1730–1784* (Oxford: The Clarendon Press, 1998), 130. On the general circumstances of the production of *An Account*, see Lock, 125–41.

59. See Goldsmith, *The Present State of the British Empire in Europe, America, Africa and Asia* (London: Printed for W. Griffin, J. Johnson, W. Nicoll, and Richardson and Urquhart, 1768), 255–391. See also R. W. Seitz, "Goldsmith and the *Present State of the British Empire*," *Modern Language Notes* 45 (1930), 434–8.

60. Thomson, "Liberty," 144.

61. See John Logan, "Robert Clive's Irish Peerage and Estate, 1761–1842," *North Munster Antiquarian Journal* 43 (2003), 1–19.

62. Austin Dobson, "A Paladin of Philanthropy," *A Paladin of Philanthropy and Other Papers* (London: Chatto and Windus, 1899), 13.

63. Philip Freneau, *The Poems*, ed. Fred Lewis Pattee, 3 vols. (New York, 1963), 382; see also William L. Andrews, "Goldsmith and Freneau in 'The American Village,'" *Early American Literature* 5 (1970): 14–23.

64. Raynal, *A Philosophical and Political History of the Settlements and Trade of the Europeans in the East and West Indies*, 5: 298.

65. [William and Edmund Burke], *An Account of the European Settlements in America*, 2: 258–64.

66. James Edward Oglethorpe, "The Adams Letters: From the MORNING CHRONICLE. To the KING. Letter I," *The Publications*, ed. Rodney M. Baine (Athens: University of Georgia Press, 1994), 313–4.

67. John Cowper, *An Essay, Proving, that Inclosing Commons, and Common-field-Lands, Is Contrary to the Interest of the Nation* (London: Printed for E. Nutt, J. Roberts, and A. Dodd, 1732), 2, 4, 23.

68. Goldsmith, Preface to *The History of Little Goody Two-Shoes*, *The Works*, ed. J. W. M. Gibbs, 5 vols. (London: G. Bell, 1884), 5: 355–56. Though it was almost certainly written by his one-time publisher John Newbery, *Goody Two-Shoes* (1765) was itself often attributed to Goldsmith. Arthur Friedman, Goldsmith's most comprehensive editor to date, does not include the story in the oeuvre. And in the most recent book-length study of Goldsmith's professional writing, Richard Taylor's *Goldsmith as Journalist* (1993), it is only mentioned as a children's book which John Newbery, Goldsmith's bookseller from 1760, introduced. See Taylor, 90. However, the edition

which Taylor calls "probably the most valuable of the collected editions before Friedman's," gives a different account of *Goody Two-Shoes*. J. W. M. Gibbs includes the story in Goldsmith's oeuvre, he explains, "in deference to the popular supposition that it was written by him. There are good grounds, it will be seen, for supposing that the Introduction and some passages, if no more, are by Goldsmith" ('Preface'). Gibbs is probably right in this supposition: the introduction certainly prefigures the politics of *The Deserted Village*. Gibbs guesses that the story itself was written by either Goldsmith, Giles Jones (brother of Griffith Jones, editor of the *Public Ledger*), or by Newbery himself. For Gibbs, the introduction suggests a disassociation of editor and author: "Do you intend this for children Mr. Newbery? Why, do you suppose this is written by Mr. Newbery, Sir? This may come from another hand" (5: 355). The Newbery story, if his it is, has been given an unmistakably Goldsmithian gloss by an introduction in which the themes of the story are brought into the adult political realm.

69. Boswell, *Life of Johnson*, 4: 170–171. Oglethorpe, notably, was court–martialed in 1746, charged with treasonable negligence for deliberately letting the Jacobites get away as the '45 petered northward to Culloden. In 1751, Horace Walpole wrote: "It was uncertain whether he was a Whig or a Jacobite, whether very brave or a coward, for he had [. . .] ran away in the rebellion." Walpole added insult to insinuation: "very certain that he was a troublesome and tiresome speaker." *Memoirs of King George II*, ed. John Brooke, 3 vols. (New Haven: Yale University Press, 1985), 1: 76.

70. Oglethorpe, "The Adams Letters," 318.

71. Austin Dobson writes of Edward Ford's "conjectural identification of Sir Wiliam Thornhill with the equally eccentric Sir George Savile" in his "Preface" to *The Vicar of Wakefield. Being a Facsimile Reproduction of the First Edition of the First Edition Published in 1766. With an Introduction by Austin Dobson, and a Bibliographical List of Editions of "The Vicar of Wakefield" Published in England and Abroad*, 2 vols. (London: Elliot Stock, 1885), xvii. Ford writes: "Sir Geo. Savile was the grandson of John Savile, rector of Thornhill, and succeeded to the baronetcy and large estates of the family, including that of Thornhill, the ancient residence of the Saviles, a parish situated about six miles from Wakefield, where Goldsmith was staying, and where he fixed his "field of action." In an old map of Yorkshire (by E. Bowen, 1750) the name is given in a marginal list of the chief landed proprietors, as "Savile of Thornhill," the property and title having devolved upon him in 1743, when he was about sixteen years old." Ford draws a parallel between the description of William Thornhill as someone whose benevolence is his undoing, with Burke's remarks that Savile's "fortune is one of the largest, which (wholly unencumbered as it is with one single charge from luxury, vanity, or excess) yet sinks under the benevolence of its dispenser." Ford, "Names and Characters in the 'Vicar of Wakefield,'" *The National Review*, no. 3 (May, 1883), 393.

72. Horace Walpole, *Journal of the Reign of King George the Third, from the Year 1771 to 1783*, ed. Dr Doran, 2 vols. (London: Richard Bentley, 1859), 1: 265.

73. Conor Cruise O'Brien, *The Great Melody: A Thematic Biography and Commented Anthology of Edmund Burke* (London: Sinclair–Stevenson, 1992), 70. The historiographical object of O'Brien's vexation is the work of Sir Lewis Namier, in particular *The Structure of Politics at the Accession of George III* (1929); and *England in the Age of the American Revolution* (1930).

74. Thomas H. D. Mahoney, *Edmund Burke and Ireland* (Cambridge: Harvard University Press, 1960), 58.
75. Edmund Burke, *The Correspondence*, ed. Thomas W. Copeland and Lucy S. Sutherland et al., 10 vols. (Cambridge: Cambridge University Press, 1960), 2: 468, 474, 476, 477–8.
76. Cited in George Thomas, Earl of Albemarle, *Memoirs of the Marquis of Rockingham and His Contemporaries. With Original Letters and Documents Now First Published*, 2 vols. (London: Samuel Bentley, 1852), 2: 232–3.
77. *Public Advertiser*, Monday, December 13, 1773, number 12058.
78. *Public Advertiser*, Wednesday, December 15, 1773, number 12060.
79. Walpole, 1: 265–266. Walpole claims that he was told of this request by the Duke of Richmond.
80. Cited in Lord Edmond Fitzmaurice, *Life of William, Earl of Shelburne, afterwards First Marquess of Lansdowne. With Extracts from His Papers and Correspondence*, 3 vols. (London: Macmillan, 1875), 2: 283–4. Such sentiments have been adduced as evidence of Shelburne's principled stance on the absentee tax issue. See Martyn J. Powell, "Shelburne and Ireland: Politician, Patriot, Absentee," in *An Enlightenment Statesman in Whig Britain: Lord Shelburne in Context, 1737–1805*, ed. Nigel Aston and Clarissa Campbell Orr (Woodbridge: The Boydell Press, 2011), 147.
81. Sheffield Archives, WWM R3/27. Goldsmith may have come to know Shelburne through Lauchlan Macleane, a mutual friend of Burke and Goldsmith's at Trinity, who became Shelburne's secretary. See Prior, 1: 149–152. When sitting beside Shelburne at Drury Lane in 1772 Goldsmith explained that he never "could conceive the reason why they call you Malagrida, *for* Malagrida was a very good sort of man?" Cited in Lord Edmond Fitzmaurice, *Life of William, Earl of Shelburne*, 2:290. Goldsmith was, as often, misunderstood: he meant that he wondered why the nickname "Malagrida" was for Shelburne's enemies a term of reproach. A reference to a Portuguese Jesuit, the nickname imputed opportunism and insincerity.
82. Mahoney, 51. See also *idem*, "Mr Burke's Imperial Mentality and the Proposed Irish Absentee Tax of 1773," *Canadian Historical Review* 37 (1956), 158–66. Burke "never willingly conceded colonial independence. To that extent, his opposition to the absentee tax can be seen as an example of his concern for the imperial system." F. P. Lock, *Edmund Burke, Volume 1, 1730–1784*, 1: 347.
83. Seamus Deane, *Celtic Revivals: Essays in Modern Irish Literature 1880–1980* (London: Faber, 1985), 23.
84. Thomas Campbell, *A Philosophical Survey of the South of Ireland, in a Series of Letters to John Watkinson, M. D.* (London: Printed for W. Strahan; and T. Cadell, 1777), 345.
85. Luke Gibbons, *Edmund Burke and Ireland: Aesthetics, Politics, and the Colonial Sublime*, xi. The paradoxical discrepancy between his earlier and later opinions is explained by Thomas McLoughlin as a symptom of the "rhetorically awkward if not ambivalent space he occupied as an Irishman in the House of Commons." McLoughlin, *Contesting Ireland: Irish Voices against England in the Eighteenth Century* (Dublin: Four Courts, 1999), 170.
86. *The Northern Star*, Number 36, from Wednesday, May 2 to Saturday, May 5, 1792.
87. Anonymous, "Irish Absentees, &c.," *Anthologia Hibernica* 2 (1793): 218–19.

NOTES

Ill Fares the Land: Conclusion

1. Tony Judt, *Ill Fares the Land: A Treatise on our Present Discontents* (London: Penguin, 2010), 1, 4, 5, 6, 28, 73.

2. Eddie Molloy, "Our national wealth far outweighs fool's gold," *The Irish Times*, Saturday, March 5, 2011.

3. Johnson, "The Bravery of the English Common Soldiers," *The Yale Edition of the Works of Samuel Johnson X: Political Writings*, ed. Donald J. Greene (New Haven: Yale University Press, 1977), 283.

4. This conversation is reconstructed from Boswell's papers in Wardle, *Oliver Goldsmith*, 256.

5. Paine, *Common Sense* (1776; Harmondsworth: Penguin, 1982), 68.

6. O'Brien, "Introduction," in Edmund Burke, *Reflections*, 38.

7. Montague, "The Sentimental Prophecy: A Study of *The Deserted Village*, in *The Art of Oliver Goldsmith*, ed. Andrew Swarbrick, 91.

8. "The Ireland which we dreamed of" is the title commonly given to the St. Patrick's Day speech given by Taoiseach Eamon de Valera on March 17, 1943. It is given in *The Field Day Anthology* (3: 747–50) as "The Undeserted Village Ireland."

BIBLIOGRAPHY

Primary Sources

Goldsmith, Oliver. *An History of the Earth, and Animated Nature*. London: Printed for John Nourse, 1774.

———. *An History of England, in a Series of Letters from a Nobleman to His Son*, 2 vols. London: Printed for J. Newbery, 1764.

———. *A Prospect of Society*, edited by Bertram Dobell. London: by the editor, 1902.

———. *A Prospect of Society*, edited by William B. Todd. Cambridge: The Water Lane Press, 1954.

———. *A Survey of Experimental Philosophy, Considered in Its Present State of Improvement*, 2 vols. London: Printed for T. Carnan and F. Newbery jun., 1776.

———. [Letter to John Bindley], in Katherine Balderston, "New Goldsmith Letters." *The Yale University Library Gazette* 39 (1964), 71–2.

———. [Letter to Sir William Chambers], in R. W. Seitz, "Goldsmith to Sir William Chambers" (1773), *Times Literary Supplement*, no. 1808 (Sept. 1936), 772.

———. *New Essays*, edited by Ronald S. Crane (Chicago: University of Chicago Press, 1927).

——— [?Anonymous]. "Reflections on National Prejudices. In Response to a Chauvinist Englishman Looking for Verification." *The British Magazine, or Monthly Repository for Gentlemen and Ladies*, 1 (1760), 460–2.

——— [?Anonymous]. Review of "*Miscellaneous Tracts Relating to Natural History, Husbandry, and Physick.*" *The Critical Review* 7 (1759), 225–41.

———. *The Collected Letters*, edited by Katherine C. Balderston. Cambridge: Cambridge University Press, 1928.

———. *The Collected Works*, edited by Arthur Friedman, 5 vols. Oxford: The Clarendon Press, 1966.

———. *The Grecian History, from the Earliest State to the Death of Alexander the Great*, 2 vols. London: Printed for J. and F. Rivington, T. Longman, G. Kearsley, W. Griffin, G. Robinson, R. Baldwin, W. Goldsmith, T. Cadell, and T. Evans, 1774.

———. *The History of England, from the Earliest Times to the Death of George II*, 4 vols. London: Printed for T. Davies; Becket and De Hondt; and T. Cadell, 1771.

———. *The Poetical Works*. London: Printed for Suttaby, Evance and Company, 1811.

———. *The Poetical Works*. London: Aldine, 1835.

———. *The Present State of the British Empire in Europe, America, Africa, and Asia*. London: Printed for W. Griffin, J. Johnson, W. Nicoll, and Richardson and Urquhart, 1768.

BIBLIOGRAPHY

———. *The Roman History, from the Foundation of the City of Rome, to the Destruction of the Western Empire*, 2 vols. London: Printed for S. Baker and G. Leigh; T. Davies; and L. Davis, 1769.

———. *The Vicar of Wakefield, with thirty-two illustrations, by William Mulready, R. A.* London: John Van Voorst, 1843.

———. *The Vicar of Wakefield. Being a Facsimile Reproduction of the First Edition of the First Edition Published I 1766. With an Introduction by Austin Dobson, and a Bibliographical List of Editions of "The Vicar of Wakefield" Published in England and Abroad*, 2 vols. London: Elliot Stock, 1885.

———. *The Vicar of Wakefield. Prefatory Memoir by George Saintsbury and One Hundred and Fourteen Coloured Illustrations by VA Poirson*. London: J. C. Nimmo, 1886.

———. *The Vicar of Wakefield, illustrated by Arthur Rackham*. London: Harrap, 1929.

———. *The Works*, edited by J. W. M. Gibbs, 5 vols. London: G. Bell, 1884.

Manuscripts

"Memoirs of the Life and Writings of the late Ch Oconor of Belanagare Esqr. M.R.I.A., to which is prefixed a short Historical Account of the Family of O'Conor From the Invasion of Henry 2. Compiled Principally from Notes and Extracts taken by Himself From Ancient Writers on Irish History And other Sources hitherto unexplored or not generally known." Gilbert Collection MS 203, Dublin City Library, Pearse Street, Dublin.

William Chambers to Edmund Burke, May 5, 1782, Rockingham MS Bk 2/543, 1/802.

Joseph Hickey to Rockingham, November 7, 1773, Sheffield Archives, WWM R3/27.

Joseph Cooper Walker to Charles O'Conor, >July 8, 1786, Huntington Library, Stowe MS 1366.

Joseph Cooper Walker to Charles O'Conor >Nov. 1787, Huntington Library, Stowe MS 1379.

Secondary Sources (a), pre-1800

Addison, Joseph. *The Miscellaneous Works*, edited by A. C. Guthkelch, 2 vols. London: G. Bell, 1914.

Addison, Joseph, and Richard Steele. *The Spectator*, edited by Donald F. Bond, 5 vols. Oxford: Oxford University Press, 1965.

Anonymous [Prior, Thomas]. *A List of the Absentees of Ireland, and the Yearly Value of Their Estates and Incomes Spent Abroad. With Observations on the Present Trade and Condition of That Kingdom*, 2nd edn. Dublin: Printed for R. Gunne, 1729.

——— [variously attributed to James Hodges, Walter Harris, Archibald Foyer, or George Ridpath]. *An Enquiry into the Causes of the Miscarriage of the Scots Colony at Darien*. Glasgow: [s.n.], 1700.

———. *An Irregular Dissertation, Occasioned by the Reading of Father Du Halde's Description of China. Which May Be Read at Any Time, Except in the Present Year 1740*. London: Printed for J. Roberts, 1740.

———. *A Table of all the Accurate Remarks and Surprising Dicoveries of the Most Learned and Ingenious Mr ADDISON, in His Book of Travels thro' Several Parts of Italy, &c.* London: Printed for the Company of Long-Bow-String-Makers, 1706.

BIBLIOGRAPHY

———. "Historical Chronicle." *The Gentleman's Magazine* 8 (1738), 161–8.

———. "Historical Chronicle." *The Gentleman's Magazine* 8 (1738), 321–8.

———. "Historical Chronicle." *The Gentleman's Magazine* 41 (1771), 329–34 .

———. "Historical Chronicle." *The Gentleman's Magazine* 43 (1773), 457–69.

———. "Irish Absentees, &c." *Anthologia Hibernica* 2 (1793): 218–9.

———. *Public Advertiser*, Monday, December 13, 1773, number 12058.

———. *Public Advertiser*, Wednesday, December 15, 1773, number 12060.

——— [John Hawkesworth?]. Review of "*The Deserted Village. A Poem. By Dr. Goldsmith*." *The Gentleman's Magazine* 15 (1770), 271–3.

———. [Review of] "*The Deserted Village. A Poem. By Dr. Goldsmith*." *The Monthly Review; or, Literary Journal* 42 (1770), 440–5.

——— [Oliver Goldsmith?]. "Reflections on National Prejudices. In Response to a Chauvinist Englishman Looking for Verification." *The British Magazine, or Monthly Repository for Gentlemen and Ladies* 1 (1760), 460–2.

——— [Oliver Goldsmith?]. Review of "*Miscellaneous Tracts Relating to Natural History, Husbandry, and Physick*." *The Critical Review* 7 (1759), 225–41.

———. [Review of] "*The Deserted Village. A Poem. By Dr.* Oliver Goldsmith." *The Critical Review* 29 (1770), 435–42.

———, [Review of] "*The Deserted Village. A Poem. By Dr.* Oliver Goldsmith." *The Town and Country Magazine; or, Universal Repository of Knowledge, Instruction, and Entertainment* 2 (1770), 268.

———. *Speculations on the State of Ireland: Shewing the Fatal Causes of Her Misery, the Evil Influence under Which She Languishes, and the Power thereof to Reduce Her to the Last Extreme of Human Wretchedness and Woe*. Dublin: Printed for the Author, 1793.

Arbuthnot, John. *An Essay Concerning the Effects of Air on Human Bodies*. London: Printed for J. Tonson, 1733.

Baretti, Joseph. *An Account of the Manners and Customs of Italy; with Observations on the Mistakes of Some Travellers, with Regard to That Country*, 2 vols. London: Printed for T. Davies, L. David, and C. Rymers, 1768.

Beeckman, Daniel. *A Voyage to and from the Island of Borneo in the East-Indies*. London: Printed for T. Warner and J. Batley, 1718.

Blackmore, Richard. *The Nature of Man. A Poem. In Three Books*. London: Printed for Sam. Buckley, 1711.

Blair, Hugh. *A Critical Dissertation on the Poems of Ossian, the Son of Fingal*. London: Printed for T. Becket and P. A. De Hondt, 1763.

Blair, John. *The History of the Rise and Progress of Geography*. London: Printed for T. Cadell and W. Gingerin, 1784.

Blumenbach, Johann Friedrich. *The Anthropological Treatises*. Translated by Thomas Bendyshe. London: Longman, 1865.

Boswell, James. *Life of* Johnson, edited by G. B. Hill and L. F. Powell, 6 vols. 1791; Oxford: The Clarendon Press, 1934–50.

———, *London Journal 1762–63*, edited by F. A. Pottle. Edinburgh: Edinburgh University Press, 1991.

Brisson, Mathurin Jacques. *Ornithologia*. 6 toms. Paris, 1760.

Brookes, Richard. *The General Gazetteer: or, Compendious Geographical Dictionary*. London: Printed for J. Newbery, 1762.

———. *A New and Accurate System of Natural History*. London: Printed for J. Newbery, 1763.

Brown, John. *A Dissertation on the Rise, Union, and Power, the Progressions, Separations, and Corruptions, of Poetry and Music*. London: Printed for L. Davis and C. Reymers, 1763.

———. *Estimate of the Manners and Principles of the Times*, 2nd edn. London: Printed for L. Davis, and C. Reymers, 1757.

———. *Thoughts on Civil Liberty. On Licentiousness, and Faction*. Dublin: Printed for A. Leathley, J. Exshaw, W. Watson, and S. Watson, 1765.

Buffon, Georges-Louis LeClerc, Comte De, *Histoire Naturelle*, 15 toms. Paris, 1749.

Burke, Edmund. *The Writings and Speeches, Volume 1: The Early Writings*, edited by T. O. McLoughlin and James T. Boulton. Oxford: The Clarendon Press, 1997.

———. *Reflections on the Revolution in France, and on the Proceedings in Certain Societies in London Relative to That Event*, edited by Conor Cruise O'Brien. 1790; Harmondsworth: Penguin, 1969.

———. *The Correspondence*, edited by Thomas W. Copeland and Lucy S. Sutherland et al., 10 vols. Cambridge: Cambridge University Press, 1960.

Burke, William [and Edmund]. *An Account of the European Settlements in America*, 2 vols. London: Printed for R. and J. Dodsley, 1757.

Campbell, Thomas. *A Philosophical Survey of the South of Ireland, in a Series of Letters to John Watkinson, M. D.* London: Printed for W. Strahan; and T. Cadell, 1777.

Chambers, William. *A Dissertation on Oriental Gardening*. London: Printed for W. Griffin, T. Davies, J. Dodsley; Wilson and Nicoll; J. Walter, and P. Elmsley, 1772.

———. *Designs of Chinese Buildings, Furniture, Dresses, Machines, and Utensils*. London: [s.n.], 1757.

Cheyne, George. *The Natural Method of Cureing the Diseases of the Body, and the Disorders of Mind Depending on the Body*. London: Printed for G. Strahan, John and Paul Knapton, 1742.

Collins, William. *Persian Eclogues*. London: Printed for J. Roberts, 1742.

Congreve, William, "Concerning Humour in Comedy" (1695). In *Critical Essays of the Seventeenth Century*, edited by J. E. Spingarn, 3 vols. 3: 242–52. Bloomington: Indiana University Press, 1957.

Cooke, William. "Table Talk; or, Characters, Anecdotes, etc. of Illustrious British Characters, during the last Fifty Years: Dr. Goldsmith." *European Magazine* 24 (1793), 93.

Cowper, John. *An Essay, Proving, that Inclosing Commons, and Common-field-Lands, Is Contrary to the Interest of the Nation*. London: Printed for E. Nutt, J. Roberts and A. Dodd, 1732.

Curwen, Samuel. *Journal and Letters, from 1775–1784*. New York: C.S. Francis and Co., 1842.

D'Argens, Jean Baptiste de Boyer, Marquis. *Chinese Letters, Being a Philosophical, Historical, and Critical Correspondence Between a Chinese Traveller at Paris, and His Countrymen in China, Muscovy, Persia and Japan*. No translator given. London: Printed for D. Browne and R. Hett, 1741.

Du Halde, J. B. *A Description of the Empire of China and Chinese–Tartary, Together with the Kingdoms of Korea, and Tibet: Containing the Geography and History (Natural as well as Civil) of those Countries*. No translator given [Samuel Johnson?], 2 vols. London: Printed by T. Gardner, 1738, 1741.

Dyer, John. *The Ruins of Rome. A Poem*. London: Printed for Lawton Gilliver, 1740.

Espiard de la Borde, François–Ignace. *The Spirit of Nations. Translated from the French*. No translator given [Thomas Nugent?]. London: Printed for Lockyer Davis and R. Baldwin, 1753.

Farquhar, George, *The Complete Works*, edited by Charles Stonehill, 2 vols. Bloomsbury: Nonesuch Press, 1930.

Freneau, Philip. *The Poems*, edited by Fred Lewis Pattee, 3 vols. New York: Russell and Russell, 1963.

Gibbon, Edward. *Memoirs of My Life*, edited by Georges A. Bonnard. 1796; London: Nelson, 1966.

Gordon, Patrick. *Geography Anatomized: Or, a Compleat Geographical Grammar*. London: Printed for Robert Morden and Thomas Cockerill, 1693.

Gray, Thomas. *The Correspondence*, edited by Paget Toynbee and Leonard Whibley, 3 vols. Oxford: The Clarendon Press, 1971.

———, William Collins and Oliver Goldsmith. *The Poems*, edited by Roger Lonsdale. London: Longman, 1969.

Hawkesworth, John [?Anonymous]. [Review of] "*The Deserted Village. A Poem. By Dr. Goldsmith.*" *The Gentleman's Magazine* 15 (1770), 271–3.

Hippocrates. *Writings*, edited by G. E. R. Lloyd. Translated by J. Chadwick et al. Harmondsworth: Penguin, 1983.

Holberg, Lewis. *A Journey to the World Underground. By Nicholas Klimius*. London: Printed for T. Astley and B. Collins, 1742.

———. *Memoirs*. No translator given. 1737; London: Hunt and Clarke, 1829.

Hughes, John. "An Essay on Allegorical Poetry. With Remarks on the Writings of Mr Edmund Spenser." In Edmund Spenser, *The Works*, 1: xxv–lvii. London: Printed for Jacob Tonson, 1715.

Hume, David. *A Treatise of Human Nature*, edited by L. A. Selby–Bigge. 1734; Oxford: Oxford University Press, 1965.

———. *Essays Moral, Political and Literary*. Oxford: Oxford University Press, 1963.

Johnson, Samuel. *A Dictionary of the English Language*. 1755; London: Times Books, 1979.

———. *London: a Poem and The Vanity of Human Wishes*. London: Etchells and Macdonald, 1930.

———. *Poems*, edited by E. L. McAdam with George Milne. New Haven: Yale University Press, 1964.

———. *Political Writings*, edited by Donald J. Greene. New Haven: Yale University Press, 1977.

———. *Prefaces and Dedications*, edited by Allen T. Hazen. New Haven: Yale University Press, 1937.

———. *The Idler and The Adventurer*, edited by W. J. Bate, John M. Bullitt and L. F. Powell. New Haven: Yale University Press, 1963.

———. *The Letters*, edited by Bruce Redford, 5 vols. Princeton: Princeton University Press, 1992–4.

Kames, Henry Home, Lord. *Sketches of the History of Man in Four Volumes*. Dublin: Printed for James Williams, 1775.

King, Anthony. *The Frequented Village. A Poem. By a Gentleman of the Middle Temple*. London: Printed for J. Godwin, 1771.

———. *The Frequented Village; A Poem, Inscribed to the Late Dr Oliver Goldsmith. A New Edition, Improved with Additions*. Dublin: Reprinted by R. Marchbank, 1784.

Le Comte, Lewis [Louis]. *Memoirs and Remarks, Geographical, Historical, Topographical, Physical, Natural, Astronomical, Mechanical, Military, Mercantile, Political and Ecclesiastical. Made in the Above*

Ten Years Travels through the Empire of China. No translator given. 1696; London: Printed for Olive Payne, E. Commins, and W. Smith, 1737.

Lithgow, William. *The Totall Discourse, of the Rare Adventures, and Painful Peregrinations of Long Nineteene Yeares Travailes from Scotland, to the Most Famous Kingdomes in Europe, Asia, and Africa*. London: I. Okes, 1640.

Lowth, Robert, *Lectures on the Sacred Poetry of the Hebrews*. Translated by G. Gregory, 2 vols. 1753; London: Printed for J. Johnson, 1787.

Lyttelton, George, Lord. *Letters from a Persian in England, to His Friends at Ispahan*, 5th edn. London: Printed for J. Millan, 1744.

———. *The Poetical Works*. London: Cadell and Davies, 1807.

Mandeville, Bernard. *The Fable of the Bees. Part II*. Edinburgh: Printed for W. Gray and W. Peter, 1755.

Mason, William. "Memoirs of the Life and Writings of Mr Gray." In Thomas Gray, *The Poems*, 2nd edn. 1–404. London: Printed for J. Dodsley and J. Dodd, 1775.

———, *Satirical Poems*. Introduced with notes by Horace Walpole, edited by Paget Toynbee. Oxford: The Clarendon Press, 1926.

[Moll, Herman]. *A Complete System of Geography*, maps by Emanuel Bowen, 2 vols. London: Printed for William Innys, Richard Ware, Aaron Ward, J. and P. Knapton, John Clarke, T. Longman and T. Shewell, Thomas Osborne, Henry Whitridge, Richard Hett, Charles Hitch, Stephen Austen, Edmund Comyns, Andrew Millar, James Hodges, Charles Corbett, and Jo. and Ja. Rivington, 1747.

Montesquieu, Charles de Secondat, Baron de. *The Spirit of Laws* [*L'Esprit des Loix*], 2 vols. Translated by Thomas Nugent. 1748; London: Printed for J. Nourse, and P. Vaillant, 1750.

———. *Persian Letters*. Translated by C. J. Betts. 1721; London: Penguin, 1993.

Murphy, Arthur. *The Orphan of China, a Tragedy*. London: Printed for P. Vaillant, 1759.

Nugent, Thomas. *The Grand Tour, Or, A Journey through the Netherlands, Germany, Italy, and France*, 4 vols. 1749; London: Printed for J. Rivington and Sons, B. Law, T. Caslon, G. Robinson, T. Cadell, W. Goldsmith, J. Bew, S. Hayes, W. Fox, and T. Evans, 1778.

Oglethorpe, James Edward. *The Publications*, edited by Rodney M. Baine. Athens: University of Georgia Press, 1994.

Paine, Thomas. *Common Sense*. 1776; Harmondsworth: Penguin, 1982.

Percy, Thomas. *Hau Kiou Choaan, or the Pleasing History. A Translation from the Chinese Language. To which are added, I. The Argument or Story of a Chinese Play, II. A Collection of Chinese Proverbs, and III. Fragments of Chinese Poetry*, 4 vols. London: Printed for R. and J. Dodsley, 1761.

———, *Life of Oliver Goldsmith*, edited by Richard L. Harp. 1801; Salzburg: Institüt f[ü]r Englische Sprache und Literatur, 1976.

Pliny (the Elder). *Natural History*, edited by E. H. Warmington. Translated by H. Rackham, 10 vols. Cambridge: Harvard University Press, 1969.

Pope, Alexander. *Epistles to Several Persons (Moral Essays)*, edited by F. W. Bateson. New Haven: Yale University Press, 1951.

Prior, Matthew. *Literary Works*, edited by H. Bunker Wright and Monroe K. Spears, 2 vols. Oxford: The Clarendon Press, 1959.

Ray, John. *The Wisdom of God Manifested in the Works of the Creation*. London: Printed for S. Smith, 1691.

Raynal, Guillaume Thomas Francois Raynal, Abbé. *A Philosophical and Political History of the Settlements and Trade of the Europeans in the East and West Indies.* Translated by J. Justamond, 5 vols. London: Printed for T. Cadell, 1776.

———. *L'Histoire philosophique et politique des etablissements et du commerce des Européens dans les deux Indes*, 4 vols. Amsterdam, 1770.

Reynolds, Joshua. *Portraits*, edited by Frederick W. Hilles. New York: McGraw-Hill, 1952.

Shenstone, William. *The Poetical Works.* Edinburgh: James Nichol, 1854.

Skelton, Philip. *The Necessity of Tillage and Granaries. In a Letter to a Member of Parliament Living in the County of _____ .* Dublin: [s.n.], 1741.

Smith, Stanley Stanhope. *An Essay on the Causes of the Variety of Complexion and Figure in the Human Species. To which are added, Strictures on Lord Kaim's Discourse, on the Original Diversity of Mankind.* London: Printed for John Stockdale, 1789.

Sterne, Laurence. *A Sentimental Journey through France and Italy.* 1768; Oxford: Oxford University Press, 1984.

———, *The Life and Opinions of Tristram Shandy, Gentleman.* 1759–67; London: Penguin, 1997.

Swift, Jonathan. *Irish Pamphlets: An Introductory Selection*, edited by Joseph McMinn. Savage, MD: Barnes and Noble Books, 1991.

———. *Journal to Stella*, edited by Harold Williams, 2 vols. Oxford: The Clarendon Press, 1948.

———. *Poems*, edited by Harold Williams, 2nd edn, 3 vols. Oxford: Oxford University Press, 1958.

———. *The Intelligencer*, edited by James Woolley. Oxford: The Clarendon Press, 1992.

Temple, William. *Essays on Ancient and Modern Learning and on Poetry*, edited by J. E. Spingarn. 1690; Oxford: The Clarendon Press, 1909.

———. "Upon the Gardens of Epicurus; or of Gardening in the Year 1685." In *Upon the Gardens of Epicurus, with Other XVIIth Century Garden Essays*, 1–65. London: Chatto and Windus, 1908.

Thomson, James. *Liberty, The Castle of Indolence, and Other Poems*, edited by James Sambrook. Oxford: The Clarendon Press, 1986.

———. *The Seasons*, edited by James Sambrook. 1730; Oxford: The Clarendon Press, 1981.

Valsas, Gulielmus. "To the Editor." *The Northern Star*, Number 36. From Wednesday, May 2 to Saturday, May 5, 1792.

Walpole, Horace. *Correspondence with Thomas Gray, Richard West and Thomas Ashton*, edited by W. S. Lewis, George L. Lam and Charles H. Bennett. New Haven: Yale University Press, 1948.

———. "Introduction" (1779). In William Mason, *Satirical Poems*, 31–33. Oxford: The Clarendon Press, 1926.

———. *Journal of the Reign of King George the Third, from the Year 1771 to 1783*, edited by Dr. Doran, 2 vols. London: Richard Bentley, 1859.

———. "Notes to the Author's Preface" [To "An Heroic Epistle to Sir William Chambers, Knight, &c. &c."]. In William Mason, *Satirical Poems*, 39–45. Oxford: The Clarendon Press, 1926.

———. *Memoirs of King George II*, edited by John Brooke, 3 vols. New Haven: Yale University Press, 1985.

Watts, Isaac. *Logick: Or, The Right Use of Reason in the Enquiry after Truth.* London: Printed for John Clark and Richard Hett, Emanuel Matthews, and Richard Ford, 1725.

———. *The Knowledge of the Heavens and the Earth Made Easy: Or, The First Principles of Astronomy and Geography*. London: Printed for J. Clark and R. Hett; E. Matthews, and R. Ford, 1716.

Whitehead, William. "Prologue." In Arthur Murphy, *The Orphan of China, a Tragedy*, no page numbers. London: Printed for P. Vaillant, 1759.

———. "The World, No. XII." *The World* 1 (1753), 67–72.

Whyte, Laurence. *Poems on Various Subjects*. Dublin: Printed for L. Dowling, T. Brown, and Ed. Hamillton, Mr. J. Hoey and Oli. Nelson, G. Falkiner; and by the author, 1740.

Whyte, Samuel. "Impromptu, written on the back of a trencher in the cottage at the crooked Wood, County Westmeath, August, 1773." In *A Georgian Celebration: Irish Poets of the Eighteenth Century*, edited by Patrick Fagan, 145. Dublin: Branar, 1989.

Wood, Robert. *An Essay on the Original Genius of Homer*. London: [s.n.], 1769.

Secondary Sources (b), Authors Post-1800

Abbott, John Lawrence. *John Hawkesworth: Eighteenth-Century Man of Letters*. Madison: University of Wisconsin Press, 1982.

Adams, Percy G. *Travelers and Travel-Liars, 1660–1800*. New York: Dover, 1980.

Ahmad, Aijaz. *In Theory: Classes, Nations, Literatures*. New York: Verso, 1992.

Allen, B. Sprague, *Tides in English Taste (1619–1800): A Background for the Study of Literature*, 2 vols. Cambridge: Harvard University Press, 1937.

Altick, Richard D. *Paintings from Books: Art and Literature in Britain, 1760–1900*. Columbus: Ohio State University Press, 1985.

Andrews, William L. "Goldsmith and Freneau in 'The American Village.'" *Early American Literature* 5 (1970): 14–23

Appleton, Jay. *The Experience of Landscape*. Chichester: Wiley, 1996.

Appleton, William W. *A Cycle of Cathay: The Chinese Vogue in England During the Seventeenth and Eighteenth Centuries*. New York: Columbia University Press, 1951.

Armitage, David. *The Ideological Origins of the British Empire*. Cambridge: Cambridge University Press, 2000.

Ashcroft, Bill and Pal Ahluwalia. *Edward Said: The Paradox of Identity*. New York: Routledge, 1999.

Ashworth, William B. "Natural History and the Emblematic World View." In *Reappraisals of the Scientific Revolution*, edited by David C. Lindberg and Robert S. Westman, 303–32. Cambridge: Cambridge University Press, 1990.

Aubin, Robert Arnold. *Topographical Poetry in XVIII-Century England*. New York: The Modern Language Association of America, 1966.

Baker, J.N.L. *The History of Geography*. Oxford: Blackwell, 1963.

Bald, R. C. "Sir William Chambers and the Chinese Garden." *Journal of the History of Ideas* 11 (1950), 287–320.

Balderston, Katherine. "New Goldsmith Letters." *The Yale University Library Gazette* 39 (1964), 71–2.

———. *The History and Sources of Percy's Memoir of Goldsmith*. Cambridge: Cambridge University Press, 1926.

Ballaster, Ros. *Fabulous Orients: Fictions of the East in England 1662–1785*. Oxford: Oxford University Press, 2005.

Barfoot, C. C. "Deserting the Village." In *The Clash of Ireland: Literary Contrasts and Connections*, edited by C. C. Barfoot and Theo d'Haen, 52–97. Amsterdam: Rodopi, 1989.

———. "'Envy, Fear, and Wonder': English Views of Holland and the Dutch 1673–1764." In *The Great Emporium: The Low Countries as a Cultural Crossroads in the Renaissance and the Eighteenth Century*, edited by C. C. Barfoot and Richard Todd, 207–47. Amsterdam: Rodopi, 1992.

Barnouw, A. J. "Goldsmith's Indebtedness to Justus Van Effen." *Modern Language Review* 8 (1913), 314–23.

Barrell, John. *English Literature in History, 1730–80: An Equal, Wide Survey*. London: Hutchinson, 1983.

———. *The Dark Side of the Landscape: The Rural Poor in English Painting 1730–1840*. Cambridge: Cambridge University Press, 1980.

Barry, Alda Milner. "A Note on the Early Literary Relations of Oliver Goldsmith and Thomas Percy." *The Review of English Studies* 2 (1926), 51–61.

Bataille, Robert C. *The Writing Life of Hugh Kelly: Politics, Journalism, and Theater in Late-Eighteenth-Century London*. Carbondale: Southern Illinois University Press, 2000.

Batey, Mavis. "Oliver Goldsmith: An Indictment of Landscape Gardening." In *Furor Hortensis*, edited by Peter Willis, 57–71. Edinburgh: Elysium Press, 1974.

Batten, Charles L. *Pleasurable Instruction: Form and Convention in Eighteenth-Century Travel Literature*. Berkeley: University of California Press, 1978.

Bell, David A. *The Cult of the Nation in France: Inventing Nationalism, 1680–1800*. Cambridge: Harvard University Press, 2001.

Bell Jr, Howard J. "*The Deserted Village* and Goldsmith's Social Doctrines." *Publications of the Modern Language Association of America* 59 (1944), 747–72.

Bissell, Benjamin. *The American Indian in English Literature of the Eighteenth Century*. New Haven: Yale University Press, 1925.

Black, Jeremy. *The British Abroad: The Grand Tour in the Eighteenth Century*. New York: St. Martin's Press, 1992.

Bohm, Arnd. "From Politics to Aesthetics: Goldsmith's 'The Traveller' and Goethe's 'Der Wandrer'." *The Germanic Review* 57 (1982), 138–42.

Bowen, Margarita. *Empiricism and Geographical Thought: From Francis Bacon to Alexander von Humboldt*. Cambridge: Cambridge University Press, 1981.

Breckenridge, Carol A. and Peter Van Der Veer, eds. *Orientalism and the Postcolonial Predicament*. Philadelphia: University of Pennsylvania Press, 1993.

Bronson, Bertrand Harris. *Facets of the Enlightenment: Studies in English Literature and Its Contexts*. Berkeley: University of California Press, 1968.

Brooks, Christopher. "Goldsmith's Citizen of the World: Knowledge and the Imposture of 'Orientalism'." *Texas Studies in Literature and Language* 35 (1993), 124–44.

Brooks–Davies, Douglas. *Pope's Dunciad and the Queen of Night: A Study in Emotional Jacobitism*. Manchester: Manchester University Press, 1985.

Brown, Jane. *The Omnipresent Magician: Lancelot "Capability" Brown, 1716–1783*. London: Chatto and Windus, 2011.

Brown, J. E. "Goldsmith's Indebtedness to Voltaire and Justus van Effen." *Modern Philology* 23 (1926), 273–84.

Brown, Keith. "A Kind of Comradeship: Goldsmith and the Late Famous Baron Holberg." *English Studies: A Journal of English Language and Literature* 61 (1980), 37–46.

Brown, Laura. *Ends of Empire: Women and Ideology in Early Eighteenth-Century English Literature*. Ithaca: Cornell University Press, 1993.

———. *Fables of Modernity: Literature and Culture in the English Eighteenth Century*. Ithaca: Cornell University Press, 2001.

Brown, Marshall. *Preromanticism*. Stanford: Stanford University Press, 1991.

Bryant, Donald Cross. *Edmund Burke and His Literary Friends*. St. Louis: Washington University Press, 1939.

Budd, Declan and Ross Hinds. *The Hist and Edmund Burke's Club: An Anthology of the College Historical Society, the Student Debating Society of Trinity College Dublin, from Its Origins in Edmund Burke's Club 1747–1997*. Dublin: Lilliput Press, 1997.

Bunbury, E. H. *A History of Ancient Geography among the Greeks and Romans from the Earliest Times to the Fall of the Roman Empire*, 2 vols. London: John Murray, 1883.

Carpenter, Andrew. "Introduction." In *Verse in English in Eighteenth-Century Ireland*, edited by Andrew Carpenter, 1–34. Cork: Cork University Press, 1998.

Carson, James. ""The Little Republic" of the Family: Goldsmith's Politics of Nostalgia." *Eighteenth-Century Fiction* 16 (2004), 173–196.

Chandler, James. "A Discipline in Shifting Perspective: Why We Need Irish Studies." *Field Day Review* 2 (2006), 19–39.

Chang, Y. Z. "A Note on Sharawadgi." *Modern Language Notes* 45 (1930), 221–4.

Chapin, Chester F. "Oliver Goldsmith and Thomas Paine." *American Notes and Queries* 11 (1998), 22–3.

———. *Personification in Eighteenth-Century Poetry*. New York: Columbia University Press, 1955.

Chase, Isabel Wakelin. *Horace Walpole: Gardenist*. Princeton: Princeton University Press, 1943.

Clarke, Desmond. *Thomas Prior, 1681–1751: Founder of the Royal Dublin Society*. Dublin: R.D.S., 1951.

Colley, Linda. *Britons: Forging the Nation, 1707–1837*. New Haven: Yale University Press, 1992.

Colton, Judith. "Merlin's Cave and Queen Caroline: Garden Art as Political Propaganda." *Eighteenth-Century Studies* 10 (1976), 1–20.

Conant, Martha Pike. *The Oriental Tale in England in the Eighteenth Century*. New York: Columbia University Press, 1908.

Connolly, Claire. "Ugly Criticism: Union and Division in Irish Literature." *Field Day Review* 4 (2008), 115–131.

Constable, W. G. *Richard Wilson*. London: Routledge, 1953.

Copley, Stephen and Peter Garside, eds. *The Politics of the Picturesque: Literature, Landscape and Aesthetics Since 1770*. Cambridge: Cambridge University Press, 1994.

Coulson, Mavis. *Southwards to Geneva: 200 Years of English Travellers*. Gloucester: A. Sutton, 1988.

Courtney, C. P. *Montesquieu and Burke*. Oxford: Blackwell, 1963.

Cox, Michael F. "The Country and Kindred of Oliver Goldsmith." *Journal of the National Literary Society* 1 (1901–03), 81–111.

———. "The 'Deserted Village' in Prose (1762)." *Times Literary Supplement*, no. 1336 (Sept. 8, 1927), 607.

——— and J. H. Warner. "Goldsmith and Voltaire's *Essai sur les moeurs*." *Modern Language Notes* 38 (1923), 65–76.

——— and H. J. Smith. "A French Influence on Goldsmith's *Citizen of the World*." *Modern Philology* 19 (1921–22), 83–92.

Crawford, Rachel. *Poetry, Enclosure, and the Vernacular Landscape, 1700–1830*. Cambridge: Cambridge University Press, 2001.

Cruickshanks, Eveline. *The Oglethorpes: A Jacobite Family 1689–1760*. London: Royal Stuart Society, 1995.

Cullen, Louis. "Catholics under the Penal Laws." *Eighteenth-Century Ireland: Iris an dá Chultúr* 1 (1986), 23–36.

Cunningham, D. J. "Anthropology in the Eighteenth Century." *Journal of the Royal Anthropological Institute* 38 (1908), 10–35.

Curley, Thomas M. *Samuel Johnson and the Age of Travel*. Athens: University of Georgia Press, 1976.

Dai, David Wei-Yang. "A Comparative Study of D'Argens *Lettres Chinoises* and Goldsmith's *Citizen of the World*." *Tamkang Review* 10 (1979), 183–97.

Darrell, Margery, ed. *Once Upon a Time: The Fairy Tale World of Arthur Rackham*. New York: Heinemann, 1972.

Davidson, Levette Jay. "Forerunners of Goldsmith's *The Citizen of the World*." *Modern Language Notes* 36 (1921), 215–20.

Davie, Donald. *The Language of Science and the Language of Literature, 1700–1740* London: Sheed and Ward, 1963.

Deane, Seamus. *A Short History of Irish Literature*. London: Random House, 1986.

———. *Celtic Revivals: Essays in Modern Irish Literature 1880–1980*. London: Faber, 1985.

———. *Foreign Affections: Essays on Edmund Burke*. Cork: Cork University Press, 2005.

———, "Oliver Goldsmith: Miscellaneous Writings 1759–74." In *The Field Day Anthology of Irish Writing*, edited by Seamus Deane, 3 vols. 1: 658–60. Derry: Field Day, 1991.

———. *Strange Country: Modernity and Nationhood in Irish Writing since 1790* Oxford: Oxford University Press, 1997.

Dickson, David. *Arctic Ireland: The Extraordinary Story of the Great Frost and Forgotten Famine of 1740–41*. Belfast: White Row Press, 1997.

———. "Jacobitism in Eighteenth-Century Ireland: A Munster Perspective." *Éire–Ireland* 39 (2004), 38–99.

———. "The Other Great Irish Famine." In *The Great Irish Famine*, edited by Cathal Póirtéir, 50–59, 259–60n. Cork: Mercier Press, 1995.

Dircks, Richard J. "The Genesis and Date of Goldsmith's *Retaliation*." *Modern Philology* 75 (1977), 48–53.

Dixon, Peter. *Oliver Goldsmith Revisited*. Boston: Twayne, 1991.

Dobson, Austin, *A Paladin of Philanthropy and Other Papers*. London: Chatto and Windus, 1899.

———. *Life of Oliver Goldsmith*. London: Books for Libraries Press, 1888.

———, "Preface." In *The Vicar of Wakefield. Being a Facsimile Reproduction of the First Edition of the First Edition Published in 1766. With an Introduction by Austin Dobson, and a Bibliographical List of Editions of "The Vicar of Wakefield" Published in England and* Abroad, by Oliver Goldsmith, 2 vols., 1: vii–xxi. London: Elliot Stock, 1885.

Downie, J. A. "1688: Pope and the Rhetoric of Jacobitism." In *Pope: New Contexts*, edited by David Fairer, 9–24. New York: Harvester Wheatsheaf, 1990.

———. "Goldsmith, Swift and Augustan Satirical Verse." In *The Art of Oliver Goldsmith*, edited by Andrew Swarbrick, 126–43. London: Vision, 1984.

———. *Jonathan Swift: Political Writer*. London: Routledge, 1984.

Drake, Michael. "The Irish Demographic Crisis of 1740–41." *Historical Studies VI*, edited by T. W. Moody 101–24. London: Routledge & Kegan Paul, 1968.

Drayton, Richard. *Nature's Government: Science, Imperial Britain, and the "Improvement" of the World*. New Haven: Yale University Press, 2000.

Drennon, Herbert. "Scientific Rationalism and James Thomson's Poetic Art." *Studies in Philology* 31 (1934), 453–71.

Driver, Felix. "Geography's Empire: Histories of Geographical Knowledge." *Environment and Planning D: Society and Space* 10 (1992), 23–40.

Durrant, Edmund. "'The Deserted Village'." *Notes and Queries*, 5th Series 10 (1878), 88.

Eagleton, Terry. *Crazy John and the Bishop, and Other Essays on Irish Culture*. Cork: Cork University Press, 1998.

Edgecombe, Rodney Stenning. "Gibbon's History of the Decline and Fall of the Roman Empire, Volume 1." *The Explicator* 53 (1995), 79–81.

———. "Regionalisms Ancient and Modern." *Classical and Modern Literature: A Quarterly* 14 (1993), 43–60.

Eliot, T. S. "Introductory Essay." In *London: A Poem and The Vanity of Human Wishes*, by Samuel Johnson, 9–17. London: Etchells and Macdonald, 1930.

Ettinger, Amos Aschbach. *Oglethorpe: A Brief Biography*. Macon: Mercer University Press, 1984.

———. *James Edward Oglethorpe: Imperial Idealist*. Hamden: Archon Books, 1968.

Eversole, Richard. "The Oratorical Design of *The Deserted Village*." *English Language Notes* 4 (1966), 99–104.

Fabricant, Carole. "Binding and Dressing Nature's Loose Tresses: The Ideology of Augustan Landscape Design." *Studies in Eighteenth-Century Culture* 8 (1979), 109–35.

———. *Swift's Landscape*. Notre Dame: University of Notre Dame Press, 1982.

Fairchild, Hoxie Neale. *The Noble Savage: A Study in Romantic Naturalism*. New York: Russell and Russell, 1928.

Fairer, David. *English Poetry of the Eighteenth Century 1700–1789*. London: Longman, 2003.

———. *Pope's Imagination*. Manchester: Manchester University Press, 1984.

Fan, T. C., "Percy and Du Halde." *The Review of English Studies* 21 (1945), 326–29.

Feingold, Richard. *Nature and Society: Later Eighteenth-Century Uses of the Pastoral and* Georgic. Hassocks: The Harvester Press, 1978.

Fenton, Seamus, *It All Happened: Reminiscences*. Dublin: M.H. Gill, 1949.

Festa, Lynn and Dan Carey. "Introduction—Some Answers to the Question: What Is Postcolonial Enlightenment?" In *The Postcolonial Enlightenment: Eighteenth-Century Colonialism and Postcolonial Theory*, edited by Daniel Carey and Lynn Festa, 1–33. Oxford: Oxford University Press, 2009.

Fielding, K. J. "*The Deserted Village* and Sir Robert Walpole." *English* 12 (1959), 130–2.

Fitzmaurice, Lord Edmond. *Life of William, Earl of Shelburne, afterwards First Marquess of Lansdowne. With Extracts from His Papers and Correspondence*, 3 vols. London: Macmillan, 1875.

Fletcher, Angus. *Allegory: The Theory of a Symbolic Mode*. Ithaca: Cornell University Press, 1964.

Ford, Edward. "Names and Characters in the 'Vicar of Wakefield'." *The National Review*, no. 3 (May 1883), 387–94.

Forster, John. *The Life and Times of Oliver Goldsmith*, 2 vols. 1848; London: Chapman and Hall, 1871.

Foucault, Michel. *Power/Knowledge: Selected Interviews and Other Writings, 1972–77*, edited by Colin Gordon et al. Brighton: Harvester Press, 1980.

———. *The Order of Things: An Archaeology of the Human Sciences*. London: Tavistock, 1970.

Fox, Christopher. "How to Prepare a Noble Savage: The Spectacle of Human Science." In *Inventing Human Science: Eighteenth-Century Domains*, edited by Christopher Fox, Roy Porter, and Robert Wokler, 1–30. Berkeley: University of California Press, 1995.

Frantz, R. W. "Swift's Yahoos and the Voyagers." *Modern Philology* 29 (1931), 49–57.

———. *The English Traveller and the Movement of Ideas, 1660–1732*. Lincoln: University of Nebraska Press, 1932.

Friedman, John Block. *The Monstrous Races in Medieval Art and Thought*. Cambridge: Harvard University Press, 1981.

Frye, Northrop. *Fables of Identity: Studies in Poetic Mythology*. New York: Harcourt, Brace & World, 1963.

Furniss, Tom. *Edmund Burke's Aesthetic Ideology: Language, Gender, and Political Economy in Revolution*. Cambridge: Cambridge University Press, 1993.

Gargett, Graham. "Plagiarism, Translation and the Problem of Identity: Oliver Goldsmith and Voltaire." *Eighteenth-Century Ireland: Iris an dá Chultúr* 16 (2001), 83–103.

Gascoigne, John. *Joseph Banks and the English Enlightenment: Useful Knowledge and Polite Culture*. Cambridge: Cambridge University Press, 1994.

Gibbons, Luke. *Ireland into Film: The Quiet Man*. Cork: Cork University Press, 2002.

———. *Edmund Burke and Ireland: Aesthetics, Politics, and the Colonial Sublime*. Cambridge: Cambridge University Press, 2003.

Ginger, John. *The Notable Man: The Life and Times of Oliver Goldsmith*. London: Hamilton, 1977.

Glacken, Clarence J. *Traces on the Rhodian Shore: Nature and Culture in Western Thought from Ancient Times to the End of the Eighteenth Century*. Berkeley: University of California Press, 1967.

Golden, Morris. "The Family-Wanderer Theme in Goldsmith." *English Literary History* 25 (1958), 181–93.

Goldstein, Laurence. *Ruins and Empire: The Evolution of a Theme in Augustan and Romantic Literature.* Pittsburgh: University of Pennsylvania Press, 1977.

Graves, Robert. *The Crowning Privilege: Collected Essays on Poetry.* New York: Books for Libraries Press, 1970.

Gregory, Derek. *Geographical Imaginations.* Oxford: Blackwell, 1994.

Griffin, Dustin. *Patriotism and Poetry in Eighteenth-Century Britain.* Cambridge: Cambridge University Press, 2002.

———. "The Visionary Scene: Vision and Allegory in the Poetry of Pope." In *Enlightening Allegory: Theory, Practice, and Contexts of Allegory in the Late Seventeenth and Eighteenth Centuries,* edited by Kevin L. Cope, 323–49. New York: AMS, 1993.

Griffin, Michael. "Oliver Goldsmith and François-Ignace Espiard de la Borde: An Instance of Plagiarism." *The Review of English Studies* 50 (1999), 59–63.

Gwynn, Stephen. *Oliver Goldsmith.* London: Thornton Butterworth, 1935.

Hammond, J. L. and Barbara Hammond. *The Village Labourer,* edited by G. E. Mingay. 1911; London: Longman, 1978.

Harman, Claire. "Partiality and Prejudice: The young Jane Austen's 'Hatred of all those people whose parties or principles do not suit with mine'." *Times Literary Supplement,* no. 5470 (February 1, 2008), 14–15.

Harp, Richard L. " Introduction." In *Life of Oliver Goldsmith,* by Thomas Percy, edited by Richard L. Harp viii–xxviii. 1801; Salzburg: Institüt f[ü]r Englische Sprache und Literatur, 1976.

Harris, John. *Sir William Chambers: Knight of the Polar Star.* London: A. Zwemmer, 1970.

Hart, Francis R. "Johnson as Philosophic Traveler: The Perfecting of an Idea." *English Literary History* 36 (1969), 679–95.

Harth, Philip. "Goldsmith and the Marquis D'Argens." *Notes and Queries* 198 (1953), 529–30.

Haskell, Ann. "Chaucerian Women, Ideal Gardens, and the Wild Woods'—in *A Wyf Ther Was: Essays in Honour of Paule Mertens–Fonck,* edited by Juliette Dor, 193–8. Liège: Liège Language and Literature, 1992.

Havens, Raymond Dexter. "Primitivism and the Idea of Progress in Thomson." *Studies in Philology* 29 (1931), 41–52.

Hawes, Clement. *The British Eighteenth Century and Global Critique.* Houndmills: Palgrave, 2005.

———. "Three Times around the Globe: Gulliver and Colonial Discourse." *Cultural Critique,* no. 18 (Spring 1991), 187–214.

Hay, Denis. *Europe: The Emergence of an Idea.* New York: Harper and Row, 1966.

Hayman, John G. "Notions on National Characters in the Eighteenth Century." *Huntington Library Quarterly* 35 (1971), 1–17.

Heawood, Edward. *A History of Geographical Discovery in the Seventeenth and Eighteenth Centuries.* Cambridge: Cambridge University Press, 1912.

Helgerson, Richard. "The Two Worlds of Oliver Goldsmith." *Studies in English Literature, 1500–1900* 13 (1973), 516–34.

Hermann, Luke. *British Landscape Painting of the Eighteenth Century.* London: Faber, 1973.

Higgins, Ian. *Swift's Politics: A Study in Disaffection.* Cambridge: Cambridge University Press, 1994.

Hilliard, Raymond F. "The Redemption of Fatherhood in *The Vicar of Wakefield*." *Studies in English Literature, 1500–1900* 23 (1983), 465–80.

Honour, Hugh. *Chinoiserie: The Vision of Cathay*. London: John Murray, 1961.

Hopkins, Robert H. *The True Genius of Oliver Goldsmith*. Baltimore: Johns Hopkins University Press, 1969.

Horkheimer, Max, and Theodor W. Adorno. *Dialectic of Enlightenment: Philosophical Fragments*. Edited by Gunzelin Schmid Noerr, translated by Edmund Jephcott. Stanford: Stanford University Press, 2002.

Horrocks, Ingrid. "'Circling Eye' and 'Houseless Stranger': The New Eighteenth-Century Wanderer (Thomson to Goldsmith)." *English Literary History* 77 (2010), 665–687.

Howes, Laura L. *Chaucer's Gardens and the Language of Convention*. Gainesville: University of Florida Press, 1997.

Hudson, Derek. *Arthur Rackham, His Life and Work*. New York: Charles Scribner, 1974.

Hudson, Nicholas. "'Britons Never Will Be Slaves': National Myth, Conservatism, and the Beginnings of British Antislavery." *Eighteenth-Century Studies* 34 (2001), 559–76.

———. "From 'Nation' to 'Race': The Origin of Racial Classification in Eighteenth-Century Thought." *Eighteenth-Century Studies* 29 (1996), 247–64.

———. *Samuel Johnson and the Making of Modern England*. Cambridge: Cambridge University Press, 2003.

Hunt, John Dixon. *The Figure in the Landscape: Poetry, Painting, and Gardening During the Eighteenth Century*. Baltimore: Johns Hopkins University Press, 1976.

——— and Peter Willis. *The Genius of the Place: The English Landscape Garden 1620–1820*. Cambridge: MIT Press, 1988.

Jaarsma, Richard J. "Ethics in the Wasteland: Image and Structure in Goldsmith's *The Deserted Village*." *Texas Studies in Language and Literature* 13 (1971), 447–59.

Jameson, Fredric. "The Politics of Utopia." *New Left Review* 25 (2004), 35–54.

———. *The Political Unconscious: Narrative as a Socially Symbolic Act*. London: Routledge, 1981.

Jarry, Madeleine. *Chinoiserie: Chinese Influence on European Decorative Art, 17th and 18th Centuries*. New York: Vendome Press, 1981.

Jemeilty, Thomas. "Dr Johnson and the Uses of Travel." *Philological Quarterly* 51 (1972), 448–59.

Joyce, James. *Letters, Volume II*. Edited by Richard Ellman. London: Viking Press, 1966.

———. *Ulysses*. 1922; London: Garland, 1984.

Judt, Tony. *Ill Fares the Land: A Treatise on our Present Discontents*. London: Penguin, 2010.

Keane, John. *Tom Paine: A Political Life*. New York: Grove, 1995.

Kelley, Theresa. *Reinventing Allegory*. Cambridge: Cambridge University Press, 1997.

Kiberd, Declan. *Irish Classics*. London: Granta, 2000.

Kirk, Clara Marburg. *Oliver Goldsmith*. New York: Twayne, 1967.

Kitching, Megan. "The Solitary Animal: Professional Authorship and Persona in Goldsmith's The Citizen of the World." *Eighteenth-Century Fiction* 25 (2012), 175–98.

Langdon, Helen. "The Imaginative Geographies of Claude Lorrain." In *Transports: Travel, Pleasure, and Imaginative Geography, 1600–1830*, edited by Chloe Chard and Helen Langdon 151–78. New Haven: Yale University Press, 1996.

Langford, Paul. *Englishness Identified: Manners and Character 1650–1850*. Oxford: Oxford University Press, 2000.

Larson, James. "Not without a Plan: Geography and Natural History in the Late Eighteenth Century." *Journal of the History of Biology* 19 (1986), 447–88.

Laurenson, Diana and Alan Swingewood. *The Sociology of Literature* (London: MacGibbon and Kee, 1972.

Leask, Nigel. *British Romantic Writers and the East: Anxieties of Empire* (Cambridge Cambridge University Press, 1992.

Lennon, Joseph. *Irish Orientalism: A Literary and Intellectual History*. Syracuse: Syracuse University Press, 2004.

Little, Ila Dawson. "Allusions to Garden Design in Poems of Goldsmith and Wordsworth." *College Language Association Journal* 39 (1995), 228–42.

Livingstone, David. "Geography, Tradition and the Scientific Revolution: An Interpretative Essay." *Transactions, The Institute of British Geographers* 15 (1990), 359–73.

———. "The Moral Discourse of Climate: Historical Considerations on Race, Place and Virtue." *Journal of Historical Geography* 17 (1991), 413–34.

——— and Charles J. Withers, "Introduction: On Geography and Enlightenment." In *Geography and Enlightenment*, edited by David N. Livingstone and Charles J. Withers, 1–28. Chicago: University of Chicago Press, 1999.

Lock, F. P. *Edmund Burke, Volume 1, 1730–1784*. Oxford: The Clarendon Press, 1998.

Logan, John. "Robert Clive's Irish Peerage and Estate, 1761–1842." *North Munster Antiquarian Journal* 43 (2003), 1–19.

Lonsdale, Roger. "A Garden and a Grave: The Poetry of Oliver Goldsmith." In *The Author in His Work: Essays on a Problem in Criticism*, edited by Louis L. Martz and Aubrey Williams, introduced by Patricia Meyer Spacks, 3–30. New Haven: Yale University Press, 1978.

Lovejoy, Arthur O. *Essays in the History of Ideas*. Baltimore: Johns Hopkins University Press, 1948.

Lucas, John. *England and Englishness: Ideas of Nationhood in English Poetry, 1688– 1900*. London: Hogarth Press, 1990.

Lutz, Alfred. "'The Deserted Village and the Politics of Genre.'" *Modern Language Quarterly* 55 (1994), 149–68.

———. "The Politics of Reception: The Case of Goldsmith's 'The Deserted Village.'" *Studies in Philology* 95 (1998), 174–96.

Lynskey, Winifred. "The Scientific Sources of Goldsmith's Animated Nature." *Studies in Philology* 40 (1943), 33–57.

———. "Pluke and Derham, New Sources of Goldsmith." *Publications of the Modern Language Association of America* 57 (1942), 435–45.

Macaulay, Thomas Babington. "Life of Goldsmith" (1856). In Walter Scott, Thomas Babington Macaulay, and William Makepeace Thackeray, *Essays on Goldsmith*, edited by G. E. Hadow and C. B. Wheeler, 20–37. Oxford: The Clarendon Press, 1918.

MacFie, A. L., ed. *Orientalism: A Reader*. Edinburgh: Edinburgh University Press, 2000.

Mahoney, Thomas H. D. *Edmund Burke and Ireland*. Cambridge: Harvard University Press, 1960.

———. "Mr Burke's Imperial Mentality and the Proposed Irish Absentee Tax of 1773." *Canadian Historical Review* 37 (1956), 158–66.

Malcolmson, Cristina. "The Garden Enclosed/The Woman Enclosed: Marvell and the Cavalier Poets." In *Enclosure Acts: Sexuality, Property, and Culture in Early Modern England*, edited by Richard Burt and John Michael Archer, 251–69. Ithaca: Cornell University Press, 1994.

Malins, Edward and The Knight of Glin. *Lost Demesnes: Irish Landscape Gardening, 1660–1845*. London: Barrie & Jenkins, 1976.

Mangin, Edward. *An Essay on Light Reading, as it may be supposed to Influence Moral Conduct and Literary Taste*. London: Printed for James Carpenter, 1808.

Mannion, David and Peter Dixon. "Authorship Attribution: The Case of Oliver Goldsmith." *The Statistician* 46 (1997), 1–18.

———. "Goldsmith and the *British Magazine*." *Literary and Linguistic Computing* 13 (1998), 37–49.

Manwaring, Elizabeth Wheeler. *Italian Landscape in England: A Study Chiefly of the Influence of Claude Lorrain and Salvator Rosa on English Taste, 1700–1800*. New York: Oxford University Press, 1925.

Maxwell, Constantia. *The English Traveller in France, 1698–1815*. London: Routledge, 1932.

Mayhew, Robert J. *Geography and Literature in Historical Context: Samuel Johnson and Eighteenth-Century English Conceptions of Geography*. Oxford: School of Geography, 1997.

McCormack, W. J. *Ascendancy and Tradition in Anglo-Irish Literary History from 1789 to 1939*. Oxford: The Clarendon Press, 1985.

———. "Goldsmith, Biography and the Phenomenology of Anglo–Irish Literature." In *The Art of Oliver Goldsmith*, edited by Andrew Swarbrick, 168–194. London: Vision, 1984.

———, "Oliver Goldsmith's *Deserted Village* (1770) and Retrospective Localism." In *Longford: History and Society. Interdisciplinary Essays on the History of an Irish County*, edited by Martin Morris and Fergus, 259–81. Dublin: Geography Publications, 2010.

McKillop, Alan D. "Local Attachment and Cosmopolitanism." In *From Sensibility to Romanticism: Essays Presented to Frederick A. Pottle*, edited by Frederick W. Hilles and Harold Bloom, 191–218. New York: Oxford University Press, 1965.

———. *The Background of Thomson's Seasons*. Hamden: Archon, 1961.

McLoughlin, Thomas. *Contesting Ireland: Irish Voices against England in the Eighteenth Century*. Dublin: Four Courts, 1999.

McMinn, Joseph. "Literature and Religion in Eighteenth-Century Ireland: A Critical Survey." In *Irish Writers and Religion*, edited by Robert Welch, 15–31. Gerrards Cross: Smythe, 1992.

McVeagh, John. "Goldsmith and Nationality." In *All Before Them: English Literature and the Wider World, Volume 1: 1660–1789*, edited by John McVeagh, 217–31. London: Ashfield, 1990.

———, "Introduction." In *All Before Them: English Literature and the Wider World, Volume 1: 1660–1789*, edited by John McVeagh, 1–47. London: Ashfield, 1990.

Mehta, Uday Singh. *Liberalism and Empire: A Study in Nineteenth-Century British Liberal Thought*. Chicago: University of Chicago Press, 1999.

Miller, Kerby A., Arnold Schrier, Bruce D. Boling, David N. Doyle (authors and editors). *Irish Immigrants in the Land of Canaan: Letters and Memoirs from Colonial and Revolutionary America, 1675–1815*. Oxford: Oxford University Press, 2003.

Miner, Earl. "The Making of *The Deserted Village.*" *The Huntingdon Library Quarterly* 12 (1959), 125–41.

Mitchell, David. "Oliver Goldsmith and His Animated Nature." *Journal of the Irish Colleges of Physicians and Surgeons* 23 (1994), 207–11.

Mitford, John. "The Life of Oliver Goldsmith." In *The Poetical Works* (1835), by Oliver Goldsmith, vii–cviii. London: Aldine, 1835.

Molloy, Eddie. "Our national wealth far outweighs fool's gold." *The Irish Times*, Saturday, March 5, 2011.

Montague, John. "The Sentimental Prophecy: A Study of *The Deserted Village.*" In *The Art of Oliver Goldsmith*, edited by Andrew Swarbrick, 90–106. London: Vision, 1984.

Moore, John Robert. "Goldsmith's Degenerate Song-Birds: An Eighteenth-Century Fallacy in Ornithology." *Isis: An International Review Devoted to the History of Science and Civilization* 34 (1943), 324–27.

Moore, Norman. "Charles O'Conor." In *The Dictionary of National Biography*, edited by Leslie Stephen and Sydney Lee, 14: 855–7. Oxford: Oxford University Press, 1917 —.

Müllenbrock, Heinz–Joachim. "The Political Implications of the Grand Tour: Aspects of a Specifically English Contribution to the European Travel Literature of the Age of Enlightenment." *Trema*, no. 9 (1984), 7–21.

Munro, Jane. "Italian Landscape Drawings by James Barry." *Master Drawings* 29 (1991), 307–310.

Murray, Ciaran. *Sharawadgi: The Romantic Return to Nature*. San Francisco: Rowman & Littlefield, 1999.

Murray, Patrick. "The Riddle of Goldsmith's Ancestry." *Studies* 63 (1974), 177–90.

Muthu, Sankar. *Enlightenment against Empire* (Princeton: Princeton University Press, 2003).

Newell, R. H. "Remarks, Attempting to Ascertain, Chiefly from Local Observation, the Actual Scene of The Deserted Village." In *The Poetical Works*, by Oliver Goldsmith, 57–81. London: Printed for Suttaby, Evance and Company, 1811.

Newey, Vincent. "Goldsmith's 'Pensive Plain': Re–viewing *The Deserted Village.*" In *Early Romantics: Perspectives in British Poetry from Pope to Wordsworth*, edited by Thomas Woodman, 93–116. Houndmills: Palgrave, 1998.

Nisbet, H. B. and Claude Rawson, eds. *The Cambridge History of English Criticism Volume 4: The Eighteenth Century*. Cambridge: Cambridge University Press, 1997.

Nussbaum, Felicity A. *Torrid Zones: Maternity, Sexuality, and Empire in Eighteenth-Century English Narratives*. Baltimore: Johns Hopkins University Press, 1995.

O'Brien, Conor Cruise. "Introduction." In *Reflections on the Revolution in France, and on the Proceedings in Certain Societies in London Relative to that Event*, by Edmund Burke, edited by Conor Cruise O'Brien, 9–76. 1790; Harmondsworth: Penguin, 1969.

———. *The Great Melody: A Thematic Biography and Commented Anthology of Edmund Burke*. London: Sinclair-Stevenson, 1992.

O'Brien, Michael J. *A Hidden Phase of American History: Ireland's Part in America's Struggle for Liberty*. New York: Dodd, Mead & Company, 1919.

Ó Ciardha, Eamonn. *Ireland and the Jacobite Cause, 1685–1766: A Fatal Attachment*. Dublin: Four Courts, 2004.

Ogborn, Miles and Charles W. J. Withers. "Introduction." In *Georgian Geographies: Essays on Space, Place and Landscape in the Eighteenth Century*, edited by Miles Ogborn and Charles W. J. Withers, 1–23. Manchester: Manchester University Press, 2004.

Ó Túama, Seán, ed. *An Duanaire—An Irish Anthology 1600–1900: Poems of the Dispossessed*. Translated by Thomas Kinsella. Philadelphia: University of Pennsylvania Press, 1981.

Pagden, Anthony. *Lords of All the World: Ideologies of Empire in Spain, Britain and France c.1500–c.1800*. New Haven: Yale University Press, 1995.

Parks, George B. "The Turn to the Romantic in the Travel Literature of the Eighteenth Century." *Modern Language Notes* 25 (1964), 22–33.

Philo, Chris "Foucault's Geography." *Environment and Planning D: Society and Space* 10 (1992), 137–61.

Pitman, James Hall *Goldsmith's Animated Nature: A Study of Goldsmith*. 1924; Hamden: Archon, 1972.

Pitofsky, Alex. "The Warden's Court Martial: James Oglethorpe and the Politics of Eighteenth-Century Prison Reform." *Eighteenth-Century Life* 24 (2000), 88–102.

Pittock, Murray. Poetry and Jacobite Politics in Eighteenth-Century Britain and Ireland. Cambridge: Cambridge University Press, 1994.

Pitts, Jennifer. *A Turn to Empire: The Rise of Imperial Liberalism in Britain and France*. Princeton: Princeton University Press, 2005.

Popkin, Richard H. "The Philosophical Basis of Eighteenth-Century Racism." In *Racism in the Eighteenth Century*, edited by Harold E. Pagliaro, 245–62. Cleveland: Case Western Reserve University Press, 1973.

Porter, Roy. *Enlightenment: Britain and the Creation of the Modern World*. London: Penguin, 2000.

———. *Flesh in the Age of Reason*. London: Penguin, 2004.

Powell, Martyn J. "Shelburne and Ireland: Politician, Patriot, Absentee." In *An Enlightenment Statesman in Whig Britain: Lord Shelburne in Context, 1737–1805*, edited by Nigel Aston and Clarissa Campbell Orr, 141–159. Woodbridge: The Boydell Press, 2011.

Pratt, Mary Louise. *Imperial Eyes: Travel Writing and Transculturation*. London: Routledge, 1992.

Pressly, William L. "On Classic Ground: James Barry's 'Memorials' of the Italian Landscape." *Record of the Art Museum, Princeton University* 54 (1995), 12–28.

Prior, James. *Life of Oliver Goldsmith, M. B.*, 2 vols. London: John Murray, 1837.

Quintana, Ricardo. *Oliver Goldsmith: A Georgian Study*. New York: Macmillan, 1967.

———. "*The Deserted Village*: Its Logical and Rhetorical Elements." *College English* 26 (1964), 204–14.

———. "*The Vicar of Wakefield*: The Problem of Critical Approach." *Modern Philology* 71 (1973–74), 59–65.

Rafroidi, Patrick. "Goldsmith ou la Géographie du Coeur." *Etudes Irlandais*, nouvelle série, no. 9 (Decembre 1984), 97–105.

Rawson, Claude. *God, Gulliver and Genocide: Barbarism and the European Imagination 1492–1945*. Oxford: Oxford University Press, 2001.

Rogers, Pat. "The Dialectic of *The Traveller*." In *The Art of Oliver Goldsmith*, edited by Andrew Swarbrick, 107–25. London: Vision, 1984.

Rousseau, G. S., ed. *Goldsmith: The Critical Heritage*. London: Routledge, 1974.

——— and Roy Porter, "Introduction." In *Exoticism in the Enlightenment*, edited by G. S. Rousseau and Roy Porter, 1–22. Manchester: Manchester University Press, 1990.

Rowbotham, Arnold H., *Missionary and Mandarin: The Jesuits at the Court of China* (Berkeley University of California Press, 1942).

Said, Edward. "Afterword to the 1995 Printing." *Orientalism: Western Conceptions of the Orient*, 329–54. London: Penguin, 1995.

———. *Culture and Imperialism*. London: Chatto and Windus, 1993.

———. *Joseph Conrad and the Fiction of Autobiography*. Cambridge: Harvard University Press, 1966.

———. *Orientalism: Western Conceptions of the Orient*. Harmondsworth: Penguin, 1978.

Samuels, Arthur P. I. *The Early Life, Correspondence and Writings of the Rt. Hon. Edmund Burke* LL.D. Cambridge: Cambridge University Press, 1923.

Schulz, Max F. "The Circuit Walk of the Eighteenth-Century Landscape Garden and the Pilgrim's Circuitous Progress." *Eighteenth-Century Studies* 15 (1981), 1–25.

Sedgwick, Romney. *The History of Parliament: The House of Commons 1715–1754*, 2 vols. New York: Oxford University Press, 1970.

Seeber, Edward D. "Goldsmith's American Tigers." *Modern Language Quarterly* 6 (1945), 417–19.

Seitz, R. W. "Goldsmith and the *Present State of the British Empire*." *Modern Language Notes* 45 (1930), 434–438.

———. "Goldsmith to Sir William Chambers" (1773). *Times Literary Supplement*, no. 1808 (Sept. 1936), 772.

———. "The Irish Background of Goldsmith's Social and Political Thought." *Publications of the Modern Language Association* 62 (1937), 405–441.

Sekora, John. *Luxury: The Concept in Western Thought from Eden to Smollett* Baltimore: Johns Hopkins University Press, 1977.

Sells, A. Lytton. *Les Sources Francaises de Goldsmith*. Paris, 1924.

———. *Oliver Goldsmith: His Life and Works*. London: Barnes and Noble, 1974.

Sewell, Elizabeth. *The Orphic Voice: Poetry and Natural History*. London: Harper and Row, 1961.

Shimada, Takua. "Is *Sharawadgi* Derived from the Japanese Word *Sorowaji*." *The Review of English Studies* 48 (1997), 350–52.

———. "The Court of Japan in Letter CXVIII in Oliver Goldsmith's *The Citizen of the World*." *Notes and Queries* 232 (1987), 345–48.

Shklar, Judith N. *Montesquieu*. Oxford: Oxford University Press, 1987.

Sirén, Osvald *China and Gardens of Europe of the Eighteenth Century*. New York: Ronald Press, 1950.

Sitter, John. *Literary Loneliness in Mid–Eighteenth-Century England*. Ithaca: Cornell University Press, 1982.

Sloan, Phillip R. "The Idea of Racial Degeneracy in Buffon's *Histoire Naturelle*." In *Racism in the Eighteenth Century*, edited by Harold E. Pagliaro, 293–321. Cleveland: Case Western Reserve University Press, 1973.

Smethurst, Colin. "Introduction." In *Romantic Geographies: Proceedings of the Glasgow Conference, September 1994*, edited by Colin Smethurst, vii–xiii. Glasgow: University of Glasgow Publications, 1996.

Smith, Bernard. *Imagining the Pacific: In the Wake of the Cook Voyages*. New Haven: Yale University Press, 1992.

Smith, Hamilton Jewett. *Oliver Goldsmith's* The Citizen of the World: *A Study*. New Haven: Yale University Press, 1926.

Sowerby, E. Millicent, ed. *Catalogue of the Library of Thomas Jefferson*, 5 vols. Washington: The Library of Congress, 1952–59.

Spector, Robert Donald. *English Literary Periodicals and the Climate of Opinion During the Seven Years' War*. The Hague: Mouton, 1966.

Spence, Jonathan. *The Chan's Great Continent: China in Western Minds*. London: Penguin, 1999.

Stafleu, Frans A. *Linnaeus and the Linnaeans: The Spreading of Their Ideas in Systematic Botany, 1735–1789*. Utrecht: Oesthoek, 1971.

Stocking, George W. "Bones, Bodies, Behaviour." In *Bones, Bodies, Behaviour: Essays on Biological Anthropology*, edited by George W. Stocking, 3–15. Madison: University of Wisconsin Press, 1988.

Stoddart, D.R. *On Geography and its History*. Oxford: Blackwell, 1986.

Storm, Leo F. "Conventional Ethics in Goldsmith's *The Traveller*." *Studies in English Literature, 1500–1900* 17 (1977), 463–76.

———. "Literary Convention in Goldsmith's *Deserted Village*." *Huntingdon Library Quarterly* 33 (1970), 243–56.

Streatfield, David C. and Alistair M. Duckworth. *Landscape in the Gardens and the Literature of Eighteenth-Century England*. Los Angeles: William Andrews Clark Memorial Library, 1981.

Stroud, Dorothy, *Capability Brown*. London: Faber & Faber, 1965.

Taylor, Richard C. *Goldsmith as Journalist*. London: Associated University Presses, 1993.

Thomas, George, Earl of Albemarle. *Memoirs of the Marquis of Rockingham and His Contemporaries. With Original Letters and Documents Now First Published*, 2 vols. London: Samuel Bentley, 1852.

Torchiana, Donald T. *W.B. Yeats & Georgian Ireland*. Washington: Catholic University of America Press, 1966.

Turner, Katherine. *British Travel Writers in Europe 1750–1800: Authorship, Gender and National Identity*. Aldershot: Ashgate, 2001.

Turner, James G. "The Sexual Politics of Landscape: Images of Venus in Eighteenth-Century English Poetry and Landscape Gardening." *Studies in Eighteenth-Century Culture* 11 (1982), 343–66.

Turner, Roger. *Capability Brown and the Eighteenth-Century English Landscape*. Chichester: Phillimore, 1999.

Turner, Stephen. "Enlightenment Topographies: Scotland, Switzerland, the South Seas." *The Eighteenth Century* 38 (1997), 231–46.

Von Erdberg, Eleanor. *Chinese Influence on European Garden Structures*. Cambridge: Harvard University Press, 1936.

Wardle, Ralph. *Oliver Goldsmith*. Lawrence: University of Kansas Press, 1957.

Watt, James. "Goldsmith's Cosmopolitanism." *Eighteenth-Century Life* 30 (2005), 56–75.

———. "Thomas Percy, China, and the Gothic." *The Eighteenth Century: Theory and Interpretation* 48 (2007), 95–109.

Welch, Robert. "The Strange Enigma of Oliver Goldsmith." In *The Sieges of Derry*, edited by William Kelly, 75–84. Dublin: Four Courts, 2001.

Wellek, René. *The Rise of English Literary History*. Chapel Hill: The University of North Carolina Press, 1941.

———. *A History of Modern Criticism: 1750–1950*, 4 vols. New Haven: Yale University Press, 1955.

Wheeler, Roxann. *The Complexion of Race: Categories of Difference in Eighteenth-Century British Culture*. Philadelphia: University of Pennsylvania Press, 2000.

Whelan, Kevin. *The Tree of Liberty: Radicalism, Catholicism and the Construction of Irish Identity 1760–1830*. Cork: Cork University Press, 1996.

Whitney, Lois. *Primitivism and the Idea of Progress in English Popular Literature of the Eighteenth Century*. Baltimore: Johns Hopkins University Press, 1934.

Wiley, Michael. *Romantic Geography: Wordsworth and Anglo–European Spaces* Houndmills: Palgrave, 1988.

Willey, Basil. *The Eighteenth-Century Background: Studies on the Idea of Nature in the Thought of the Period*. Harmondsworth: Penguin, 1962.

Williams, Glyndwr, "The Pacific: Exploration and Exploitation." In *The Oxford History of the British Empire, Volume II: The Eighteenth Century*, edited by P. J. Marshall, 556–65. Oxford: Oxford University Press, 1998.

Williams, Raymond. "Nature's Threads." *Eighteenth-Century Studies* 2 (1968), 45–57.

———. *The Country and the City*. London: Chatto and Windus, 1973.

Wilson, Kathleen, ed. *A New Imperial History: Culture, Identity and Modernity in Britain and the Empire 1660–1840*. Cambridge: Cambridge University Press, 2004.

Winchcombe, George. *Oliver Goldsmith and the Moonrakers*. London: Thab, 1972.

Withers, Charles J. and Robert J. Mayhew. "Geography: Space, Place and Intellectual History in the Eighteenth Century." *Journal for Eighteenth-Century Studies* 34 (2011), 445–452.

Wittkower, Rudolf. "English Neo–Palladianism, The Landscape Garden, China, and the Enlightenment." *L'Arte* 2 (1969), 18–35.

Wood, Nigel. "Goldsmith's English Malady." *Studies in the Literary Imagination* 44 (2011), 63–83.

Wood, Paul B. "The Science of Man." In *Cultures of Natural History*, edited by Nicholas Jardine, J. A. Secord, and Emma Spary, 197–210. Cambridge: Cambridge University Press, 1996.

Woods, Samuel H., Jr. "Images of the Orient: Goldsmith and the Philosophes." *Studies in Eighteenth-Century Culture* 15 (1986), 257–70.

———. *Oliver Goldsmith: A Reference Guide*. Boston: G.K. Hall, 1982.

———. "*The Vicar of Wakefield* and Recent Goldsmith Scholarship." *Eighteenth-Century Studies* 9 (1976), 429–43.

Yeats, W. B. *The Poems*, edited by Daniel Albright. London: Everyman, 1990.

Zach, Wolfgang. "Oliver Goldsmith on Ireland and the Irish: Personal Views, Shifting Attitudes, Literary Stereotypes." In *Studies in Anglo-Irish Literature*, edited by Heinz Kosok, 23–36. Bonn: Bouvier Verlag, 1982.

Zhijian, Tao. "Citizen of Whose World? Goldsmith's Orientalism." *Comparative Literature Studies* 33 (1996), 15–34.

INDEX

absentee landlordism, 114, 120–27, 132, 134–51
Addison, Joseph, 53, 54–6, 59–61, 101, 162n6, 162n11, 170n35
Adorno, Theodor, 6, 154n15
Ahluwalia, Pal, 5–6, 154n13
aisling, symbol in literature, 89, 91, 112, 172n61
allegory, 87–112
Allen, B. Sprague, 94, 168n19
America, 48–9, 113–45
Anglican nationalism, 11–12
Anne, Queen, 23
Anstey, Christopher, 106
Anthologia Hibernica, 144, 179n87
anti-imperialism, 7, 9, 17
d'Argens, Jean-Baptiste de Boyer, Marquis, 92, 167nn12–3
Ashcroft, Bill 5–6, 154n13
Asiatic writing, 97–100
Asiatics, 35, 40, 47, 49, 98
Auburn (poetic village), 89, 112, 113–20, 143–7, 151, 172–3n6
Augusta, Princess Dowager of Wales, 107
Austen, Jane, 26, 157n56

Ballaster, Ros, 94, 168n21
Baretti, Joseph, 55–6, 162n10
Barnouw, A. J., 66, 164n41
Barrell, John, 15, 155n34
Barry, James, 60–61, 163n24
Bataille, Robert, 26–7, 157n57
The Bee, 92
Beeckman, Daniel, 48, 161n36
Bell, David, 34, 39, 158n6
Bentivoglio, Cardinal, 63
Bindley, John, 43, 160n30
Bingham, Charles, 138–9
Bissell, Benjamin, 48, 161n39
Blackmore, Sir Richard, 53, 56, 67, 162n12

Blaquiere, Colonel John, 137
Brett, John, Bishop of Elphin, 115
British Magazine, 21
Britons, character of, 41, 68
Brookes, Richard, 41, 159n18, 160n29, 169n29
Brooks, Christopher, 91, 167n9
Brown, John, 127, 176n45–6
Brown, Lancelot "Capability," 102, 106, 171n51, 173n6,177n44
Brown, Laura, 129, 177n54
Brown, Marshall, 114, 172n5
Bryanton, Robert, 92
Buffon, Georges-Louis LeClerc, Comte de, 31, 42–4, 129, 159n22
Burke, Edmund, 8, 9, 10–12, 15, 60, 80, 101, 102, 106, 109–10, 118, 119, 120–30, 133, 134–43, 148, 154n20, 155n29, 170n36, 170nn39–40, 171n54, 172nn57–9, 175nn35–6, 175n40, 175n44, 177nn57–8, 177n65, 178n71, 178n73, 179n74–5, 179n81–2, 179n85
Burke, William, 130–31, 133

Campbell, John, 130
Campbell, Thomas, 142, 179n84
Carey, Daniel, 8, 155n21
Cave, Edward, 92
Celtic Tiger, 147–8
Chambers, John, 102
Chambers, William, 102–3, 106–8, 170–1nn42–3, 171nn45–6, 171n48, 171nn52–3
Chandler, James, 10, 155n28
Charles XII of Sweden, 102, 170n41
Cheyne, George, 113, 172n2
China, 91–112
Chinoiserie, 96–9
climate, 28, 32, 34–41
Clive, Lord, 131
Colonialism, 4–5, 69–70, 127–34 *see also* imperialism

[203]

INDEX

Comte, Louis Le, 92, 95, 168n24
Condamine, Charles–Marie de la, 130
Confucianism, 95, 100
Congreve, William, 36, 159n11
Contarine, Thomas, 21, 52, 115, 157n50, 164n39
Cooke, William, 115, 162n16, 173n12
cosmopolitanism, 2, 9, 52, 55
Cowper, John, 135, 177n67
Crabbe, George, 118, 173n16
Crawford, Rachel, 118, 155n27, 174n18
Critical Review, 98
Cruickshank, George, 74
Cullen, L. M., 20, 156n44

Deane, Seamus, 10, 14–15, 17, 119, 142, 155n29, 155n33, 156n38, 174n23
DeValera, Éamon, 151, 180n8
Dickson, David, 22, 157n51, 174n25
Diderot, Denis, 7, 133
Dobson, Austin, 132, 177n62, 178n71
Downie, J. A., 18, 155n32, 156n39
Dublin, 3, 18, 102, 105,114, 121–3, 138–9
Duck, Stephen, 118
du Halde, Jean–Baptiste, 92, 94, 168n22, 168n24, 169n29
Dyer, John, 61,163n25

Eagleton, Terry, 120, 174n26
economics, 113–14, 147–8, 151
Edgecombe, Rodney Stenning, 57, 162n14
Effen, Justus Van, 66, 164n41
Elphin, 115
emigration, 28, 114–35, 142–4
enclosure, 115, 128, 134–51
enlightenment, 2–10, 35, 54–5, 63, 82, 92, 94, 113, 150–51
Espiard de la Borde, François–Ignace, 38–40, 159n19, 159n21, 160n24
ethnography, 52, 56
Eurocentricism, 3, 5, 150

Fabricant, Carole, 10, 15, 89, 105, 155n29, 155n35, 166n7, 171n47, 172n60
Fairer, David, 117, 173n16, 156n40
Farquhar, George, 36, 159n12
fashion, 60, 65, 90–91, 93, 95–7, 101–2, 107, 111–12, 144
Fenton, Seamus, 19–20, 156n43, 156n47
Festa, Lynn, 89, 155n21
The Field Day Anthology of Irish Writing, 14, 174n23, 180n8
Fletcher, Angus, 108, 172n55
Foucault, Michael, 5–6, 8, 154n10, 154n13

Fox, Christopher, 5, 154n9, 160n31
France, 3, 6, 31, 52, 57, 65–6, 91, 126
freedom, 6, 8, 16–17, 24–5, 36, 61–3, 68, 79, 80–82, 100, 118, 131, 148–9
Freneau, Philip, 132, 177n63
Frézier, Amédée–Francois, 130
Friedman, Arthur, 10, 153n8, 158n5, 164n40, 165n53, 167n13, 168n24, 172n56, 177–8n68
Frith, William, P., 74

garden design, 101–3, 106–7
Gargett, Graham, 26. 157n53
Gentleman's Magazine 103, 113
geography, 4–5, 8, 10, 27, 35, 44, 56, 59, 61, 64, 83, 113–45, 150
George I, 24
George II, 24
George III, 18, 20, 57
Georgia, 127–34
Gibbon, Edward, 63, 163n29
Gibbons, Luke, 10, 143, 155n29, 155n34, 175n41, 179n85
Ginger, John, 71, 164n45
Glorious Revolution, 17, 20, 22, 71, 136, 149
see also Jacobitism
Goethe, Johan Wolfgang von, 62, 74, 163n28
Goldsmith, Francis, 19
Goldsmith, Henry, 57–8
Goldsmith, John, 19
Goldsmith, Maurice, 18
Goldsmith, Oliver: as Anglo–Irish, 19–20, 147–51; *The Citizen of the World*, 27–8, 41, 58, 77, 84, 90, 91–112, 150; "A Comparative View of Races and Nations," 31, 32, 35, 37, 50, 53; cosmopolitanism of, 2, 9, 33–4, 52; *The Deserted Village*, 1–2, 12, 13–14, 15, 27–8, 40–41, 49, 61, 64, 70, 78, 87–89, 101, 112, 113–51; "The Effects Which Climates have upon Men, and Other Animals," 38, 130; and the enlightenment, 2–3, 7–9; *An Enquiry into the Present State of Polite Learning in Europe*, 37–8, 65–6, 71; family, 18–20; geographies of, 3–5, 10, 27, 34, 113–45, 150; *The Good Natur'd Man*, 78, 88; "The History of a Poet's Garden," 111; *History of England, from the Earliest Times to the Death of George II*, 23–6, 131; *An History of the Earth and Animated Nature*, 42–50; "On the Instability of Worldly Grandeur," 92–3; Irishness of, 3, 10–28, 89, 91, 112; liberty in his works, 2–3, 10, 17, 25, 51–84, 117–18; on monarchy, 25, 79–80, 149; nationality and, 3, 7–8, 11–12,

[204]

14–15; as pastoral poet, 12, 15, 116; politics of, 2, 3, 10, 14–15, 17–19, 20–28, 82–3, 105–6, 128, 149; *The Present State of the British Empire in Europe, America, Africa and Asia*, 131; *Retaliation*, 120; "On the Several Conditions of Life," 123–5; *She Stoops to Conquer* 54, 83–4, 87–8, 106; *Survey of Experimental Philosophy*, 113; *The Traveller, or, a Prospect of Society* 15, 16–17, 27, 51–84, 91, 124, 125, 129, 131, 145, 150; at Trinity College 3, 18, 102, 120–23; *The Vicar of Wakefield* 13, 27, 28, 52–65, 72–84, 128, 137
Goldstein, Laurence, 32, 130, 157n2, 177n56
Gordon, Patrick, 4, 153n2
Gordon riots, 139
Grand Tour, 53, 57, 62
Graves, Richard, 111
Graves, Robert, 88–9, 166n3
Griffin, Dustin, 10, 155n26
Griffin, William, 42

Haller, Albrecht von, 63
Hawes, Clement, 8–9, 152n22, 161n36
Hawkesworth, John, 113, 172n4
Hayman, John G., 53, 54, 162n4, 162n7
Heawood, Edward, 4, 153n5
Helgerson, Richard, 77, 165n54
Hickey, Joseph, 141
Higgins, Ian, 18, 156n39, 170n41
Hippocrates, 34–5, 47, 158nn7–8
Hoare, Henry, 111
Hodson, Daniel, 58, 90
Holberg, Baron Lewis (Ludvig), 71–2, 84, 164n47
Holland, 4, 40, 52, 66–7, 70–71, 81, 91
Honour, Hugh, 97, 169n26
Horkheimer, Max, 6, 154n15
Hudson, Nicholas, 44, 156n40, 160n32
Hughes, John, 91, 167n10
Hume, David, 25, 26, 36–7, 53, 159nn15–6

illustrations in *The Vicar of Wakefield*, 74
imperialism, 4–10, 16, 17, 40, 41, 50, 82, 88, 131–2, 134
Ireland, 3, 12–15, 17–22, 25, 27, 31–2, 35, 48, 50, 57–8, 69, 74, 87–112, 113–22, 125, 127–8, 136–44, 147–51
Irish Times, 148, 180n2
irony, 13, 74, 77, 97
Italy, 38, 52, 54–7, 59, 60–65, 91

Jacobitism 3, 10, 17, 18, 21, 24, 100, 105, 112, 122, 136, 145, 149–50

James II, 22, 23
Jameson, Fredric, 118, 174n19
Johnson, Samuel, 5, 9, 18, 20–21, 26, 42, 58, 136, 148–9, 153n7, 156n40, 163n20, 168n16, 180n3
Joyce, James, 73, 165n48
Judt, Tony, 147, 180n1

Kames, Henry Home, Lord, 159n16
Kelly, Hugh, 27, 157n57
Kew gardens, 107
King, Anthony, 117–18, 119, 174n17

Lafitau, 132
landscape gardening, *see* garden design
Langford, Paul, 62, 163n27
Leask, Nigel, 93–4, 168n18
Liebniz, Gottfried Wilhelm, 95
Lennon, Joseph, 6, 154n14
Levellers, 79
liberty, 1–3, 10–11, 15–17, 23–5, 28, 35–6, 38–40, 51–84, 101, 106, 117–18, 127, 131, 134,139, 144, 147, 150
Linnaeus, Carl 43–4, 160nn29–30
Literary Magazine, 103
Lithgow, William, 48, 161n37
Lock, F. P., 130–31, 177n58, 179n82
Lonsdale, Roger, 27, 157n58, 162n17, 174n28
Lucas, John, 16, 156n37, 164n43
Lyotard, Francois, 9
Lyttelton, George, Lord, 92, 162n6, 163n26, 167n13, 169n25

Macauley, Thomas Babington, 20, 116–17, 156n46, 173n15
MacGabhann, Sean, 19
Mackenzie, Henry, 77
Maclise, Daniel, 74
Mahoney, Thomas, 138, 142, 179n74, 179n82
Mandeville, Bernard, 144
Mangin, Edward, 115, 173n9
mankind, categories of, 45–50
Martin, John, 74
Mason, William, 106, 171nn48–9
McCormack, W. J., 20, 124, 156n45, 175n41
McMinn, Joseph, 89, 166n2, 166n5
McVeagh, John, 10, 155n24
Montague, John, 89, 151, 166n4, 180n7
Monthly Review, 93, 100, 110
Montesquieu, Baron (Charles de Secondat), 7, 31, 37–40, 52, 53, 92–4, 154n18, 159n14, 159n17, 160n25, 161n1, 167n12, 168n15
Moran, Thomas, 20
Morning Chronicle, 134

INDEX

Müllenbrock, Heinz–Joachim, 55, 162n8
Mulready, William, 74, 75, 165n50
Murphy, Arthur, 94, 169n28
Murray, Ciaran, 55, 162n9, 170n36
Murray, Patrick, 19, 156n41
Muthu, Sankar, 6–7, 154n17

Napier (Napper), Robert, 115
Nash, Richard "Beau," 77
national characteristics, 8, 14, 31, 45, 50, 94
native Americans, 132
natural history, 31–50
Newbery, John, 135, 177–8n68
Newell, R. H., 115, 173n10
Newton, Gilbert Stuart, 74
Northern Star, 143, 179n86
Nourse, John, 42
Nugent, Thomas, 38, 164n39
Nussbaum, Felicity, 45, 161n33

O'Brien, Conor Cruise, 137, 149, 170n36, 178n73, 180n6
O'Carolan, Turlough, 21
O'Ciardha, Eamonn, 21, 156n49, 176n51
O'Conor, Charles, 21, 114, 157n50
O'Donovan, John, 19, 156n42
Oglethorpe, James Edward, 128, 131–6, 143, 176nn49–50, 177n66, 178nn69–70
Ó Rathaille, Aogán, 89
Ordnance Survey (1837), 19, 156n42
Orientalism, 5–6, 28, 39–40, 90–91, 93, 94, 96, 97, 112

Paine, Thomas, 1–3, 148–50, 153n1, 180n5
Paterson, William, 128
Percy, Thomas, 18, 26, 100, 107, 157n55, 169nn29–32
"Philo-Marius," 140, 143
Pierson, William, 102
Pitt, William, First Earl of Chatham, 140
Pittock, Murray, 112, 156n40, 172n62
Polo, Marco, 91–2
Pope, Alexander, 88, 124, 156n40, 172n60, 176n49
Porter, Roy, 6, 94, 113, 154n9, 154n16, 160n31, 168n20, 172n3
postcolonialism, 8–10, 90
Poyning, Sir Edward, 141
primitivism, 50, 63, 65, 134
Prior, James, 19, 71–2, 115–16, 122, 164n31, 179n81
Prior, Thomas, 121, 123, 174n29
Public Advertiser, 140, 143
Public Ledger, 92

Quintana, Ricardo, 13, 155nn31–2

Race, 44–50, *see also* national characteristics
Rackham, Arthur, 74, 76, 165n51
Raynal, Abbé, 7–8, 9, 133, 154n19, 160n3, 177n64
Rea, John, 128
Reynolds, Joshua, 107, 116
Rockingham, Charles Watson-Wentworth, Marquess of, 120, 137–43, 171–2n54, 179n76
Romanticism, 65, 78, 93, 124, 132
Romero, Juan, 18
Rousseau, G. S., 94, 168n20
Rousseau, Jean–Jacques, 94
Rowlandson, Thomas, 74
Royal Magazine, 32
Rusticello, of Pisa, 91–2
Ryley, Charles, 74

Said, Edward, 5–6, 93, 119, 154nn11–3
Samuels, A. P. I., 124, 175n40
Savile, George, 136, 139–40, 178n71
Scotland, 24, 32, 34, 128, 135–6
Scottish clans, 135–6
Scottish enlightenment, 32
Seitz, R. W., 10, 106, 155n25, 171n52–3
Sells, A. Lytton, 65, 164n36, 172n56
"The Seven Sages," 11, 12
Seven Years' War, 22, 32, 34–5, 54, 132–3
Shackleton, Richard, 118
Sharawadgi, 101
Sharp, Samuel, 55, 60
Shelburne, William Petty, Earl of, 140–1, 179nn80–1
Shenstone, William, 110–11, 172n60
Skelton, Philip, 119–20, 174n24
Smethurst, Colin, 5, 162n6
The Spectator, 101
Spence, Jonathan, 92, 167n11
Sterne, Laurence, 74, 84, 165n48
Storm, Leo, 57, 162n13
Stothard, Thomas, 74
Strean, Dr Annesley, 115
Swift, Jonathan, 3, 9, 10, 13, 15–17, 18, 35, 36, 48, 88–90, 121–3, 125, 155n29, 155n32, 156n39, 159n13, 161n36, 165n48, 166n2, 174nn30–1, 176n49
Switzerland, 52, 57, 58, 63–5, 68–9, 70, 91, 145

Temple, Sir William, 36, 101, 158–9nn9–10, 170n34, 170n38
Thomson, James, 53, 55, 59, 61, 68–9, 131–2, 134, 163n25, 164n34, 164n42, 177n60

[206]

INDEX

Tone, Wolfe, 137
Toryism, 18, 23–5, 124, 127
travel writing, 55–6
Trinity College, 3, 18, 102, 120–23, 144
Turner, James, 89, 166n7, 172n60
Turner, Katherine, 52–3, 162n3, 162n6
Turner, Steven, 63, 163n30

United Irishmen, 143, 145
Unwins, Thomas, 74

"Valsas, Guilelmus," 143, 144
Voltaire (François–Marie d'Arouet), 63, 93, 157n53, 164n32, 167n12, 168n15, 169n27

Walker, Joseph Cooper, 114–15, 173nn7–8
Walpole, Horace, 54, 106, 137, 140, 162n6, 167n13, 171n48, 171n49, 178n69, 178n72, 179n79
Walpole, Robert, 24, 172–3n6

Watt, James, 9, 100, 155n23, 169n31
Weekly Magazine, 22
Wentworth, Thomas, 19
Westminster Magazine, 111
Whelan, Kevin, 120, 174n27
Whiggery, 4, 11, 12, 17, 23–25, 28, 32, 54–6, 59, 101, 106, 131–2, 137, 139, 141, 143
Whiteboy disturbances, 136
Whitehead, William, 99–100, 169n28
Whyte, Laurence, 121–2, 145, 175n34, 175n42
William III, 23, 24
Williams, Raymond, 118–19, 174n21
Wilson, Richard, 60, 63, 163n23
Wittkower, Rudolf, 106 , 171n50

Year of Victories (1759), 22, 32
Yeats, W. B., 11–12, 119, 155n30

Zach, Wolfgang, 32, 157n3
Zhijian, Tao, 90, 167n8

ABOUT THE AUTHOR

Michael Griffin lectures in eighteenth-century and Irish studies at the University of Limerick, where he is director of the Eighteenth Century Research Group. He has published widely on eighteenth-century studies, utopian satire, and Irish writing in English. His critical edition of *The Selected Writings of Thomas Dermody* was published by Field Day Press in 2012.